Alan Sanders

Football Apprenticeships in England

GW00599416

Alan Sanders

Football Apprenticeships in England

The vocational socialisation process

VDM Verlag Dr. Müller

Impressum/Imprint (nur für Deutschland/ only for Germany)

Bibliografische Information der Deutschen Nationalbibliothek: Die Deutsche Nationalbibliothek verzeichnet diese Publikation in der Deutschen Nationalbibliografie; detaillierte bibliografische Daten sind im Internet über http://dnb.d-nb.de abrufbar.
Alle in diesem Buch genannten Marken und Produktnamen unterliegen warenzeichen-, marken- oder patentrechtlichem Schutz bzw. sind Warenzeichen oder eingetragene Warenzeichen der jeweiligen Inhaber. Die Wiedergabe von Marken, Produktnamen, Gebrauchsnamen, Handelsnamen, Warenbezeichnungen u.s.w. in diesem Werk berechtigt auch ohne besondere Kennzeichnung nicht zu der Annahme, dass solche Namen im Sinne der Warenzeichen- und Markenschutzgesetzgebung als frei zu betrachten wären und daher von jedermann benutzt werden dürften.

Coverbild: www.purestockx.com

Verlag: VDM Verlag Dr. Müller Aktiengesellschaft & Co. KG
Dudweiler Landstr. 99, 66123 Saarbrücken, Deutschland
Telefon +49 681 9100-698, Telefax +49 681 9100-988, Email: info@vdm-verlag.de

Herstellung in Deutschland:
Schaltungsdienst Lange o.H.G., Berlin
Books on Demand GmbH, Norderstedt
Reha GmbH, Saarbrücken
Amazon Distribution GmbH, Leipzig
ISBN: 978-3-639-15672-0

Imprint (only for USA, GB)

Bibliographic information published by the Deutsche Nationalbibliothek: The Deutsche Nationalbibliothek lists this publication in the Deutsche Nationalbibliografie; detailed bibliographic data are available in the Internet at http://dnb.d-nb.de.
Any brand names and product names mentioned in this book are subject to trademark, brand or patent protection and are trademarks or registered trademarks of their respective holders. The use of brand names, product names, common names, trade names, product descriptions etc. even without a particular marking in this works is in no way to be construed to mean that such names may be regarded as unrestricted in respect of trademark and brand protection legislation and could thus be used by anyone.

Cover image: www.purestockx.com

Publisher:
VDM Verlag Dr. Müller Aktiengesellschaft & Co. KG
Dudweiler Landstr. 99, 66123 Saarbrücken, Germany
Phone +49 681 9100-698, Fax +49 681 9100-988, Email: info@vdm-verlag.de

Printed in the U.S.A.
Printed in the U.K. by (see last page)
ISBN: 978-3-639-15672-0

CONTENTS

1

2

ACKNOWLEDGEMENTS

Thank you to John Sugden and Alan Tomlinson for all their expertise and advice.

DEDICATION
For Inger, Gabriella and Julia.

3

Figures

INTRODUCTION

The research for this book was undertaken between 1998 and 2004 for a thesis as part fulfilment for a Ph.D in Social and Applied Sports Studies at the University of Brighton.

1. Football as a vocation

Football is the most popular sport in the world (Reilly and Williams 2003). The most widespread code is association football (or soccer) and this was formalised in England by the establishment of the Football Association (F.A.) in 1863. Since then, the sport has become an integral part of our culture (Hopcraft 1968), whereby comprehensive media coverage of football at an elite level has become part of everyday life in this country. The attraction of football as a sport to young people is beyond comparison. Reilly, Williams and Richardson (2003:307) describe this attraction as follows. "Many thousands of youngsters who participate in soccer aspire to play at an elite level. The dream to become a star player and compete on the international stage may even be the foremost motive for playing from an early age".

However, the reality is that only a very small number of those who aspire to become a professional footballer ever achieve their ambition, because by the very nature of professional sport, there is only space for an elite few.

The issues and problems that aspiring young footballers face can be compared and contrasted to those experienced by young people in other performance-based professions, such as acting, ballet and classical music. Comparisons can also be made between the processes the industries use to cater for the high demand of young people wishing to enter into them and also the ways they deal with the high failure rates.

Recent changes within professional football at youth level, mainly instigated by the F.A.'s 'Charter for Quality' (1997), have looked to address the issues that arise from and for a young person trying to get into a highly competitive industry. Entrance into this industry requires that a young person embarks upon various vocational socialisation processes – and it is upon this journey that this work is based.

2. Habitus

Integrated within these processes for the aspiring elite performer is the gradual acquisition of 'habitus'. Bourdieu describes (1995) habitus as being similar to habit, except that habit is 'repetitive' and 'mechanical' rather than 'productive'. He also sees habitus as 'powerfully generative' and (1995:87). "A product of conditionings which tends to reproduce the objective logic of these conditionings while transforming it." Bourdieu (1984) engages the idea that an individual through conscious and sub conscious means develops an understanding for the bodily requirements in order to perform. Jarvie and Maguire (1994:189) explain this in the following way. "The knowledge of what it is to be a boxer, for example, involves the development of a body habitus. Here lessons are absorbed about manners, customs, style, and deportment that become so ingrained in the boxer that they are forgotten in any conscious sense."

Of course, the development of body habitus for a professional footballer would evolve in a similar manner to boxing, albeit within a football environment, whereby lessons of a comparable nature would be absorbed. These could include for example, the way an aspiring young footballer behaves within and outside a football environment and his lifestyle. A crucial point for this book, and in particular the fieldwork related to it, is to establish the extent to which the development of body habitus affects the chances of an individual becoming a professional footballer.

3. Aims and Objectives

The main aim of this work is to analyse the necessary processes that aspiring young footballers need to go through in order to embark on a professional career. The key questions will be to discover:

- What career path must an aspiring young footballer follow in order to become a professional footballer?
- What comparisons can be made between professional football and other performance-based professions?
- What is the vehicle used by professional football to establish young players for the future?

- What problems does an aspiring young footballer face whilst attending a professional football club as a player?
- What are the socio-psychological and sociological factors that assist a young person becoming a professional footballer?
- How do those that attend cope with the prospect of failure?
- How the youth system at Brighton and Hove Albion compares with two other professional clubs?
- What can be learnt from this study?

4. The Research Design

The purpose of this research is to investigate whether the changes made over recent years by the Football Association with regard to professional football at youth team level are beneficial to the aspiring young player, and how this balances with the requirements of the professional football clubs. The intended primary audience are individuals in the field of professional football who deal with policy-making decisions at youth team level. However, the audience may also include those in the social science community who solely wish to gain knowledge for understanding of the processes involved with becoming a professional footballer, and therefore the work should be considered as a combination of policy and theoretical research.

The fieldwork for this book is mainly based upon qualitative research in the form of participant observation undertaken at a professional football club as outlined in Chapter 5. The club selected as the case study is Brighton & Hove Albion, and this is supported later in the research by informal interviews with staff at Bristol City and Charlton Athletic Football Clubs. The approach used is therefore of a qualitative nature, which mainly "involves observing the informants over a period of time" (Creswell 1994:6) and according to Hakim (1997:26) offers, "descriptive reports of individuals' perceptions, attitudes, beliefs, views and feelings, the meanings and interpretations given to events and things as well their behaviour".

Discussion about the findings of this research are then followed by conclusions which look at the development of aspiring elite professional footballers in the wider context of sports development and government strategy in this country.

This publication can be viewed as an original piece of work , as to date, there has been no academic research based upon participant observation within a youth system at an English professional football club over a significant period of tine (in this case, three years) since the changes brought about by the Charter for Quality (1997).

However, one significant study undertaken in the area prior to 1997 was conducted by Parker (1996) entitled 'Chasing the Big Dream. Football Apprenticeships in the 1990's'. This work draws upon Parker's research (particularly in Chapter 3 and Chapter 10) in an attempt to analyse comparative and contrasting issues in research design, methods and findings._

Figure 1

Schematic outline of research design

Research Phase	Objectives of Research Phase	Method	Chapter
Phase I – Secondary Research	* To outline recent developments within professional football apprenticeships	Literature Review	1
	* To outline the major influences and potential barriers that youngsters encounter in their journey towards a chosen career		2
	* To analyse the psychological, socio-psychological and sociological factors that can affect the likelihood of a career in sport as an elite performer		3
	* To compare professional football with other performance-based careers		4
	* To examine the effect of the recent changes within youth systems at professional football club		5
Phase II – Primary Research Methodology	* To identify the most appropriate research strategy to achieve the research objectives		6
	* To outline the adopted methods selected for primary research		
Phase III – Research Findings	* To describe and discuss the emergent themes from the data collected	Case Studies, Participant observation & semi-structured interviews	7 & 8
Phase IV - Conclusions		Integration of overall findings	
	* To develop an overall evaluation of the vocational socialisation of young people into professional football		9
	* To assess the development of aspiring elite professional footballers in the wider context of sports development and government strategy in this country		10

5. The Structure of this Publication

The first part of this publication is based upon a survey of relevant literature (Chapters 1, 2, 3, 4 and 5) relevant to the area. This is followed by discussion of the research method of participant observation and the actual methods (Chapter 6) used for the primary research. The main part of the research is based upon fieldwork undertaken at one professional football club (Chapter 7) followed by short case studies at two others (Chapter 8). The final sections (Chapter 9 and 10) are used to analyse the empirical material generated by the fieldwork, to discuss the key issues and to assess the findings of this work in the context of sports development and government strategy in this country.

Chapter 1 sets the scene by highlighting the reasons that in 1997 led to the reorganisation and restructuring of professional football at youth team level in England, and the changes that are now in place.

This is followed by Chapter 2, which looks at a much broader area of study by highlighting the various theories that attempt to identify psychological and sociological reasons that influence young people's vocational/career choice. From a psychological point of view, a number of different theories are examined, including those based upon trait and factor, personality, developmental and autonomy. Many of the sociological issues discussed can be divided between intentional (with the specific aim of promoting learning) and incidental sources (learning based upon chance rather than design) of information that occur throughout a child's life. These are discussed along with factors such as class, education, gender and ethnicity. The chapter concludes with a brief look at the influence of the economic and political climate.

Chapter 3 examines the psychological, social psychological and sociological factors that can affect aspiring young elite sports performers and a list of all the key factors are given in a diagrammatic format. Many of the psychological theories are based upon efforts to match personality with physical activity. Although this type of matching is not a new concept, an attempt is made to look at the latest research in this area. The social psychological factors concentrate upon the individual as a participant and the influences of the underlying processes that occur within that situation. Examples of this include the effect of parents, coaches, teachers and friends. The sociological factors link with some of the issues discussed in Chapter 2, such as class and ethnicity, but with particular reference to the way they may play a part in the success or failure of an aspiring elite performer.

Chapter 4 is a comparison between the career structure and the requirements of some performance-based professions (ballet, classical music, drama and football). Special attention is given to the issue of body culture, with the performance of the body being the tool that will often be the decisive factor in determining the level of success a performer achieves. Contrasts and comparisons of factors that performers hoping to get into these professions face - such as the need to practice from an early age, length of career, coping with failure, prejudice and financial hardship - are all considered.

Chapter 5 concentrates solely upon professional football at youth level and the farm systems that lead into it. The issues that are discussed include the level of importance that the clubs give to these systems and the young people who are part of them (for example, the education and welfare of the individual). In addition, detail is given about the direct pressures put upon the young players, such as the fear of rejection, and the indirect pressures that include the sudden influx of foreign players at professional level which will mean a reduction of places available at the highest club level.

Before the presentation of any fieldwork material was undertaken, an examination of ethical matters and moral issues that relate to participant observation is covered. Literature and examples of research relating to this are discussed in Chapter 6 with particular attention being given to the type of participant observation that would best suit research in this area. This is followed by specific detail of the methods used for this research. In addition, attention is given to the problems that occur for a researcher who becomes a full-time employee at the club and at the same time attempts to produce valid and objective data from fieldwork based at that club.

Chapter 7 comprises a detailed case study of three years of fieldwork at Brighton and Hove Albion Football Club. The two key areas of study are based upon the club's Centre of Excellence and the Scholarship Scheme. This is preceded by a brief background of the club's recent history. The research covers from a broad perspective all youth players who were at the Club between 2000-03, and special attention is given to one-year group from the crucial stage of the last two years at the Centre of Excellence to the end of the first year of the Scholarship Scheme. Inevitably, whilst the research focuses upon youth team players, other issues and events that occur at the club which have both a direct and

11

indirect impact upon the young players, such as a change in personnel of the first team manager's post, are discussed.

Chapter 8 focuses on two other professional football clubs, Bristol City and Charlton Athletic, in the form of small case studies. As they are only small case studies, it is not possible to make a full comparison between the three clubs, however some similarities and differences do become apparent that generate areas of discussion.

The overall evaluations and conclusions are discussed in Chapter 9. Here reflections are made on the study, the strengths and weaknesses of the research are considered and recommendations for future research are given.

Finally, Chapter 10 considers how the structure and processes of youth systems within professional football fit within the wider context of government strategy and elite sports development of young people in this country.

CHAPTER 1
RECENT DEVELOPMENTS IN FOOTBALL APPRENTICESHIPS

In 1997, the Football Association's Technical Department, under the guidance of Howard Wilkinson (Technical Director), produced a document entitled 'Football for Young Players – A Charter for Quality'. Within this were the proposed regulations for the setting up of two types of recognised centres, Football Academies and Centres of Excellence, upon which all professional clubs would be expected to base their apprenticeship schemes around. Before discussing the structure of these centres, in order to put them into their proper context, it is worth briefly establishing why the Football Association (FA) felt it necessary to attempt to influence a change in direction of professional football at youth level.

There is little doubt that in 1994 there was a mood of despondency throughout football circles in England at the failure of national senior side to reach the World Cup finals being held in the U.S.A. Initially, under sensational tabloid newspaper headings, journalists looked for quick answers and apportioned the blame on the out-going manager, Graham Taylor. A journalist for the Daily Mirror newspaper, Nigel Clarke said (cited in Taylor and Ward 1995:349), "we (the Daily Mirror) got after him and The Sun got after him, and of course he became nationally known as 'Taylor the Turnip'". However, it was also felt, not least by leading coaches, that there may be more deeply entrenched reasons for a lack of achievement by the national side that could be found within English football. So great was the feeling, that the Professional Football Association (PFA) Management Committee set up a working party to investigate ways forward and "make recommendations to improve the provision of coaching and provision for coaches in the English professional game in an attempt to improve the level of skill, technique and game understanding amongst all English football players. (1996:7)".

The study 'A Kick in the Right Direction' covered a wide range of issues including; the national youth selection process, youth coaches, the professional game, the F.A., coaching qualifications, education and facilities. It is interesting to note that of these issues, two dealt solely with youth football whilst others (coaching qualifications and education) also broached this key area. It is clear that this working party saw the

13

development of youth football as central to footballing success in this country, and it is this area that for the football authorities has been of particular concern.

Historically, the football industry has had an unenviable reputation as one that has not looked after the young trainees hoping to enter into it. Up until the 1960's it was illegal for a club to take on any player under the age of seventeen, and so a way around this was for the club to employ boys at the age of fifteen in the capacity of, for example, 'ground-staff'. Monk and Russell (2000:64) state that,

> "It is undeniable that many clubs saw their young charges as
> a source of cheap labour for the servicing of senior players'
> equipment, the stadium and other club property. Moreover,
> no consideration was given to their educational needs which
> were only met formally by individual initiative and
> informally through the acquisition of any practical skills
> that accrued from the time spent on ground-staff
> or office duty".

In 1960 the F.A. allowed apprentice players to join a club at 15 as a trainee footballer, and in1965 a further development took place when the Football League, in an attempt to decrease exploitation of boys still at school, introduced its own rule which stated that clubs were allowed to sign players over the age of thirteen "for the purposes of training and coaching provided that priority be given to school activities". Those players under fifteen were not allowed to play for the clubs, and pupils over fifteen were only allowed to play with the headmaster's consent. Also, clubs were not allowed to put "undue pressure" on players to sign, and no registration of apprenticeship would be accepted without the agreement of both the headmaster and the local authority. In addition, during the 1960's the FA were keen for clubs to allow players time to take up educational courses during their apprenticeships, although in reality, few bothered to do so.

In 1978, the PFA established the Footballers' Further Education and Vocational Training Scheme (FFEVTS), which was set up to help both current and past players. According to Harding (cited in Monk and Russell 2000:64) this originally involved little formal education and a large amount of enforced labour. However, the situation was soon to get better with the introduction of the government's Youth Training Scheme (YTS) in 1984, which provided much needed cash into this area. This normally meant the apprentice

14

players were allowed day release to study once a week, and often it would be for example, a City and Guilds in Leisure. In1990, the YTS was replaced by Youth Training (YT), which was a two-year programme that had more of an educational bias. For this, the players would often study the General National Vocational Qualification (GNVQ) in Leisure and Tourism at either intermediate or advanced level, according to their General Certificate of Secondary Education (GCSE) results.

There was a general feeling in football circles during the nineties that more help should be given to trainees, particularly for the players that were not successful and faced being released after their trainee period. In Garry Nelson's best-selling book, 'Left Foot Forward' (1995:256), as the PFA's representative to his club Charlton Athletic in 1994, he described the limited advice was given to the young players that were to be released.

> "The PFA can give him general careers advice; can try to
> interest a (minor) club abroad in giving him a contract;
> can set up a trial game for him in front of spectating
> representatives from American colleges handing out
> scholarships. There's not much hope in that lot".

The issue of the high drop out rate within the football industry during and at the end of the trainee period is also a concern of the Football League, which stated in their annual handbook (1997:292): "Clubs should be cautious about signing players and vet much more thoroughly before doing so. Too many are disappointed at present because of the high wastage rate from signings".

As already mentioned, the PFA (1995:18) highlighted youth football as a key area for development. Amongst its concerns on this topic were that "football for the younger age groups should be limited to smaller pitches and that the ultimate aim is to reduce the age at which players can be coached at professional clubs to six years old", – an idea supported by the successful Dutch youth system. The report quoted from an interview with ex-Dutch international, Arnold Muhren in The Sunday Telegraph (21.11.93). "England don't have as many skilful players as the Dutch. That's because you don't teach the kids the basics until 12 or 13 – six years too late".

This raises a very important issue (looked at in more detail in Chapter 3) - at what age do children need to become part of the 'farm system' in order to have the best opportunity of becoming a professional footballer?

The PFA were also concerned that football within schools had not developed as much as it might, due to lack of time, lack of space available and lack of primary school teachers with sufficient knowledge or desire to adequately coach football skills. An example is used of a survey in Leicestershire, Nottingham and Derbyshire that showed that 163 unqualified parents were taking responsibility for coaching children within schools (ibid: 17).

The underlying belief of the PFA was (and probably still is), that ex-professionals should take a major role in the development of coaching children, and that these coaches should attend courses that will help them with such aspects as methods of teaching, supervisory and responsibility skills. A cynic may say that this view is founded on the PFA attempting to look after its members after they have finished their playing career, although on a more positive note, there is little doubt that ex-professionals' playing experience could be seen as irreplaceable. The PFA suggested that a specific youth coach qualification should be introduced so that specific coaches would be responsible for players aged nine to fourteen, fifteen to eighteen and a reserve coach for eighteen to twenty one. Many examples of systems similar to these ideas were cited from other countries for supporting evidence.

It seems likely that Howard Wilkinson gave the ideas of the PFA close scrutiny when devising 'A Charter for Quality'. Indeed, an F.A. spokesman from his department confirmed this (Field Notes 18/9/98) and added that a great deal of research and consultation with other bodies including the Football League, the English Schools Football Association as well as many other foreign football authorities, had taken place before the Charter was finalised.

The crucial changes that were proposed within the 'Charter for Quality' really concerned the establishment of Football Academies and Centres of Excellence. Essentially, the better youth players would be encouraged to join the Academies, and the F.A. stressed that Premier clubs would be expected to operate these. The F.A. thought that all other professional clubs, excluding those that ran an Academy, should run Centres of Excellence. Also the Associate schoolboy scheme was abolished in 1997 and this was replaced with the Academies and Centres of Excellence that were now to cater for players aged nine to twenty one.

The two main differences between the two structures are that firstly, players who attend an Academy can only play in matches organised by the F.A. against other Academies or Centres of Excellence. They are not allowed to play in any other competitive matches. On the other hand, those who attend Centre of Excellence can play for the centre, representative football, (country, county and district), as well as their school. Secondly, that an Academy has a responsibility to provide 'educational and technical programmes'. Educational provision is to be available for each academy player including primary, secondary, further and higher education. The Charter states (1997:12): "The players' technical and academic potential must be catered for and not compromised".

In reality, some non-Premier clubs set up an Academy (for example Watford), that was approved by the F.A., and it is likely that many smaller clubs would do if they had the finances to do so, but this often entails an educational centre with classrooms, and the following full time staff; a Director of Academy, two Assistant Directors, two Physiotherapists, a Doctor (on call) and an Education Welfare advisor. For a Centre of Excellence only a Director and Coaches are necessary. It should also be added that some non-professional clubs, (for example Hythe) have been able to set up Centres of Excellence.

The developments to the game that the 'Charter for Quality' brought from grassroots to the highest level followed an overall change to the FA coaching course structure in 1996. (Table 1).

The change has meant that the English FA has moved from an insular programme to one that is incorporated within a European coaching structure. In this way it is hoped that the level of coaching will be brought up to the level of the best of our European neighbours. All head coaches within academies and centres of excellences, as well as those in charge of professional youth teams are required to have the UEFA 'A' Coaching Award, and all other coaches at the clubs must have a UEFA 'B' Coaching Award.

According to Rich (2002:27), Dave Richardson, the Premier League's Director of Youth said: "Nowadays, nobody can take a youth side without qualifications, whereas a few years ago the milkman could run it".

At a lower level, successive British Governments have also supported the new initiatives brought about by the F.A. In 1996, £1 million was given to schools in the form of coaching videos and equipment through a 'Football in the Community' project. This was aimed at assisting primary schoolteachers and came as a direct response to Prime Minister John Major's 'Raising the Game' initiative (1996), which called for greater commitment to sports in schools, particularly team games. Although the purpose of this was not to cater for the elite, it was aimed at encouraging more children to take part in the

Changes in the FA coaching course structure

Level	FA Courses/awards pre 1996	FA Courses/awards pre 1996	UEFA awards
5	-	FA Coaching Diploma	UEFA 'Pro Coaching Award
4	FA Advanced Coaching Licence	FA Advanced Coaching Licence Youth/Senior Coaching	UEFA 'A' Award
3	FA Preparatory Course/ FA Intermediate Award	FA Coaching Licence UEFA 'B'	Coaching Award
2	FA Preliminary Award	FA Coaching Certificate	-
1	Football Leaders Award	FA Junior Team	-
FA Teachers Certificate	FA Teaching Certificate	Managers' Award	-

Table 1

sport, and thereby indirectly enabling them to live part of the dream of becoming a professional footballer. This was particularly enhanced with the development in the late 1980's and early 1990's of the 'Football in the Community' schemes - by now a common feature within all professional football clubs. It is now seen as regular practice for clubs to send coaches, and sometimes players, into local schools to coach.

In 1999, the FA Premiership agreed to put £50 million (5% of their revenue) into grass root football, with schools a priority. This award scheme (Slater 1999:1): "coincided with a new award scheme - the Charter Standard - to identify schools which provide high quality coaching and good facilities.

The Government and the F.A. were keen to show their commitment to increasing participation and this is highlighted by the awards only been made available to schools that could offer equal access to girls.

At the elite level, the FA in 1992 established the National School of Excellence that was based at Lilleshall, Shropshire. Seventeen boys, considered to be the best fourteen year olds age in the country, were selected to attend this boarding school. Within five years this scheme was abandoned as it was deemed unsuccessful, and figures explain the reason why. Granada Television (2001) followed the careers of the group of boys that started in 1995 and taking them as typical example, only five of the original seventeen still remained in professional football. When one considers that these were seen as the best players in the country for their age group, this could be regarded as a very low return. By 1997, the with the introduction of the F.A.'s Charter for Quality, new initiatives within the Football in the Community Scheme and increased Government involvement, professional football faced major changes. How this affected young people hoping to get into the profession is a key feature of this work.

CHAPTER 2
THE VOCATIONAL SOCIALISATION OF YOUNG PEOPLE INTO THEIR CHOSEN CAREER

On the premise that for many young people, professional football is an attractive industry to be part of, important questions arise such as what are the major influences and potential barriers that a youngster encounters in his journey towards this as a chosen career? In order to fully understand the processes involved it is necessary to look at career choice as a topic in its own right.

It is widely thought that both psychological and sociological factors play a major role in determining career choice and vocational development. Although this work is written from a social scientist's (and professional in the field's) perspective, failure to consider psychological factors would give an incomplete overview of the issues involved due to the overlapping nature of sociological factors.

Psychological factors have been a major influence on occupational choices. Related to this, one of the most established psychological concepts is trait and factor, which is based on the examination of individual differences, often referred to as differential psychology. Some of the earliest and leading proponents of this position were Paterson and Williamson in the 1960's, who between them developed aptitude tests for use in vocational guidance "and helped to establish its widespread practice" (Gothard 1985:10). It was based on the premise that an individual's traits are correlated with the requirements of certain jobs.

Rodger (1971:11) developed this general theory and applied it to vocational guidance in the UK. This was known as *The Seven Point Plan.* The seven points were; physiological make-up, attainments, general intelligence, special aptitudes, interests, disposition and circumstances.

In terms of physiological make-up, Rodger argued that some jobs require a specific body type, for example a jockey clearly needs to weigh as little as possible in order for the horse to be able to benefit in terms of its racing ability. Individuals who are considered heavy by the horse's owners would be seen as unsuitable. Other examples could include a person's appearance or speech, and factors such as these are largely judged by the values and prejudices of the employer. In this respect 'unfair' discrimination may occur.

20

In terms of attainment, Rodger (1971) argues that people are considered suitable to certain jobs because of their demonstrated academic capabilities. This is often one of the first criteria considered by potential employers, and to them, knowledge of employees' weaknesses is just as important as knowledge of their strengths.

Often linked to an individual's level of attainment is the level of their intelligence - wrongly so in many cases. Assumptions are sometimes made concerning the correlation between numbers of G.C.S.E's and grades at 'A' levels and an individual's intellect. It is conceivable that many are disadvantaged because they have under performed at examinations, and solely for this reason are not able to enter into their chosen professions. Yet the reason for them being unable to pass their 'A' levels may purely have been their inability to cope with sitting examinations. In order to overcome this problem, part of the selection process for the nursing profession includes the D.C test. The five sections in this test cover verbal, spatial, number, non-verbal and comprehension skills. According to Child (1997: 412), about a third of those who failed to attain five GCSE's at C or above succeeded at this test, thus increasing the potential entrants to nursing.

There is no doubt that certain individuals have special aptitudes in one or more areas and little in others. This need not necessarily be a problem for an individual who wishes to use his talent for a particular career. For example a writer, although being a best selling novelist, does not necessarily need a degree in English to be successful. And a successful accountant with a particular aptitude for figures need not necessarily have studied mathematics at university.

When considering the occupational 'interests' of an individual and how this may affect decisions concerning a chosen career, Super (1957:413) states that these interests can be sub-divided into four categories: expressed, inventoried, tested and manifest. With regard to expressed interest, a person is asked to name his or her choice directly, although particularly with children the choice is liable to change from time to time and is not considered very accurate. Inventoried interests are based upon comparing interests of individuals who are being assessed and those who are already successful in that career. It is thought that if an individual has similar interests then there is a good chance that he will be deemed suitable for that career. For the tested interest category, a person who is suitable is one who will already have gained some knowledge about that area, particularly

21

compared to one who knows little about it. The fourth category is manifest interest where, for example, a child has such an interest in sport that he regularly plays that particular sport - although it is accepted again by Super that this is subject to change. There are many well-established inventories that attempt to take into account an individual's disposition. The most frequently used is Cattell's 16PF (16 personality factors), (Gothard 1985) which scores individuals as a basis for occupational profiles relating to specific jobs.

The final element in Rodger's model is circumstance, in which he believes it is only by analyzing an individual's social and economic background that one can make a realistic forecast about the kind of work which might appeal to them.

Obviously, in order to draw an accurate psychological picture of the individual's possible career path a combination of all of Rodger's *Seven Point Plan* should be taken into consideration as opposed to relying too heavily on one or two of the categories.

In contrast to the trait and factor theories, Holland's work, which dates back to 1957 but still provides a common phenomenon in career practice (Arthur, Hall and Lawrence. 1989), is based on personality theories. He considers an individual to have a lifestyle that is centred upon values, interest, aptitudes, personality factors, intelligence and self-concept.

These help steer the person towards one of six possible occupational environments which he lists as realistic (for example labourer, truck driver etc.), investigatorary (anthropologist, biologist), artistic (musicians, actor), social (teacher, social worker), conventional (secretary, book keeper) and enterprising (salesman, publicity officer). Holland associates each of these occupational environments with a personality type. For example in the social category a person might be, amongst other factors, sociable, disorderly and idealistic.

In addition to the trait and factor and personality theories are developmental theories, and the most outstanding contributors, according to Child (1997:415), are Ginsberg and Super. Ginsberg et al. (1951) based their research on a small unrepresentative study that was conducted over a period of years, with a series of interviews. The conclusions were that individuals move through a series of three stages: the fantasy period, which lasts until eleven and is based on needs and impulses; the tentative period, from eleven to seventeen - based on interests, ambitions and values; and the realistic period which begins at seventeen where compromises based on reality take place.

They felt that the process of occupational choice takes place between a period of six to ten years and that the decision making process is irreversible. The actual occupational choice had the quality of compromise once reality had set in.

In 1972 Ginsberg modified the original theory with the following key points. He felt that the idea of irreversibility was incorrect, and that people try to keep their options open as long as possible - indeed the actual process of choice is life-long. Also, that in fact people do not necessarily compromise, instead they make what they see as the most of what is on offer to them.

Whilst Super (1981:25) criticised Ginsberg's theory as speculative, he did adhere to the idea that it was stimulating and that many of the ideas were worth further analysis. Super also looked at different phases of vocational development and at Ginsberg's original theory of an individual life cycle. He divided the whole of life into five major stages: growth (age 0-15), exploration (16-25), establishment (26-45), maintenance (46-64) and decline (65+).

In addition he made some major propositions which he felt were central to the theory. They are; that individual differences such as personality should be considered and that everyone has potential in a number of occupations. Every individual is more suited to certain occupations than he or she is to others, although vocational preferences change over time and adjustment is a continuous process. This process is represented in the life stages previously mentioned. Throughout the stages a career pattern is determined by external factors, such as work applications, and internal factors, for example achievements. Progress through the stages can be guided by counselling in which increased knowledge about one's own abilities and options is encouraged.

Super (1981) feels that vocational development is centred upon the implementing of a self-concept, and that is built from playing a variety of roles throughout one's career. This is done through Super (1981:14) "matching one's picture of oneself against one's picture of people in occupations that one knows and in which one is interested in". This self-development will then be influenced by the extent of approval accorded by superiors and one's own peers. The role-playing is then a comparison between one's own self-concept and the realities of external social affairs. Finally Super sees work as a way of life and the degree of satisfaction one gains from it is proportionate to the degree to which he or she has been able to implement his or her own goals.

The key to all of this is Super's argument that personal and social factors interact to form a self-concept, and that the development of them is a life long issue. It is essential for a careers counsellor to know what life stage an individual has reached in order to offer any credible advice.

Social learning theory was applied to vocational choice by Mitchell, Jones and Grumboltz (1979:24). They felt that an individual arrives at knowledge of preferred work through instrumental and associative learning experiences. Instrumental learning is when the individual sees work as either rewarding or disappointing and then reinforces an interest or lack of interest in that chosen field. In contrast associative learning occurs when an individual sees others (for example role models) being rewarded for or disenchanted with work that they do. Together these lead to self-analysis and decision making about work.

More recently Hodkinson and Sparks (1997:32) formulated what they considered to be a more updated model that attempted to blend social and cultural factors with personal choices and to merge individual preferences with opportunity structures in a form that incorporates serendipity. This is supported by Jencks *et al*, (cited in Keil1981:174) who saw "life chances as much a matter of luck, personality and on-the job competence as anything else".

Finally, another established psychological theory about the process of occupational choice is known as 'autonomy'. For this an individual is seen to have control of his or her own actions. Law (1981:334) uses a scale of autonomy where at one extreme the individual has no autonomy and at the other he or she is able to reach chosen targets. Prior to this, Roberts (1977:32) felt that individuals do not actually choose, as they are much more likely to enter into a job or profession due to factors such as availability of jobs, and the type of education they have received.

In all, psychological factors have become increasingly important (Arthur, Hall and Lawrence 1989) to careers advisors in helping youngsters determine their future. However, coupled with this is the widespread belief that sociological aspects can have just as big an influence and that the two are often intertwined.

For example, Kidd (1981:64-5) sees an individual encountering a combination of 'intentional' and 'incidental' sources of information that vary throughout a child's life. The intentional factors or influences, with specific the aim of promoting learning, include schools, for example careers officers, teachers, careers literature and also the mass media (such as the internet and newspapers) where careers literature can be found. The incidental factors, where learning about jobs is more about chance than design, are mainly centred upon the parents of the individual, and again the media where for example, television programmes and teenage magazines can individually carry an enormous influence without actually setting out to try to do so.

Clearly there is much overlap between intentional and incidental sources. For example, a parent can affect a child's perception both by directly advising or inadvertently influencing on such matters.

In a study by Taylor (1996) that was based upon a representative sample of Year 11 pupils from ten schools, there is clear evidence that schools can influence many of its pupils' choice of career. Taylor found that at least 60% of the pupils felt that they were helped by the school in learning more about jobs, school courses (for Years 12 and 13), college courses and interviews. Worryingly, the study also showed that a high percentage (28.6) felt that they had no help, and 42% said they had had no help in learning about Youth Trainee schemes.

However, Fergusson and Unwin (1996:78) feel that schools have the potential to play a major role in the decision making process. They conclude:

> "Objective differences in academic performance, academic
> preferences and social economic characterisation are
> demonstrably influential in determining outcomes; but so
> apparently are the culture of the school, its policies regarding
> staying on, perceived conditions in the labour market (informal
> as well as formal), the reputation of the local YT schemes and
> the influence of parents and peers. Schools and career staff have
> powers to affect these".

According to Morgan (2000: 217), this potential is not always realised. In a study that examined the extent of influence of people in relation to decisions about career and course choices, he found two significant patterns. Firstly, that the pupil's (aged between

25

14 and 16) own environment reflected by self, family and friends are all more influential than school-based influences, such as specialist support from careers and careers officers; secondly, that the influence of specialist help from the school decreases as the pupil gets older. Boreham & Arthur (1993:37) support these views and refer to this in terms of the pupil's 'disinterested information' whereby the pupil perceives that the influence of the school is less than that of parents and friends in helping them to make career choices. Therefore, the formal process of lessons and careers interviews within a school could obviously have an effect on career decisions made by pupils, but does not always do so. This is not to say that the school does not have an effect on a pupil's choice as many of these friends would be fellow pupils, and this furthers the argument that even indirectly, the school as an institution plays a major role.

Of course, one should not assume that the norms and values the school wishes to portray are the same as those held within various peers groups - indeed they are very often to the contrary. In a small-scale but classically ethnographic study of a Midlands secondary school, Willis (1977) looked at what he saw as two different groups of pupils; the 'ear 'oles' who accepted the authority of the school and the 'lads' who rejected it. Willis used participant observation techniques to gain an insight into the subjective world of the group which consisted of the twelve 'lads'.

He concluded that cultural influences within the school reflected society at large – essentially the differences between the skilled and unskilled. The 'lads' through perceived expressions of masculinity sought to defy authority, as a form of escapism from their 'oppressors'. Willis's study, which was based upon social-class cultural reproduction, concluded that the conservative nature of the school system only reinforced class division and that working class boys end up in working class jobs partly because of this. Hence when choosing a job, they were far more likely to be influenced by the leaders of their group, than by teachers within the school.

However according to Taylor's study, far more students felt that they received more valuable advice from their own family (65%) than their friends (18%),(although the study fails to state whether the subjects acted upon this advice). Many believe (Willis (1977), Halsey (1981), Gothard (1985), Cole (1989)), that family background and socio economic class have even more of an effect on choice of career then the education system.

26

Gain and George (1998:35) make the point that Britain's class system has changed significantly over the past thirty years, due to a number of factors including the disappearance of working class communities around traditional industries, the appearance of greater social mobility, and the overall rise in living standards. In addition, classification of social class is often arrived at by using the father's occupation as the sole factor. In times where occupation of both parents plays an important role, and where there in an ever increasing number of children living with the mother only, this type of classification becomes less and less appropriate.

Although this change has taken place, Gain and George state that (1998:35):

> "many working class parents will want a wider range of
> opportunities for their children than they have experienced
> themselves, many will socialise their children into the world they
> know (just like middle-class parents do) and many inculcate
> attitudes of short-termism and relatively restrictive horizons".

Indeed there is much empirical material to support Gain and George's conclusions, one of the most well known being Halsey's study (1980) of social mobility. Results from this showed that when analysing class of origin, based on a father's occupation and the class of destination of an individual, more than half of the middle class sons resumed that social status, whereas only one in nine working class sons moved up into the middle class.

Other sections of our society that are often seen as having less opportunity than others in the work place are minority ethnic groups (all those other then white). Jones (1997) states that there is an increasing disparity between the circumstances in specific groups. Therefore if one is to accept this argument it is difficult to make broad assumptions about ethnic groups and prospects of employment. Take for example the South Asian population which, according to Jones, has the most (African, Asian and Indian) and least (Pakistani and Bangladeshi) successful of ethnic minority groups he studied.

The Afro Caribbean population tends to fall into a position somewhere between the two extremes, whereas the Chinese appear to be in a similar position to the African-Asians and the Indians. The lower end of Jones's scale would be those people who are unemployed and without formal qualifications, whereas at the other end groups would have high proportions of well qualified people comparable to whites. Many reasons have

27

been offered as to why some ethnic groups do not in proportion fill managerial posts, for example poor self-image, poor provision of education facilities and lack of job opportunities in inner cities. However, there is no doubt that the problem is complex. Kowalozewski (1982:52) stated that research has been:

"contradictory, unclear, without any systematic study of factors
such as the selective and classificatory processes, teachers'
attitudes to race and colour, school ethos, or any explanation as
to why a number of ethnic minority children are not
underachieving or attaining relatively high results".

In support of this view, Jones (1997:247) concludes that "varied findings are open to alternative interpretations" and that further research is needed.

In addition to individual psychological and sociological influences there are also economic and political factors. In the 1930's, industrial economies based on 'Fordism' had a considerable effect on the nature of peoples working lives and the possibilities that were open to them. The term 'Fordism' comes from the American giant car company and, according to Newman and Williams (1995:109), it has principles based upon mass production, mass markets, a mass labour force and functional specialization. This meant very distinct divisions of labour for the workforce whose work was characterised by a semi-automatic assembly line.

Today, the UK economy can be considered to be in a phase known as production methods, niche markets, a flexible labour force and multi-skilling. According to Newman and Williams (ibid) the effect post-Fordism has had on the modern day workforce is quite considerable. The idea that an individual has to be flexible implies that he has to be able to respond to the markets demands that may mean being able to adapt skills and knowledge and even career. Hodkinson and Sparkes (1997) see this as a transfer of the concept of 'career for life' to 'careership', in which decision-making and a flexible approach are ongoing.

From a political perspective, Hodkinson, Sparkes and Hodkinson (1996:9) believe that post-Fordist beliefs form an integral part of Vocational Education Training (VET) in Britain, which was widely accepted by the government and main opposition party of the day (the mid-1990's), as well as by the Confederation of British Industry (CBI) and the Trades Union Congress (TUC). They add that post-Fordist enthusiasts often over simplify the nature and extent of changes from Fordism stating that in today's society, there is no clear-cut division between the two.

Kenway (1993:115) sees the post-Fordism influence as having negative implications upon our society. She sees (ibid: 119) post- modernity, which is linked to globalisation and multi-national companies as helping to "shape and reshape our individual and collective identities as we plug in at various points to their cultural and economic networks".

Whitty, Power and Halpin (1998:42) sympathise with the view that the push for the change and diversity that is taking place is causing problems, particularly within education, where there are more being created than are being solved, stating that in schools, "there is growing empirical evidence that rather than benefiting the disadvantaged, the emphasis on parental choice and school autonomy is further disadvantaging the least able to compete in the market".

Whatever the views on globalisation and the effects that it has upon our society, the Government strives to keep pace with the changes it brings. The Department for Education and Employment (DfEE) (1999:1) states that "We live in a world of unprecedented competitive challenge....Our national competitiveness and future prosperity depends on us having a highly flexible and motivated workforce capable of meeting that challenge".

This leaves the student embarking upon a new career faced with the prospect of having to be multi-skilled and able to change careers if necessary. This therefore complicates the overall picture when trying to establish the vocational socialisation of young people into their chosen career, when a single career choice may not be sufficient for the twenty first century. This is particularly relevant for a young footballer attempting to enter (or already entered into) professional football, as the career span in this field normally lasts less than twenty years, as will be discussed later.

Overall, it is clear that influences on occupational choice from both a psychological and sociological view are quite complex, and the impact of all of the factors discussed will vary according to the individual. Trait and factor, personality and developmental theories all play a significant part in helping to understand individual choice, and all of these areas are constantly evolving based upon new research. The important issue, conclude Arthur, Hall and Lawrence (1989:20), is that one should be aware that career theory "will always be engaged on a struggle of viewpoints" and that "only the spirit behind the development of career theory can remain constant".

Knowledge of these theories as well as an awareness of the sociological influences (class, education, ethnicity and political climate*), will all assist theorists and practitioners in helping to understand the whole process of career choice.

*Footnote. The issue of gender as a sociological influence as a choice of career has been omitted because of the lack of relevance of this issue in professional football in this country

CHAPTER 3
PSYCHOLOGICAL AND SOCIOLOGICAL FACTORS THAT
CAN AFFECT AN ASPIRING ELITE PERFORMER

Many of the influences and barriers that a youngster faces when choosing a career, as discussed in the previous chapter, are also at the forefront as deciding factors when assessing the likelihood of a career in sport as an elite performer. These can be divided into three types: psychological, social psychological and sociological. The key areas within these types can be shown in diagrammatic form (Figure 2).

3.1 Psychological Aspects

Psychologists have written much about the measurement of personality and performance and to a similar extent, sociologists have analysed the potential problems elite sporting individuals face with factors such as gender, class and race. Analysis of both psychological and sociological factors is necessary in order to gain a complete perspective on the processes and problems a potential elite performer goes through in order to reach and survive at the very top level.

Attempting to match personality and physical activity is not a new area of research. Sheldon and Stevens (1942) developed a widely recognised system for assessing body build or somatatype. This involves rating a person's physique alongside the three somatatypes of ectomorph, endomorph and mesomorph, with personality type. They saw ectomorphs (linearity) as tense and introverted, endomorphs (roundness) as sociable and affectionate and mesomorphs (muscular) as risk takers and adventure seekers. In the past this theory "attracted several sport and physical educational researchers" (Gill 1996:25), although in more recent times few contemporary personality psychologists adhere to this view as subsequent research failed to confirm his findings.

In 1973, Hardman looked at twenty seven studies conducted between 1952 –68 which had been based on sportsmen using a Cattell's 16PF personality test. From these he concluded that participation in sport was associated with high intelligence, instability, assertiveness, enthusiasm, low super ego, strength, shyness, suspiciousness and tension, and was also associated with low anxiety and independence. Further to this, Morgan (1980:66) stated "research reviewed in this section shows that athletes differ from non-

Factors that can affect an aspiring elite performer

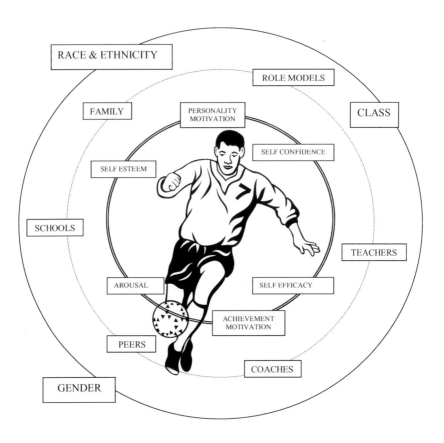

RACE & ETHNICITY

ROLE MODELS

FAMILY

CLASS

PERSONALITY
MOTIVATION

SELF CONFIDENCE

SELF ESTEEM

SCHOOLS

TEACHERS

AROUSAL

SELF EFFICACY

ACHIEVEMENT
MOTIVATION

PEERS

COACHES

GENDER

═══ Psychological   ·········· Socio-psychological   ——— Sociological

Figure 2

athletes on a variety of psychological states and traits, and these differences become most noticeable when the elite performer is considered".

However, Bull (1998) claims that in spite of trait theory tests being generally valid and reliable, they do not appear to predict behaviour consistently. An example of this may be a sports performer being assertive in some situations but shy in others. The main problem with trait theories, according to their critics, is that they do not take into account that we learn from our environment. It is therefore seen as too simplistic despite the fact that the strength of this theory is that it allows at least on the surface objective measurement of personality through inventories. Morris (1995:23) disputes the relevance of trait theories when he states: "The attempt to explain sports behaviour on the basis of traits alone has devoured vast amounts of research energy for little in the way of outcome".

In contrast to the trait theories are the social learning theories – which are also based upon behaviour and personality. Bandura (1977) acknowledges the role of personality in behaviour in that an individual arrives at situations with preconceptions. However, he also claims that people learn to deal with situations by observing others. In this way social approval or disapproval reinforces our responses to the way an individual behaves, thus lessening the importance played by personality. One could argue that the stronger the personality, the less likely this is to happen. Skinner's theory on 'behaviourism' discounts personality altogether. For example, a sports performer will act in an assertive manner, because that is what is expected of him in that situation.

Over recent years, according to Bull (1998), most sport psychologists have moved away from the idea that traits are the sole determinants of behaviour, likewise that social theories are not the only factors. Instead, more widespread beliefs today are centred upon the interactionist approach. In simple terms, this is formularised into B=f(P,E), where behaviour is equal to the function of personality and the environment. An example of this may be a sportsman who is anxious about highly competitive situations and consistently under-performs but is normally a very confident and successful individual. There are numerous possibilities as to why this may be the case, but based upon the interactionist approach it is likely to be a combination of personality and the situation that the individual is placed in, not solely one or the other.

Many researchers have attempted to answer whether there is an athletic type, in other words, do their personalities differ from a non-athletic type? Is one of the 'gateways' to becoming a top performer based upon a specific type of personality? Gill (1996) describes this area as one of the most popular areas in sports psychological research. As far back as the 1920's Griffith (cited in Gill) examined the personality profiles of successful USA college and professional sportsmen. He observed that they had "ruggedness, courage, intelligence, exuberance, buoyance, emotional adjustment, optimism, conscientiousness, alertness, loyalty, and respect of authority."(Gill 1996:31) However, Gill casts doubt on the legitimacy of Griffith's work by stating that (ibid), "Griffith's list was more of a global observation than a scientifically derived conclusion". In more recent times, Bull (1998:316) concludes that, "what does seem to emerge is that both male and female sports people have traits of extroversion, dominance, enthusiasm, confidence, aggression and high activity levels".

This conclusion is based upon the work of Butt (1997) who according to Bull "reviewed a great wealth of variety and data". (Ibid: 316)

To support this general view, Cooper (1969) described a sportsman as being more confident competitive and socially outgoing, and Kane (1976) and Morgan (1980) conclude that a sportsman is likely to be an extrovert and less anxious.

However, there are numerous problems concerned in particular with making such generalisations about the personalities of elite sportspeople. For example, what is the definition of an elite sportsperson? Is there a tendency for personalities to differ according to the sports they play or the position they play in? Does personality change as a result of participating in and/or being successful in sport or is it a certain prerequisite to regular participation or success?

In answer to the first question, Cox (1994:34) sees lack of consistency in defining categories of people as a major obstacle when attempting to use this area of research. He goes on to say: "Until some unifying system is adopted, it will always be difficult to compare results from one study with those of another".

Therefore, definitions of sportsmen or non-sportsmen and elite performers (do they play for club or country?) remains at the discretion of the researcher.

Many studies have attempted to compare personality types from different sports. Kroll and Crenshaw (cited in Cox 1994) concluded that wrestlers and American footballers had similar profiles whilst karate specialists and gymnasts differed from each other as well as wrestlers and footballers. Schurr, Ashley and Joy (1977) found that team players were

34

more likely to be anxious, dependent and extrovert, but less sensitive and imaginative than individual sports players. Clingham and Hilliard (1987) concluded that super adherers (runners, swimmers, cyclists – those who were dedicated to endurance events), differ greatly from the population norm in personality traits of, for example, achievement, dominance, harm avoidance and play.

Despite all of this evidence many current sports psychologists (Cox 1996, Gill 1996, Bull 1998), are keenly aware that it is difficult to categorise sportspeople according to their sports on the basis of personality profiles. Gill (1996: 36) concludes: "Coaches and others working with sports participants can probably learn more about individual differences through observations and talking with participants than through existing personality profiles".

The final question of whether personality changes as a result of participating in sport in itself possibly poses as many questions as it gives answers. Folkin and Sime (1981), having reviewed this area of research, conclude that participation in general sports activities does not affect personalities, whereas those sports that involve vigorous activity do have positive effect with regard to mood, self concept and general mental health. However, according to Gill (1996), even among those researchers who argue that exercise and fitness may improve mental health, relatively few agree on an explanation, their many attempts, ranging from the suggestion that the chemical release of endorphins account for some psychological change, to the belief that exercise increases an individual's sense of control.

Perhaps from the point of view of a social learning theorist, an individual's personality may be affected by the expectation of others towards him whilst taking part in sport, or at least affected by what he perceives his role should be. For example, an aspiring young sportsman may well respond to aggression from an opponent with aggression of his own if persuaded to do so by his peers. If faced with a similar situation in the future, would he see that as being the correct response and hence become part of his personality? Clearly this could be different for each individual, for whilst one person may repeat this response on such future occasions as he sees that this is what he thinks is expected of him, another may bitterly regret his initial response.

Another area of psychological research that is thought to have implications for one's suitability towards achieving success at sports is motivation, and of course this in itself is linked to personality. Gill (1986) sees motivation being made up of two components: firstly, intensity of behaviour, often referred to as arousal, and secondly, direction of behaviour, for example, self-concept and self-esteem.

Arousal, which is a state of mental and physical preparedness for action, can either enhance or inhibit performance. The drive theory proposes that an expert performer plays better as arousal increases, which for example could due to playing in front of large crowds. Whereas a novice, who has not yet perfected technique, is more likely to make mistakes in the presence of a crowd than he would do when performing with no onlookers. Further to this there is the inverted-U theory, which states that there is an optimal arousal level for all – although this varies according to the individual. If an individual becomes over aroused then the performance will suffer. Clearly these as with many theories are very generalised, as they do not take into account those, who regardless of ability thrive upon attention. Neither do they take into account the variation that may occur according to the requirements of each sport that is being played. Oxendine (1970) attempted to solve this particular problem by determining the optimal arousal levels of various sports tasks. He stated that for tasks such as those involving strength, endurance and speed, a high level of arousal is required in order to perform at a maximum level. On the other hand the same level of arousal is detrimental to performance involving complex skills, coordination, steadiness and general concentration. And for all motor skills a slightly above average level of arousal is preferable.

Oxendine's research has been criticised by Landers (1978) on the basis of lacking existing research and Gill (1996) supports this view, concluding that as we cannot predict precise optimal arousal levels for each performer and each task, performers are better spending their time concentrating on performing to the arousal level that is best for them. A useful method for attempting to ensure that one does not exceed the optimum arousal level is to apply stress management. The procedure chosen should be suitable for the individual where stress does not inhibit performance.

The motivation of an individual can be affected by self-concept and self-esteem in the following ways. If an individual deems himself as having the necessary physical attributes and ability (self-concept) as well as valuing himself, particularly in this context (self-esteem), then the likelihood is that his motivation to do well will be higher than that of a person who has low self concept and low self esteem, despite being of similar ability.

Butt (1997) claims that different levels of self-esteem can have a direct effect on personality profile, for example people with high self-esteem are often optimistic and enjoy challenges whereas people with low self-esteem tend to lack confidence and be to be self-protective.

The level of self-confidence and self-efficacy can have a direct result on one's performance in sport. Weinburg and Gould (1995) considered confidence as a major factor in arousing emotion, enhancing concentration, positively affecting goal setting, increasing effort and enhancing psychological momentum. Obviously, excessiveness can have a detrimental effect on performance if it leads to over-confidence. However, so important is self-confidence to a successful participant, that Gill (1996) sees it as possibly the most critical cognitive factor in sport. She goes on to state (1996:155) that "research indicates that the most consistent difference between elite and the less successful athletes is that elite athletes profess greater confidence."

Indeed a low level of confidence can also be linked to competitive stress and anxiety. Jones (1998:43) claims that anecdotal reports strongly suggest that "a high level of cognitive anxiety is associated with a low level of self-confidence in competition." Clearly this is something that should be avoided by elite performers.

Of course, the coach or teacher can have a significant effect on the confidence of an individual and this may lead to a self-fulfilling prophecy – which means "expecting something to happen actually causes it to happen". (Weinburg and Gould 1995:301). Martens (1987:153) explains that a negative spiral can ensue whereby low expectation leads to failure which in turn leads to diffidence. This cycle can repeat itself – all of which leads to low levels of performance. Clearly, a positive self-fulfilling prophecy can work in complete reverse to this downwards spiral, and Martens (ibid.) describes how athletes can work this to their advantage.

Childs (2004) discusses the process in which a child performs to the level he or she envisages that the teacher expects them to perform. There are links here with relationships between the child and teacher, and the performer and coach. For an aspiring elite sportsman, being 'labelled' by a coach in a positive or negative way, is likely to have a profound effect on their motivation and overall performance.

Another aspect of motivation that is considered to be of major importance in the search for success is termed 'achievement motivation'. Atkinson (1974), a leading theorist in

37

this area, put forward a theory which targeted two areas for consideration; the need to achieve (Nach) and the need avoid failure (Naf). He concluded that high achievers had a greater motivation to succeed and in turn a higher tendency to achieve, whereas low achievers have a tendency to avoid situations which can result in failure as perceived by themselves or others.

According to Gill (1996), achievement motivation measures are often used alongside trait anxiety measures. In these cases individuals who score high on the achievement measure and low on the anxiety scale are not surprisingly high achievers, whereas the opposite for both is found for low achievers.

Forzoni (2001(a) and 2001(b)) analyses the role of intrinsic motivation in football whereby a high level of one's own will to win is an essential element for success at an elite level and reliance upon extrinsic factors, such as pleasing parents or coaches and winning medals, is much less likely. He develops this theme by explaining the Cognitive Evaluation Theory and stating that (2001(b): 31) "players have an innate need to feel personally competent and self-determining". Elite players have a strong need to demonstrate their own ability and also choose to set themselves difficult and demanding goals. A good coach can obviously help to develop a young player's confidence through appropriate target setting.

Overall, from a psychological perspective, despite all of the research that has been done, it is difficult to make any assumptions about what aspects of personality an aspiring sportsman possesses, and there appears to be no conclusive evidence that there is a particular sporting personality type. (Although many researches would argue, particularly those from the social learning and interactionist schools of thought, that there is no substitute for experience of dealing with situations within the chosen sport.) Sanderson (1996:277) writes that: "There are no are no identified personality profile patterns which are a prerequisite for successful participation in sport in general and soccer in particular, even at the highest levels".

However, Priestley, Richardson and Eubank (2002:49) in their research based upon the psychological characteristics and development of player's within Premiership academies, claim that the players' interviews highlighted "some psychological characteristics essential for elite performance". To support this view, some professionals within football would argue that aspects of personality are considered desirable in the pursuit of success at high-level sport. For example, Colin Murphy, (Chief Scout for the Football Association) states (2001:55) that when identifying young talent, the key areas to consider are: confidence, composure, concentration, ability to be tough minded and enthusiasm.

The important issue here is that not only is there disagreement within academic circles, but that practitioners are applying their own judgements upon the psychological profile of players in order to find elite performers.

A final point worth considering here is that there is insufficient research to date to indicate whether an elite performer's personality changes significantly as a result of success in sport, or whether success in sport instigated the significant change. Clearly, there are a lot of unanswered questions in this area.

3.2 Social Psychological Aspects

As with any member of society, no aspiring elite performer develops in total isolation without any external influences. Carron (1981) describes the subject of social psychology as being centred upon an individual as a participant within a social situation and also upon the influences of the underlying processes that occur within that situation. For example, with regard to sport, how the individual relates to the presence of team -mates, competitors, crowds officials and spectators.

Byrne (1999) sees the child surrounded by a 'circle of influences', for example parents, coaches and teachers, all of whom may have a bearing on their choice and relative level of success at sport. It is the relationships with these groups that help provide an insight into the child's sporting development.

Hellstad (1987) argues that parent's level of involvement in their child's sporting activities can be divided into three categories: under-involvement, (which includes uninterested or misinformed parents), moderate involvement, (which Hellstad describes as the 'comfort zone'), and over-involvement, (which includes the excitable and fanatical parent). From these categories, it is clear that under-involved and over-involved parents are more likely to have in their own way an adverse affect on the child's progress in sport and that according to Hellstad the ideal level of parental involvement would be moderate. Of course, the involvement of a parent may change significantly as the child becomes older and Coté (1999) saw the committed parent changing from a leadership role during what he described as the 'sampling years' (6-13), through to follower and supporter in the 'investment years' (15-18). During the 'sampling years', the parent would try to provide opportunities to enjoy sport, whereas in the 'investment years', parents are keen to help their offspring fight any setbacks and also offer moral support. In between these two stages, the 'specialising years', (13-15) the parent develops a commitment to the child's interest in a limited number of sports. Clearly, for optimal performance for an aspiring elite sportsman, all of these stages would take place for parents situated in what Hellstad termed the 'comfort zone'.

Research has also shown (Scanlan and Lewthwaite (1986), Brustad (1988) and Scanlan, Stein & Ravizza (1989), that there is a likelihood that children will have positive outcomes within sport, for example enjoyment, if parents show their approval. Byrne (1999:46) view this from another perspective, as he states that: "Youth sports participation can provide parents and their children with common interests. It can also lead to tensions between them".

Indeed, McGuire and Cook (1983) go further by stating that those who are forced to play sport by their parents are more likely to give up at an early age. They based their conclusion on a study ("The influence of others and the decision to participate in youth sports") that looked at the responses of youth sports participants aged between 10 and 13. In addition to the role that parents can influence performance, other significant adults can also include coaches. Smith and Smoll (1995:125) state that: "Coaches influence the effects that youth sport participation has on children through the inter-personal behaviours they engage in, the value and attitudes they transmit both verbally and through example, and the goal priorities they establish (for example, winning versus equal participation and fun)".

They go on to say that because many youth coaches are volunteers and therefore amateurs, very often the influences they have on the children are inappropriate. The reason for this is that the mass media often portray professional coaches as having a win-at-all costs attitude, and they base successful coaching on this model.

To a similar degree much has been written about the role peer groups can play in affecting the involvement of youngsters in sport, although this was a factor strangely missing from Byrne's 'circle of influences'. Smith (1999:346), when researching the perceptions of peer relationships and physical activity participation in children found that: "Early adolescence is a developmental period in which important decisions are made about health behaviours. The findings of this study suggest that perceptions of both friendship and peer acceptance in physical activity settings can contribute to the formation of physical activity attitudes in the behaviour of young adolescents".

In support of this research, Brustad (1996) claims that there is a transfer at about the age of 10 for children to change from their preference to rely on adult feedback on their physical competence to feedback provided by their peers. Brustad (ibid) also claims that research has shown that sports ability is an important contributor to social status and peer acceptance for children and adolescents, thus making the playing of sport that much more attractive. The relevance to an aspiring performer is that it will give them more incentive to remain one of the elite. However, it is widely shown (Alder et al., 1992, Chase & Dummer, 1992, Eder & Parker, 1987) that it is boys rather than girls that link high social status with sport, as girls often regard physical appearance as the major factor.

Cratty (1981:35) emphasises the effects older people have upon children and this is obviously a much wider field than sport: "Younger children usually find themselves in an environment containing powerful figures who almost completely dominate their every move and thought".

Of course the older people within the immediate family may not just be confined to parents, as an individual may well have older brothers and sisters. This highlights another field of study – does the birth order of siblings affect the sport chosen for participation, and can it have an influence upon chances of success?

Attempts have been made, Wilson and Edington (1981) and Dunn (1984), to classify the affects birth order can have upon the personality of an individual, and Cratty (1981:47) believes that birth order can play a part in the type of sport chosen: "In most studies (…) first borns are seen to be as likely participants in sports in general as are late borns. The differences seem to lie in just what sport is chosen. The first-born, perhaps over protected, fearing failure because of achievement related child-rearing behaviours, is less likely to risk either failure or injury in sports".

Lewko and Greendorfer (1988:292) state that parents have more influence upon the sports socialisation of a child than the siblings, although they do point to the lack of research done on the influence of siblings. They conclude that older siblings are also "subordinate to the power of adults" and although they may have some influence in their

41

own right, often it is '"monitored and defined in part by their parents". Following on from this line of thought, it would seem that siblings do not necessarily have a major role in the sports socialisation of each other, although it would be wrong to totally disregard as a possibility.

Overall, the youngster's self perception will be affected by feedback and reinforcement from significant adults and peers in response to performance, and this could lead to further success in sport or to ultimately choosing not to participate.

Recent research, Helsen, Williams, Van Winckel and Ward (2003) and Simmons (2002a), has suggested that within youth systems in English professional football, boys born in the earlier months of the academic year have a significant advantage over those from the same age group born in the latter months. Further, that this does not just occur in England but also in the nine other European countries they researched (all leading football nations). According to Helsen, Williams, Van Winckel and Ward (2003) their research has shown that is also the case in other professional sports such as baseball, cricket and ice hockey. They state that there are a few possible explanations for this, the most important being the apparent variance in physique between the older and younger children. From a psychological perspective, they think it is likely that older players will experience success earlier on than younger ones and therefore the latter may suffer from lack of motivation due to difficulty in achieving initial success. They also claim that older boys may have practiced up to 700 hours more than those born earlier in the year and therefore been at a distinct advantage.

Simmons's (2002(b): 31) research, which looked at boys aged between 9 and 16 involved with professional clubs, supported this view. He states that "Statistics for players in professional and grass roots clubs show an obvious bias towards birthdays in the September to December third of the year", a point also raised by Paull (1999) and Paull and Simmons (1999). He strengthens this by arguing that general population births within this country show no evidence of bias towards any given period.

The conclusion to this must be that professional football in this and other European countries loses young talented players to the game purely due to their date of birth. A player born on the last day of the academic year (31st August) will have much less chance of becoming a footballer than one born on the first day of the next (1st September). This is a factor that is not confined to young footballers as Simmons cites research (Bell and

42

Daniels 1990, Hauck and Finch 1993, Sharp et al 1994, Sharp and Benefield 1995, and Sharp 1995) that has shown (2002:31) "the eldest achieve better results within a year group when compared to the youngest children."

3.3 Sociological Aspects

As the title of this book suggests, the main thrust of this research is related to sociological issues. Some of the most crucial of these with regard to professional football are; habitus, social class, masculinity and racism. In addition, other issues (religion and schooling) are briefly discussed in the latter part of this section.

3.3.1 Habitus and sport

Bourdieu (1986) argues that the main factors governing an individual's choice of sport are based upon social reasons. The choice is initiated at an early childhood stage and is influenced by habitus – a combination for example of the individual's attitudes, tastes, preferences in sport and all other aspects and influences of cultural participation and consumption. A key question here is how is this choice formulated?

Bourdieu (1995:130) sees choice and 'transformation of sporting practices and consumption' being related to changes in supply and demand. The suppliers are seen as; the organisers and governing bodies of the sport, the producers and vendors of the sport (for example the equipment and special clothing), and those involved in the services required in order to pursue the sport (for example the teachers and coaches). He goes on to state that changes in the supply arise through competition; between sports and within each sport, between established and new sports and also between the categories of agents involved, including teachers, coaches and equipment manufacturers.

Bourdieu (ibid.) highlights the transformation of lifestyles as one aspect of the change in demand for sport. He argues that the suppliers have the power 'to produce or impose new practices or even new forms of old practices' upon the public at large.

From this, the individual makes his own evaluations, tastes and preferences towards activities, although these are developed upon what is available to him. For Bourdieu, to state that an explanation of differential participation in sport is related to how expensive the sport is would be far too simplistic – and this is discussed further in this next section.

3.3.2 Social class and sport

In many ways, social stratification has been closely linked to sport throughout modern history. Throughout the nineteenth century through to the present time, the type of sport played has been strongly linked to the social background of the participants. According to Polley (1998:111), the limitation of leisure activities and sport "has historically been constrained by time, space and disposable income, all of which are variable across class lines". Further to this, these limitations have been far more acute for the working classes and many sports have been associated with certain groups. Obvious examples would be football, rugby union and polo for the working, middle and upper classes respectively. Bourdieu (1985) argues that the main factors governing an individual's choice of sport are based upon social reasons. This choice is initiated at an early childhood stage and is influenced by habitus - a combination for example of the individual's attitudes, tastes, preferences in sport and all other aspects and influences of cultural participation and consumption. From this standpoint, the individual makes his own evaluations, tastes and preferences towards activities, although these are developed upon what is available to them. (Shilling1993). For Bourdieu, to state that an explanation of differential participation in sport is related to how expensive the sport is would be far too simplistic – and there are many examples of sports and recreational activities that would support this view.

Take for instance rambling, which can be considered a middle class activity and yet is comparatively inexpensive to take part in. To Bourdieu it is more to do with the different classes' perception of costs, (economic, cultural and physical) and benefits attached to different sports. For costs, he sees economic and cultural benefits as association of a sport within a particular class grouping – for example, golf and the middle class and access to socially exclusive groups. Physical benefits might be the visual effect one could get from changes in personal appearance through participation in activities such as use of the gymnasium. Here Bourdieu differentiates between the middle classes (and working class women) who use the gymnasium for fitness and suppleness and working class men who use it solely for muscular strength that leads to visible signs of masculinity.

A further point by Bourdieu worth mentioning is that he sees popular team sports as being more accessible to all classes than individual sports, as they require bodily and cultural competences that can be fairly easily acquired. He argues that many individual sports involve a high investment of time and early learning – as well as often taking place in exclusive venues, which disadvantages the working classes. His work is used and applied further in forthcoming chapters.

When considering the position of an aspiring elite performer of a popular team game, one can take for granted that the individual has already acquired the necessary bodily and perhaps cultural competences. In other words, they may already have reached the stage where people are describing them as talented. Also, even though many of the people that hold most power within the game are from the higher social categories, it seems unlikely that young people, once they have reached a certain level of performance and have acquired the habitus of a professional footballer, are disadvantaged due to social status – certainly as far as player status is concerned.

Ironically, the most popular reference to social class difficulties in top level football has been about those players who are considered either by themselves or by others, to have come from a middle class or superior educational background. Viner (2000), in an article entitled 'Outcasts who only want to be liked', discusses the problems faced by past footballers and even present, such as English international Graeme Le Saux, who have faced ridicule by their team mates for their comparatively successful educational background. Although it is true that Le Saux played at international level and therefore cannot been disadvantaged too much, it does not necessarily follow that people from all social backgrounds are readily accepted into the game at professional level. Indeed, Parker, when discussing how values are installed to young aspiring footballers within professional clubs, states (2001:61) that they "strongly reflect a masculine working class legacy which has come to shape the historical contours of professional football".

3.3.3 Parker, masculinity and sport

At the heart of the habitus of football then, is a deeply rooted masculinist culture, in which a traditional notion of masculinity is celebrated. Parker (1996:198) found the professional football club he researched a "strictly gendered affair. Its relational dynamics, its working practices, its commercial ventures, its promotional interests are replete with images of maleness". He also describes (ibid.) how "manliness was cultivated" within the workplace environment of the club and how the "issues of consumption and personal identity dominated masculine concern".

For him, the club officials were instrumental in promoting the social expectations of the male culture. The lifestyle expected of the professional footballer according to Parker included (1996:232) "sexual endeavour, conspicuous consumption and socializing". For an individual to fail to live up to these expectations would clearly leave him in a disadvantaged position. To support this, the sad experiences in professional football of the late Justin Fashanu in which his own manager, Brian Clough, ostracized him for being gay are well documented

Indeed, Parker's found the term 'homosexuality' a problematic notion for the trainees to accept and that heterosexuality and homophobia were key aspects of 'masculine construction' at the club. He states (1996:229): "Males failing to enact the basic physical and verbal masculine expectations of footballing life – excessive drinking, sporting prowess and the vehement pursuit of women and sex –necessarily received a barrage of criticism as regards their 'queer bastard' potential".

One of the underlying themes within this work is to establish how much of a role, if at all, the masculine culture within the youth system at a professional football club still plays.

3.3.4 Racism and sport

This ranges from 'stacking', (the disproportional (under) representation of ethnic minorities in certain positions in a team), lack of opportunity to participate or progress in a sport, to open personal abuse between players and from spectators to players of an ethnic minority background. Long and Spracklen (1996), in a study which looked at racial stereotyping in rugby league, identified players who had given up because it was not worth the 'aggro' caused by encountering and having to deal with racism. Significantly, all of the black players in their study, as well as some of the white players, were aware of racist abuse coming from opposition players in order to put players off their game.

In an article, 'Racism in football: A victim's perspective', Moran (2000:190) an ex-professional footballer cites some defining moments in his professional football career that made him 'quit the game' – all of which involved racial abuse directed at him from his own various managers. He emphasises (2000:194) that there is little value in a player being told to 'rise above' it by various well-meaning individuals. He states (2000:194) that, "surely, facing up to racism is the best way to counter it, rather than doing nothing by subscribing to an ill-defined and vague notion of 'rising above' it".

Moran goes on to describe numerous incidents of racism that were reported in the national press in the late 1990's, all of which would make depressing reading for an aspiring elite performer who is non-Caucasian.

In a recent article by Burt (2003), professional black players spanning six decades are asked about their experiences concerning racism within the game. The players spanning from the 1950-80's tell of stories and incidents that relate closely to those told by Moran. However, Robbie Earle who played throughout the nineties sees racism in football as being subtler since those days, citing the fact that there are so few black people in positions of authority and management. Joel McAnuff, a current player for Wimbledon, describes a more positive experience stating that (2003:5): "To be honest, there is not a lot of racism now on the terraces and any abuse you get from the fans does not tend to be about your colour. I've been subject to racist abuse only once in five years, when I was in the youth team".

A lot of recent literature has also concentrated upon the problems faced by Asians, which seem to mirror those faced by black players. Further to this, they also face the additional problems that blacks were facing up to until early 1990's. Chaudhary (1994) claimed that there were only sixty Asian footballers playing in semi-professional or high level amateur teams and just six professional apprentices during the 1993-4 season. This compared to black players who made up 20% of the two thousand professionals playing at the time in the English Premier and Football League. This number is still on the increase as in 1997-8 the number had risen to 25%. Yet the number of Asian players has barely increased since the early 1990's. Brown (1997:80) attempts to explain this: "Too many football club scouts and officials believe Asians don't or can't play, claiming it's not in their culture; that their parents put them off and push them into academia or the family business that they eat the wrong foods and don't have the hunger".

In addition to the racial bigotry some players may face from the clubs, officials and supporters, Parker (1996:229) found that in the minds of the white trainees, "boys of alternative ethnicities appeared to be regarded as some kind of masculine threat who irritated the trainees by the way in which they adopted a casual laid-back lifestyle demeanour and communicated more effectively with a range of female students".

47

Steps to eradicate racism in sport have been taken by the Government by way of laws on discrimination including the power of arrest and prosecution to the police for any spectator using racial abuse. Also, over recent years there have been a number of initiatives and campaigns to deal with this issue. For example, the Commission for Racial Equality's 'Let's Kick Racism Out of Football' campaign (1993), the Football Task Force's report 'Eliminating Racism from Football' (1998) and by a new independent organisation, 'Kick it Out (1999).

These developments should give some hope for the next generation of potential non-white professional footballers, although as Moran (2000:199) states, "there is still much work to be done, both in and out of sport, before it can be said to have been truly tackled."

Bains and Johal (1998:50) talk of the 'confident' predictions that a small number of Asian players will make a breakthrough into professional football and of certain individuals within clubs that are working hard towards this. Khan (2000:51) looks at four professional clubs that have embarked upon schemes that demonstrate 'good practice'. However, he also states that although clubs "are attempting to work and attract Asian players" the work in general tends to be "sporadic and conducted in isolation". Garland and Rowe (2001:195) place the lack of progress squarely on the shoulders of the majority of those working within professional football clubs: "Campaigning groups and some journalists might raise questions about chronic under representation of minority ethnic groups within institutions of the game, but few individual clubs seem inclined to reorganise the problem as racism continues to be addressed in its narrowest forms".

Of course, stereotyping according to people's race does not help towards integration and McCarthy, Jones and Potrac's study (2003) that looked at the way football commentators interpreted the game they were watching gave worrying indications of the problems that are still faced. They stated (2003:234): "Black players were praised in terms of their physical capabilities considerably more than the whites by the commentators examined". Perhaps more worryingly, they went on to state that: "The findings suggest that both the black and white respondents within the study perceived an emphasis within the football commentary to be the physical attributes of the black player and the cognitive abilities of whites".

48

The findings of this research are quite disturbing, due to the power of television and the amount of air time stations give to professional football. Stereotyping of this nature is being reinforced to the next generation on a massive scale and this will inevitably have an effect upon participation and the positions people play. The 'stacking 'of players in certain positions is not a new concept, but has little chance of disappearing according to the findings of McCarthy, Jones and Potrac.

3.3.5 Other issues and sport

There have been some occasions in recent years when participation in high-level sport has clashed with an individual's religious beliefs, for example the rugby union All Black international, Michael Jones, who refused to play for his country on Sundays. However, such instances have been few and far between. This according to Coakley (1998: 484-485) is because, "sports have been increasingly incorporated into Christian organisations and beliefs because they emphasise a rationally controlled lifestyle, characterised by discipline, hard work, sacrifice, and the endurance of pain in the pursuit of success2. With regard to football in England, it is less likely for an individual to suffer inequality purely on religious grounds. It is far more likely that if inequalities do exist, then they would be heavily linked to racist or even nationalistic reasons where there has been hostility between England (or UK) and the area or country of origin of an individual. For example the abuse Osvaldo Ardiles received from football crowds when the UK were at war with Argentina in 1982, and more recently towards the Leicester City player Muzzy Isset, whose father is Turkish, in the light of problems between Galatasaray and various English clubs.

Finally, it is worth briefly mentioning some other inequalities an aspiring young footballer may face in attempting to enter into this profession. These include the role his school plays in his development. For example, he may attend a school that does not have football within the physical education curriculum, does not run any football teams and has no links with professional clubs. A student attending a school that has a strong footballing tradition will obviously have distinct advantages over someone attending the previous type of school. Also, schools situated in large urban areas are more likely to have links with the local professional clubs than schools situated in rural areas where there are no nearby clubs of similar status. Therefore, living in a large city may well be advantageous.

Overall, there is evidence from psychological (albeit, arguable), socio-psychological and sociological research that shows there are limiting and advantageous factors that determine the likelihood of an individual's chances of success of becoming a professional footballer. The part they play can override the importance of an individual's ability to play football.

CHAPTER 4
THE VOCATIONAL SOCIALISATION OF YOUNG PEOPLE
INTO PERFORMANCED- BASED CAREERS

Although the aim of this research is centred towards football, the very fact that as a profession it has so many similarities with other sports and performance based careers offers an opportunity for comparison with other careers. Indeed, Hudson (1997) described football as the working man's ballet. Failure to make comparisons may give the impression that football as a career is unique in the potential successes and problems that an individual may face. In this regard, what follows can be considered as part of an important contextual framing of the main focus of this study.

Faulkner (1975:531) stated in his research based on the comparative occupations of professional ice hockey players and professional orchestral musicians that both rely upon "the output of their respective 'farm systems' for the socialisation and training of aspirants into the occupational culture and its work roles". The key aim of my research focuses upon professional football and follows the necessary training and career path that youngsters need to follow in order to successfully pass through their respective 'farm system'.

However, before confining the research to football, there are a number of either sporting or non- sporting occupations that have similar processes and barriers, which for example, accompany career mobility and also those which are associated with rejection, that are worthy of comparison in a similar way to the research done by Faulkner. The three chosen for consideration here are ballet, classical music and acting.

Entering into all of these activities at professional level and maintaining a career in the relevant field will involve high levels of competition with other performers. In all, an individual has to be considered better than others to be given the role of performer. The footballer is not only faced with the internal competition from his own team mates but with the external competition of the opposition. Gruneau, when discussing sport in general, states (1975:169), "the fact that the high levels of athletic expertise that are the most enjoyable to watch are closely associated with an accelerated importance of rationalised competition and accompanying non-egalitarianism poses an interesting dilemma for even the most radical and egalitarian critics of inequality".

It seems that the apparent high levels of competition within all of these professions fall perfectly within a post industrialised society based upon meritocracy. Conversely, Gruneau (1975:147) discusses the view of modern multi-dimensional theorists who claim that individuals do not occupy a single position within the reward structure, but can occupy several positions. He says (1975:147) that "an individual may be a highly skilled athlete yet comparatively uneducated; he may make a high income but be black and be discriminated against; and finally he may feel some anxieties over the 'status' inconsistencies that permeate his life".

The inequalities and discriminations that high-level performers encounter in the aforementioned professions will be discussed a little later. However, according to the advice given to aspiring young people hoping to get into these professions and to play or perform at a high level, they must be 'a natural' or have a 'gift' (Cashmore 1990:2) or talent (Glasstone 1976, Sussex Careers Service 2002:1 (a) and Sussex Careers Service 2002:1(b)). These words are commonly used when discussing the necessary requirements, but why are some people associated with them whilst others are not? Perhaps the answer can be found within theories based upon the body.

To emphasise this point, one common aspect for the professions mentioned is that the key tool for all is the human body and that in varying degrees, performance is based on audience consumption of the presentation and manipulation in tandem of physical and intellectual attributes and indeed, the success of career mobility may well depend upon. Dirk Bogarde (1978:13) stated in his autobiography that actors are expected to see themselves as instruments "and we tend to have to keep reassuring ourselves - and looking for reassurance – as to how good that instrument is". Clearly, Bogarde realised the importance of his body as a tool (whether that be for example, through the use of his voice or through physical movements) and the success of which depended upon the reaction of other people's response to his performance.

An aspiring young actor might ask the question, how did Bogarde come to learn how to perform to a successful level? The answer to this can be linked to the theories of Bourdieu (1977) on body culture, whereby the body can be seen as a site for social memory. This involves a complex system of interaction between the individual and the society within which he lives as well as conscious and unconscious aspects of the person's social make-up. Therefore, for an aspiring actor it goes "beyond the limits of

52

what has been directly learnt" (Bourdieu 1986:170) and extends to the transformation into the "distinctive lifestyle of the necessities and facilities characteristic of a condition and a position" (ibid) – in this case, an actor. For Bourdieu, "it is not solely a question of nature versus nurture but rather, the dialectical aspects of nurture" (Jarvie and Maguire 1994:186).

Perhaps then, social memory and development of the body habitus combine to help formulate what Cashmore (1990:2) refers to as possessing a gift for performance-related activities.

Over recent years there has been much academic focus on types of employment that rely on 'body capital'. Bourdieu (1986:65) described body capital as accumulated labour that allows an individual to appropriate social energy in the form of reified or living labour. In return, the employer will attempt to make as much economic capital as he can from the individual's essential asset, in other words his body. This expectancy from employers must be all too familiar to the demands that are sometimes placed upon the high level players who are involved in the performance-based industries.

In general terms, Eichberg (1998:143) in his essays on 'Body Culture', sees today's typical sportsman as having a "streamlined body" which is suitable for "quick and dynamic exercises", like football and boxing, as opposed to those games in the past that have needed to be suitable for either just strength or endurance. Whether one accepts this or not, it is now generally recognised (Wacquant 1995; Blake 1996; Turner 1996) that the question of 'embodiment' is fundamental to much of the sociology of sport. From a sportsman's point of view this obviously has serious implications, for he must realise the position he is now in once he enters into the professional game. For example, in Wacquant's (1995:65) study based on the ethnography of a boxing gym and on participant observation of the daily routines of boxers, he stated that: "Like much fixed capital and like all living organisms, the body of fighters has inherent structural limitations including a limited life expectancy…This explains why boxers must carefully manage the investment of their physical assets over time".

For the footballer, there are obviously similarities here. He is expected to keep himself fit throughout the season. The English football season is often criticised for being too lengthy and involving too many games. This in itself will take a toll on the body and could have a damaging effect on the length of a playing career. Added to this are the physical demands the club places upon the player. According to Guilianotti (1999:110): "Some players are effectively instructed that their body is a weapon, for stopping opponents, winning possession or scoring a goal".

Few would doubt that similar requirements are part of everyday life for an international rugby player (whichever code he is playing). Will Carling (1998:151), ex-England rugby union captain, described the attitude and physical demands needed to beat France in 1991:

> "This was rugby on the edge, our flat-out response a matter
> of reacting as quickly and effectively as possible. Fingers-
> in-the-dam rugby, filling holes, patching cracks. In
> moments like these tactics and strategy go out of the
> window to be replaced by character and guts. Only players
> who have had that experience know the demands it makes
> on you physically and mentally".

Requirements such as those mentioned by Carling and Guilianotti, expose the physical extremes sports players are prepared to put their bodies through in order to be successful. Although demands that go to such extremes are not common outside of the sporting arena, other professions by their very nature require physical demands of their own. According to the highly acclaimed conductor, the late Sir Adrian Boult (1973:44), it is vital for any top classical musician not to come to the peak of his performance in rehearsal, as he is unlikely to be able to repeat it again due to both the physical and mental demands required. He states, "We are sporting people and I cannot see why our artistic processes should not be managed in a way similar to the main roles of sports training".

However, generally neither in sport or music is physical appearance a pre-requisite to success, as can often be the case for performing arts. In a documentary entitled 'Fame School' (Brinkworth 2000), which looked at life at a performing arts college, one of the students was constantly warned about her weight. She had given the role of lead singer in a pop group that, according to her college director Bruce Rogers, "could be the next Spice Girls"'. However, the record company they were dealing with, whilst being happy with the song, was less than impressed with her appearance. In a frank meeting with the girl in which he gave the record company's evaluation of her performance Rogers told her: "They were really impressed with the way you did it, and the way it was handled, but they weren't impressed with your weight."

Despite several attempts, the girl did not manage to lose weight, and Rogers made it clear to her that opportunities for success may well disappear as a result, thus confirming the demands placed upon performing artists.

According to Foster (1997:110), ballerinas often become so obsessed with their body image and looking in the mirror that it is as if they 'co-exist' with their image as if it were their partner. She also describes (ibid) the extremes to which many aspiring ballerinas will push themselves towards in order to cultivate and maintain a specific physical appearance: "They may undertake surgery to enhance the size of their lips, the curvature of the arch or to remove unwanted cellulite tissue. In order to maintain their substandard weight, stipulated as part of the contracts in many ballet companies, they engage in intentional dehydration, laxative abuse, self induced vomiting and extended fasting". Foster (ibid) goes on to discuss the effects this has on a large number of those that follow these practices. Many will apparently become bulimic and anorexic which will require medical attention – a factor, she claims, parents should be aware of before sending their daughters to ballet school.

In contrast, Mackrell (1992:136) describes how the requirements of the performer in modern dance, termed 'New Dance', vary drastically in comparison with those of the more traditional forms, for example ballet. She states that many of the dancers bear little resemblance to the physical stereotypes that used to dominate dance companies, and no longer are dancers expected to be 'sylph-like'.

There is no doubting that body image also has an extra dimension to play in the success of some elite performers. For example, in sport whilst appearance is unlikely to have an effect on actual performance it can have an effect upon financial gain. It is well documented (Herzog: 2004) that during Wimbledon week the woman who in the late 1990's - early 21st Century constantly featured in advertisements, and whose face appeared on the front of the tabloid newspapers due to her beauty, is Russian tennis player Anna Kournikova. The financial gains that she is able to make because of this are likely to easily exceed the prize money she is capable of earning, particularly as she is rarely rated in the top ten of the world rankings and has to date never won a major singles tournament.

For someone like Anna Kournikova, apart from maintaining her physical fitness in order to play tennis, it is unlikely that she needs to go to any extremes to maintain her looks. For other elite sports people, because the standards required to enter into and maintain one's position in high-level sport, is often increasing, so is the need to push oneself to physical limits. The descriptions given by Guilanotti (ibid) and Carling (ibid) show that the number of years one can perform at the highest level could become shorter. Wacquant's concerns about boxers' need to manage their physical investment (in other words their body) over time, is just as relevant to the aspiring footballer or rugby player. To counter this, most people involved in high-level sports are increasingly aware of the need for a healthy diet and monitored fitness regimes. As a result, a playing career can be extended, and this can be considered as part of the vocational socialisation process. For the ballerina, the answer is not so simple, as performance is often inextricably linked to their physique, and as long as the requirement is for them to be of substandard weight, cases of bulimia and anorexia will continue to occur.

On the subject of the physical demands placed upon ballerinas, Patterson, Smith, Everett and Ptacek (1998) found that there is a direct link between the pressures that are associated with professional ballet, the support they receive and injuries. They conclude (1998:111): "Certainly, the ballet environment is a highly demanding one that contains endemic stress".

For some performance professions, success at the highest level can depend upon the gender, and the problem could be exacerbated by age. Oddey (1999:9) found in her interviews with twenty-two top British female actresses, that the older women became the harder it was to find work: "Performers have discovered a certain kind of work for women in their thirties, followed by disappointment with what is available in their forties and a real lack of good parts in their fifties, particularly in television".

Even for women entering into the profession after completing courses at drama schools or universities, the problem of finding work is not necessarily easy, again particularly for women. In a B.B.C. documentary entitled 'Theatre School' based on The Drama Centre, London, it stated (Barnes 1998) that of "the twenty five that embarked upon the three year course, less than half found employment within a year of leaving and only three of these were women." Twelve women had initially started the course. With examples such as these one might expect there to be a shortage of women wishing to enter into the profession, but according to the documentary, this is not the case - applications for places on their courses is often close to being even.

Traditionally, women have never been the dominant gender in terms of numbers within classical orchestras. A major breakthrough occurred during the Second World War due to a large number of men having to leave the profession to join the forces – and at the end of the war many of the women were able to hold on to their positions within the orchestras. However, there were still a number of traditionalists who were vehemently opposed to women being involved. Perhaps Great Britain's most famous conductor of the twentieth century, Sir Thomas Beecham (cited in Atkins and Newman 1981:70) was reported to have said in 1959: "The trouble with women in an orchestra is that if they are attractive it will upset my players and if they are not, it will upset me".

Despite the numbers of mixed orchestras increasing, a professional orchestra with as many or more women is yet to be seen. Green (1996:42) states that although at present women work in a variety of fields within entertainment including classical music, concertgoers would "raise a few eyebrows" if there were more women than men. In terms of equal opportunity, it would be difficult to ascertain whether it is currently harder to gain a place in a top orchestra purely because of gender.

Maidlow (1998:45) suggests that women within orchestras are often more likely to be found in the string section rather than the brass and that gender associations with instruments are likely to be reinforced by mentors and role models available to the young musicians, and this is a cycle that will take a long time to erode. Although this is not discriminatory, it does highlight another barrier to youngsters, in that it is a perception within our society that women ought to play certain instruments rather than others.

In sport in Great Britain, with the exception of doubles tennis, there are no female full-time professional team game players. With women's football, as the country's fastest growing sport, this may well change in the near future. However, at present it is not possible for a girl to enter into professional football in a playing capacity, and until it is, football will be regarded by many as a male preserve.

To a similar degree, boys who wish to take up music (McQuattie 1986) and ballet (Sayers 1997) often face the same problem and perhaps it is due to this that according to Sayers (1997:140) "there are still very few boys" in comparison to girls that can be found in ballet classes. Glasstone (1980:10) claims the reason why boys being drawn away from

57

ballet, is because they may be seen as effeminate: "In an age which glorifies sport, it is ironical that the male dancer - who can vie with any athlete or sportsman in physical agility as in sheer strength and stamina – should sometimes be looked down on as being 'soft'".

Burt (1995:30) sees the issue of homosexuality in ballet as a longstanding problem and one that should be broached and not avoided. For him, the subject should be openly discussed, as for too long there has been silence about gay male dancers due to the fear that fund raising and sponsorship from individuals and businesses may be affected.

Burt (ibid) believes that one of the results of this prejudice against male dancers is that men often do not discover dance as a profession until their late teens or early twenties. Also, as fewer men go into professional dance training than women, it is easier for men to find employment in dance than women.

However, perhaps the image of men entering into the profession of ballet is beginning to change. Gilbert (2001:7) cites the recent examples of the film 'Billy Elliot', which was seen as successful in box office terms and the Channel 4 documentary, 'Ballet Boyz'. 'Billy Elliot' which used lines like "Ballet is for poofs", was a film set in the 1980's, and according to Gilbert included attitudes that "wouldn't be plausible today". She goes onto to describe 'macho' image of the professional ballet stars featured in the documentary 'Ballet Boyz'. On this issue she concludes: "Slowly but surely, the hard personal and physical discipline demanded by dance is beginning to be seen on a par with, say, that of professional football. It's understood that dancers have to be muscular and tough".

Although this change in attitude may be apparent in certain sections of British society, it may not yet have reached the confines of the professional football dressing room.

The problems faced by people from ethnic minorities and from low socio-economic status groups can also be of a discriminatory nature within performance-based occupations. For example, in acting Woolfe (1998:22) states that "leading drama schools are suffering from a talent shortage as high fees exclude students from poor backgrounds and ethnic minorities".

And with many local authorities not giving discretionary grants (Morrison 1998), it seemed that people from low income would find it increasingly difficult to get into this profession. However, in order to alleviate this problem, in 1999 the DfEE set up the 'Dance and Drama Awards'. These would allow up to 820 students (aged 16 and over for dance and 18 and over for drama), to attend twenty-nine of the country's top drama and dance schools with some form of financial support.

This new initiative may help people entering the profession, but there are still other problems faced by those people from within. When black actress, Marianne Jean-Baptiste, was asked (Oddey 1999:91), if she felt her colour stopped her from getting certain parts, she replied: "Of course it has, but I refuse to allow it to be a problem. It is what it is. It happens all the time". Further to this, Baptiste's problems of finding parts are likely to get decidedly worse once she gets into middle and old age.

For music, there is a different problem. Music within British schools has traditionally been classically based (Kwami 1998). There have been steps over the past twenty-five years to broaden music taught within the curriculum, but it still is mainly of Western origin (ibid). There is a distinct danger here that by keeping to these traditions, schools are not coping very well with a multi-cultural society. In this respect many pupils may feel they are studying a type of music that holds no interest to them. Therefore, whilst it is difficult to state whether our orchestra's are accommodating ethnic minority players, it is perhaps more pertinent to ask if British society is helping young people to develop their musical talents in a way that they may wish.

Clearly, until equality exists and prejudices disappear within our society, some performance-based professions will always be dominated by a specific gender, others by class and others by ethnic groups. To some aspiring performers, this will inevitably create enormous advantages, but to others there will be insurmountable barriers.

Those that do manage to make it into these highly attractive professions may also face problems from those they work with. Hoel and Cooper's (2000) study looked at intimidation in the workplace, based upon 5,300 workers in 70 occupations. Of these, only teachers, communications workers and prison officer suffer more intimidation in the workplace than dancers. It found that because most are freelance or on short-term contracts, many were too worried about challenging their superiors. (Professional musicians and sportsmen were not included in this study).

There are some similarities here with Brinkworth's (1997) study on prospective professional footballers at Chelsea Football Club. This highlighted the oppressive regime that the young players were subjected to, both on and off the field. The daily admonishments received by the players from coach Graham Rix for not cleaning first team player's boots to the required standard, certainly verged on intimidation.

Some of the most interesting commonalities that occur within these highly competitive performance-based professions, are often the need for an individual to follow a defined career path (see Figure 3) and the need to be making career-based decisions in the early years, or what Ginsberg (1951) described as the 'fantasy period' (which generally lasts up until the age of eleven). Few would argue that from a psychological point of view this is not a good time to be making such important decisions, particularly when the prospect of failure is so great.

Jonathon Cape, one of Britain's top male ballet performers claims (cited in Craine 2003:13) that he had to have a two year break from the profession when he was in his late twenties due to the fact that until then he had had lifetime solely devoted to ballet: "You start ballet when you are six and you go right through and never stop. That is all you know and all you do".

The Arts Council (1998:2) states that, potential top ballet dancers start training as early as five, (usually at the local dance school) and then go on to a major ballet school. Without this early formal training it is difficult to see how a ballet dancer could hold realistic ambitions of becoming a top performer. The advice given by the Sussex Service Careers (S.C.S) (2002(a):1) is that, "unless you have already begun serious training by the age of 16, you are unlikely to succeed".

For dance careers other than ballet, for example modern dance, this early training may not be seen as so important. The first year intake for the London School of Contemporary Dance (L.S.C.D) established in the mid-1960's for people over eighteen, did include some students with classical training, but also there were others without any dance background. This could be seen as a deliberate attempt to step away from the more traditional formalities of training for ballet. The policy of allowing people from a range of backgrounds to join has continued, and the advice given by the S.C.S (ibid) for anyone wanting a career in modern dance is that training is important "but does not need such an early start as ballet. You can start in your early twenties, especially if you are male".

For classical musicians, formal training at an early age is normally a pre-requisite to high-level performance. According to the Incorporated Society of Musicians (I.S.M) (1998:4), performers will be expected to have reached advanced levels of performance (at least Grade Eight) by the time they leave school. From there, musicians either go to specialist music colleges, such as The Royal College of Music, or go to a university to take a degree in music where technical mastery of the instrument or voice, and general musicianship is taken for granted. In a similar vein, aspiring professional sportsmen will be expected to have mastery of the skills linked to their game at an early age. Rarely, do top performers who have not acquired skills at this stage age ever reach the highest level. According to Simmons (2000:55): "Research on the development of top class sportsmen and women found that the only common trait was that they had practised for at least 10 years and had usually started very young. This suggests that the opportunity to play at a very young age was more important in the development of elite performers than having natural talent".

Although Simmons is not specific about the research that shows this, it is nevertheless a comment worthy of consideration.

To become a professional actor, the career-based decisions during the 'fantasy period' are by no means essential. Undoubtedly, many youngsters will attend stage school at an early age, either on a full or part-time basis, and this may give them an advantage when going to auditions for employment in acting during childhood. However, many aspiring actors will follow a more traditional educational path, without attending stage school even on a part-time basis, and either wait until they attend drama school or take a drama degree at university after leaving school. It should be added here that in order to become a professional actor in theatre or television, it is almost essential to belong to 'Equity' and in order to obtain an 'Equity' card, one must take courses accredited by the National Council for Drama Training (N.C.D.T).

For all of these careers, it is the occupational attractiveness that makes jobs in the performance industry so sought after at an early age. Although, even for the successful, high levels of income do not necessarily follow. Advice to aspiring performers is constantly being given. The Arts Council (1998:2) state that: "The idea of working in dance may seem glamorous but the reality is often very ordinary. In addition, a great deal of commitment is required and early on your income may not be high".

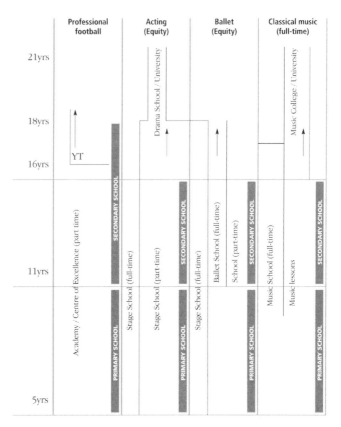

Figure 3: Career pathways

This sentiment is echoed by the Conference of Drama Schools (C.C.S) (1999:6), which not only warns of low income but also the long and unsocial hours and the unlikelihood of regular employment, and the S.C.S (2002 (b):1) states that most musicians have to use skills besides their musical talents in order to make a living.

Often associated with high levels of occupational attractiveness comes disappointment to the many that try to enter into the profession but fail. According to Nicholls (1994:13), trying to get a place at drama school is very difficult: "Every year, around 1,500 aspiring young thespians apply for 30 places at the Royal Academy of Dramatic Art (RADA), and there is similar competition for the 20 or so drama schools around the country".

And in classical music, only about 2,000 classical musicians can get full-time work in British orchestras, and there are very few openings each year (SCS 2002 (b):1).

Glasstone (1986:217) states that in his experience, children who train to become professional dancers are "remarkably resilient" and soon adapt to a different way of life once they have been rejected. He sees the bigger problem being the parents who find it difficult to cope with the 'loss of face'. Indeed McQuattie (1986:209), when referring to young classical musicians, sees proud parents as a "destructive force", claiming that there is a thin line between "support and push".

For some of these professions, performance at the highest level is limited to a few years due to the physical requirements. It is well known that a professional footballer will not normally play at this level much beyond his mid-thirties, although the career span has gradually extended over recent years due to improved health regimes and better fitness levels. The S.C.S. (2002 (a):1) claim that in any type of dance, few people go on past the age of 35.

In acting, although the problem of age is not necessarily of major importance, (with the exception being the problems women face, as has already been discussed), estimates of between 70% (S.C.S: 1998) and 90% (Nicholls: 1994) of performers are unemployed at any one time. For professional classical musicians, many are unable to find work on a full-time basis, and so they have to rely on contract work (SCS: 2002(a)).

Like many other professions, it is not uncommon for children whose parents have had a career in a performance-based profession to follow their mother or father's choice. The names of Redknapp, Lampard and Summerbee have been familiar within football circles for thirty years because fathers and sons from the same family have played at a professional level. Harry Redknapp stated in a recent BBC documentary (1998) that he allowed his son Jamie to miss school when he was in his early teens so that he could train with the professionals at the club (Bournemouth) that he managed, whilst Jamie stated that the only topic he ever seriously discussed with his father was football. According to Richardson (1995:9), acting can often follow a similar pattern: "Acting like other talents, does seem to run in families – like the Redgraves and the Cusacks – and as with other jobs, it is not uncommon to follow in the mother's or father's footsteps".

Of course, these are only a few examples of families who have followed this tradition, and there are many thousands of people in performance-based industries that have not done so. The key question here is how much, if any, of an advantage do the offspring of parents have within these industries? For example, do the parents know influential people within these industries, and if they do, will it help make the pathway for their offspring into these professions easier? Have the offspring just inherited a natural talent or has the parent helped (consciously or sub-consciously) to develop their child's habitus? The answers to contentious questions such as these are worthy of debate, though there may be no definitive answers.

All four of the selected activities (acting, ballet, playing classical music and football) are discussed within Bourdieu's oeuvre either as leisure pursuits or professions. Their relevance within this context is the attraction of each towards specific social groups. Going to the theatre (acting), watching ballet and listening to classical music all feature in the lifestyle of the petite bourgeoisie, whilst watching and playing football appears most commonly as an interest of the lower classes. This is supported by the research already discussed in Woolfe (1998) (acting) and Parker (2001) (football) as well as Sherlock (1993:38) who claims that "ballet has a minority appeal for a select group of mainly professional and semi-professionals, predominantly females".

However, Bourdieu (1986) also accepts that we live in a changing world and appreciates that taste and career opportunities of social groups alter between generations over time, due to factors such as increased opportunity through education and qualifications. Warde (1997:10) develops this argument when he argues that social class plays a negligible part in modern society: "A problem of modernity and post modernity is the requirement that individuals construct their own selves. No longer are people placed in society by way of their lineage, caste or class but each must invent and conspicuously create a personal Identity".

It follows that if this is indeed the case, it is quite conceivable that for all four selected activities, their specific farm systems could change quite drastically over time with regard to the type of person entering into them. Overall, comparisons can be drawn about all of the professions discussed, for all performers, whether due to a short career, part-time or the unpredictability of work, need to become adaptable and flexible enough to work within a post-Fordist society. For if they do not, they face the prospect of periods of unemployment. In addition, aspiring performers will find that entry into one of these industries in the first place is likely to be extremely difficult due to occupational attractiveness; and if they have not made some crucial decisions by their early teens, very often it will be too late.

The barriers to enter into these careers can be enormous and can range from discrimination against many sections of society to heightened physical stresses of the body. For a variety of reasons, all can be described to young hopefuls as extremely risky businesses.

CHAPTER 5

THE EFFECTS OF RECENT CHANGES IN FOOTBALL APPRENTICESHIPS – POST CHARTER FOR QUALITY

Since the introduction of the Scholarship Scheme 1997 (via the 'Charter for Quality'), there has been a wide amount of media interest through television programmes and newspaper articles. What follows, is a selection of the main issues raised within this coverage, together with a survey of some related academic literature and information gained through an educational arm of the PFA, the Football Further Education and Vocational Training Society (FFE&VTS).

One of the main ideas behind the National School of Excellence, when it was set up in 1992, was to allow elite footballers to spend frequent periods of time being coached together. This idea was supported by Howard Wilkinson when he introduced the 'Charter for Quality'. When commenting upon the difference the Scholarship Scheme would have upon the youth team players at professional football clubs, he stated on Channel 4's documentary 'Football Academy' (Dower 2001) that:

> "The fundamental difference is people together for the right
> amount of time and it's the access to the kids and it's time that
> matters. This won't work for two nights a week for an hour and a
> quarter. For this to be effective it's got to be an all week thing –
> not all of the week all of the time – but the boys have got to
> realise that if they are going to improve they've got to practice".

For parents, the theory that their son should be asked to spend so much of their spare time playing football could create a conflict of interests between them and the club. For example, it may be seen by them to have a detrimental effect on the time spent doing homework. However, according to Tim Devine, Education Officer at Liverpool Football Club, the boy's welfare is paramount. He insists the club views the boys as "people first – players second" (ibid) and this is supported by the boys themselves who claim that the club keep in close contact with the schools to ensure that the boys football is not adversely affecting their education (ibid).

Of course, it does not necessarily follow that all football clubs attempt to take such care as Liverpool. The mere fact that Liverpool recently spent £12 million on the establishment of their new Academy would suggest that the club take their youth policy seriously and are likely to be at the forefront of new ideas or developments. For the club, the justification for this high level of spending is that the discovery and nurturing of only one potential international player would still leave the club in profit. Gerard Houllier, manager of Liverpool, stated (1999:37) that his aim was to have three quarters of the first team coming from the academy. Indeed, Houllier has made no secret of his belief in a strong youth system. Richardson (cited in Rich 2002: 27) states: "When Gerard Houllier, who was then French technical director, addressed a managers' and coaches' conference a few years ago, he said it would be six to eight years before we would see the fruits of our labour and on those terms we still have a few years to go".

Everton Football Club have realised since the introduction of the F.A.'s Charter for Quality the importance of adapting to changes that have occurred with regard to recruitment. Ray Hall (Academy Director at Everton) claims that (2003:53):

> "The result is that there are less players (sic) from a smaller
> recruitment area. Everton Football Club has reorganised its
> recruitment policy with the emphasis upon recruiting
> local players. Should there be any deficiency in the quality
> of our players we would compensate for this by looking
> Nationally (sic) or internationally."

He goes on to discuss the high level of importance Everton gives to the young players attending the Club's academy in order to make sure they stay and are not tempted away by other clubs. Hall cites (2003:53) several reasons why the Club has been able to keep child prodigy Wayne Rooney. These include him being a local boy, having joined Everton when he was eight and being given the opportunity to develop although cynics may say the final reason listed, 'satisfactory financial arrangement' could well be the most important.

However, the general shift of emphasis within football concerning the overall welfare of the player is also helping to broaden the appeal of football as a potential career. Goodbody and Lee (1999:20) state that "The invasion of football by the middle classes is spreading from the hospitality box to the pitch, led by a new breed of young players from comfortable backgrounds."

For evidence of this, Goodbody and Lee (ibid) point to Peterborough United, which reports that half of the boys within the club's academy are from a middle class background. The club's Education Officer Dan Ashworth, is quoted as saying that the stereotypical view of the footballer as inarticulate is changing, and there is going to be a much greater mix of classes within the professional game in the future. It is likely that one of the major reasons for this is because the PFA currently insist that all full-time youth players are given ten hours of education per week over three years (between the ages of 16-19). In this way it is possible in theory for brighter students to study for up to four 'A.S.' levels and then three 'A' levels during that period, and therefore they do not miss out on their education.

In addition, Goodbody and Lee (ibid) list six traditional public schools that over recent years have included football as part of their curriculum due to the increased popularity of the sport. The knock-on effect of this trend could see a much higher percentage of ex-public schoolboys attending academies and centres of excellence, and then succeeding into the professional game.

The current emphasis both from the FA and within the clubs is to look after all of the players ranging from the full professionals to the young boys from the age of 8 or 9 who attend the academies or centres of excellence. Nutrition and diet are regarded as key to the avoidance of injury and illness and to the lengthening of playing careers (Smith 2001: 'Football Academy'). In addition, education is seen to as a back up for those who are not offered professional terms and to help find a new career for the successful ones after they have finished their playing career. Improvements in working conditions and the way players are treated are also seen as important. In a recent circular from the FFEVTS (4.11.01) to all clubs it stated: "Scholars are not to undertake menial tasks such as cleaning dressing rooms, cleaning boots, maintenance work etc".

Tony Carr, West Ham's Academy Director, in the documentary 'Football Academy' (ibid) says that making youth team players feel at home at the club is essential for producing their best on the pitch, as they will be much more confident to try to express themselves, something that is important for their development.

68

All of this attention to the development to youth team players is a far cry from professional clubs in the late 1980's and early 1990's as other current and ex-professionals testify (Adams 1998, Nelson 1995, Redknapp, cited in Dower 2001). There is however an issue regarding the power of football agents that is sometimes seen by clubs as detrimental to the player's development and one that is becoming increasingly common within football circles. Linked to this is the pressure some parents place upon clubs to give financial inducements to keep the players.

In Alan Hansen's documentary 'Football Dream Factory' (Cabb 2001), an agent claims that some parents demand and receive between £30,000 and £50,000 from the club, despite the fact that officially clubs are not allowed to pay money. The purpose of the football agent is to look after the interests of the boy and his family and to try to broker the best possible deal. He may well then take a percentage of that money. To an extent, the choice of club can be limited, depending upon where the family live, as boys can only play for clubs that are within one and a half hours travelling distance of their home. One way of overcoming this has been for families to move house at the suggestion of the club. In London competition is fierce, with clubs competing to attract players as young as six (ibid).

It could be argued that the pressure this puts upon youngsters is unacceptable. For them, to be central to the large financial inducements at such an early age can be damaging to their overall perspective of the value of money. Also, the practice of agents and parents bargaining with clubs, can lead to players going to clubs they are unhappy with. Parental pressure can also lead to pushing clubs into making false promises, for example, guaranteeing the child that they will become a professional player if they go to their club (ibid). Premiership managers Bobby Robson and David O'Leary agree (ibid) that some parents do not act within the interests of their child and are purely concerned with financial gain.

Clearly, professional football by its very nature is a competitive industry. For the FA, raising the standard of the sport within this country and ultimately winning the World Cup have got to be two of its main priorities. For professional clubs, winning for prestige and commercial success are the ultimate aims and if clubs such as Liverpool can have a first team made up of three quarters of home grown talent, as is the aim of manager

69

Gerard Houllier, then massive savings on the transfer market will obviously be made. The clubs' measure of success for its youth system is how many players can make through to the first team (ibid). In addition, financial rewards are given to the scouts from the clubs and agents of players that discover talent. Where does this leave the aspiring young player? This and other related questions are worthy of investigation.

An additional problem for young British players hoping to make the professional grade has been the influx of foreign players, particularly into the Premiership. Research by Richardson and Littlewood (1999) and Littlewood, Richardson, Lees and Peiser (2001), has shown the extent of this problem. English player recruitment by clubs from the Premiership has decreased from 61 in 1990/1 to 48 in 1999/00. Players acquired from other countries (outside of the British Isles) have increased from 1 in 1990/1 to 22 in 1999/00. This of course has an effect on the whole of professional football, as young aspiring English players who may have been good enough for the Premiership either resort to playing for clubs in the Football League, thus denying others the opportunity, or never actually become professional players.

By the very fact that currently few of those sixteen year olds who actually get into academies and centres of excellence will make the professional grade shows that clubs are catering for a high percentage of potential failures within the youth system. In this sense, is it the clubs' responsibility to concentrate on teaching the youngsters how to cope with failure?

A young player must wait until he reaches the age of sixteen, and normally the end of Year 11 at school, in order to gain entry into a club's academy or centre of excellence on a full-time basis. The FA will fund up to six players for each club in order to make this transition, although clubs are allowed to fund more if they wish. Many of the clubs' squad for that particular age group will be released. What do the clubs do in order to prepare the boy and his family to cope with such rejection and do they feel as if they have been fairly treated?

Garside (2003) describes the tension involved whilst a player waits to hear of his fate, whilst Conn (2000) discusses the actual issue of rejection: "The dramatic increase, now to nearly 200 foreign players in the Premiership, has coincided with about £110m spent establishing club-based youth academies, suggesting that the academies' cost, in terms rejected young players, are likely to be very high indeed".

Adam Crozier, FA Chief Executive, talked of the need to educate young players in the professional clubs into being 'well rounded individuals' (Cabb 2001), and many others involved in various clubs youth systems share this view (cited in Cabb 2001: Carr, Devine, and Rees). The ultimate question is whether clubs are achieving what they are claiming to be trying to do or is it purely a cosmetic exercise that just makes professional football a more fashionable, modern and attractive industry to be part of.

A report by the FFE&VTS gives details of the boys who took part in the Football Scholarship programme based upon Wilkinson's 'Charter for Quality' in 1998 and those who completed in 2001. According to this (2001:3) 541 scholars from 64 clubs had embarked upon the scheme. Keith Waldon, (FFE&VTS Representative for the South East) claims (Field Notes 27/10/02) that the reason all 92 professional clubs did not take part in the Scheme was because some preferred the previous system which meant that they could totally discard the players after two years and not have to worry about their education in the third year.

Of the 541 scholars, 55% had 5 GCSE's at 'C' or above (and 17% had 5 or more GCSE's with A*, A or B grades). This compares to figures in 1991 that show only 10% of those entering into professional football had similar qualifications, and in 1996 this had increased to 45%. Clearly, there is a trend here that demonstrates how increasing numbers of better-educated individuals are entering into football.

The retention rate for the 2001 cohort showed that 32% were released after two years and a further 32% were released after three years with 36% being offered a professional contract. Mickey Burns (Chief Executive for the FFEVTS) claims (Field Notes 20/10/02) that FFEVTS has been particularly concerned about the number of boys being taken on by clubs for the Scholarship Scheme and then releasing them after two or three years. In the Football Scholarship Report, the FFEVTS state (2001:2):

> "The Society at onset of the Scholarship attempted to make
> clubs more selective with boys entering the football industry
> on a full-time basis at 16 years of age in order to improve
> the retention rate. This was done by the Society only funding

71

18 scholars over any 3-year period (average of 6 per year, but
clubs could have differing numbers in each year as long as
this did not exceed 18)".

Many Clubs not only take up their full quota of PFA funded players but also pay others
themselves. For example, in the 2001 third year group, Blackburn Rovers had 15 players
in their Scheme, whilst Bristol City, Coventry and Sheffield United all had 14 and
Manchester United and Newcastle United both had 13. However, the following table
shows that the recruitment trend has been to the liking of the FFEVTS.

YEAR OF INTAKE	NUMBER OF SCHOLARS	NUMBER OF CLUBS	AVERAGE
1998	541	64	8.45
1999	671	83	8.01
2000	605	85	7.11
2001	594	87	6.8

Number of Scholars (1998-2001)

(The Football Scholarship Report 2001)

Table 2

Of course, this trend could be seen in both a positive and negative light. On the one hand
it shows that by the time they are sixteen fewer players are being led to believe that they
have a future in professional football and are therefore not being lured out of mainstream
education. However, players do develop at different rates, and it could be argued that
those who are late developers between the ages of sixteen and nineteen are not being
given the opportunity to shine at a professional club.

For the 2001 cohort, the Scholarship players undertook the following courses:

TYPE OF COURSE	NUMBER OF PLAYERS	PERCENTAGE
'A' Level programmes	49	9
B/TEC National Diploma	41	7.5
B/TEC National Certificate	196	36
GNVQ Advanced Certificate	70	13
GNVQ Intermediate Certificate or B/TEC 1st	85	16
NVQ Programmes	80	15
Learning Needs	20	3.5

Courses taken by first cohort of Scholars (1998-2001)

(The Football Scholarship Report 2001)

Table 3

Those scholars (65.5%) who embarked upon the 'A' level, B/TEC National Diploma, B/TEC National Certificate or the GNVQ Advanced Certificate followed courses that were direct academic routes to university qualifications.

At first glance, these figures make impressive reading. However, the actual outcomes for the courses are not quite as encouraging. This is not totally surprising considering other pressures placed upon the young footballers. Of the 776 courses undertaken, 158 were not completed, 49 had no result or were failed. In all there was a 73% pass rate. The difference between clubs in terms of course completion is quite staggering. For example, two high profile London clubs failed to get any of their scholars to complete a course and a Premiership club from the North West only had three courses finished out of seventeen. In comparison, other clubs had all scholars passing all courses.

Of the 541 scholars from the first cohort, 192 were given professional contract as can be seen from the table below.

PATHWAY	NUMBER	PERCENTAGE
Professional Contract	192	35.5
University	59	11
Employment	58	11
Further Education	18	3
Extended Scholarship	7	1.5
Part-time football (looking for another club)	31	5.5
Other*	14	2.5
Unknown**	162	30

* This figure includes a large number of the 14 who left for disciplinary reasons

**This figure includes 73 boys who were early leavers through for example, mutual consent and/or injury

Destination of scholars from first cohort (1998-2001)

(The Football Scholarship Report 2001)

Table 4

Therefore, on average about two players from every six in the year group for each club will eventually make the final step into professional football, but Burns estimates (Field Notes 20/10/02) that only one of those two players survives beyond a one year contract. To put this into context, only one boy from the hundreds that go through a club's centre of excellence or academy will make a living at the game. As most people would recognise, the process that Parker described as "Chasing the Big Dream" (1996), is highly likely to end in failure.

So what are professional football clubs actually looking for when choosing young players who they see may become full time players, either to be kept or sold on?

From a coach's perspective, the traditional way to decide whether a player has a future in professional football is to assess his ability. Roger Smith former Director of Wimbledon Football Club describes (2002:82) how scouts identify a player by seeing if "he looks and moves" like a professional football player. He goes on to say that more detail is required and he highlights other qualities that he categorises. They are: pace and ability, understanding and awareness, attitude and application, determination, shooting and finishing and finally, defending. He goes on (2002:82): "Clearly you would not expect to find some of these attributes in the real young ones, but you would want to consider such items when choosing potential trainees for selection at a professional club".

However, some now see a list of playing qualities on the field involved as only part of the requirement. Craig Simmons, the F.A. Player Development Advisor, highlights three other areas in addition to football ability that are worthy of consideration. They are: psychological maturity, physiological development and social influence – all very broad areas of study. Simmons (2002:48) sees these three areas as "maybe more aligned to ongoing development than the initial identification of football ability".

For many years, Dutch football has been admired by people throughout the football world for the style of play and the success of the club sides and the national team, and according to an FA spokesman (Field Notes 18/9/98), the Netherlands was one of the countries visited by Howard Wilkinson in a fact finding mission before formulating the Charter for Quality.

According to Simmons (2003) though, there has been disruption in Dutch football during the 1990's due to changes in organisational strategy. However, this has not affected the reputation of Ajax, one of Holland's leading professional clubs, as a producer of world-class footballers. One of the club's strategies (Barwick et al 1998) for finding the best young players is to invite 7, 8 and 9 year olds to attend 'talent weeks'. In 1997, 2640 boys attended one such week, with only 4 boys selected. Ajax expects 90% of those who are with the club at Under 12 level to still be with them at Under18. The coaching staff are particularly keen to take players on at the club who possess more than just the required amount of football ability. The primary qualities they look for during selection are: technique, intelligence, personality and speed, thus incorporating ability within a more holistic framework.

To date there has been little by way of criticism towards the youth system for professional football set up by Howard Wilkinson through the Charter for Quality. Much easier to find has been the high level of support from those within football. Les Reed, Technical Director for the FA, (cited in Football Association 2003:3) stated: "Howard has paved the way for a bright future. He has developed a philosophy which puts the player at the centre. We have established a policy of continuity, consistency and stability as the basis of our development and learning programmes".

One of the aims of this work is to look in detail at the main vehicle, in this case the youth system at Brighton and Hove Albion Football Club, which paves the way towards professional football for those young boys living in Sussex – a product based upon the Charter for Quality.

CHAPTER 6

METHODOLOGY

Before undertaking any fieldwork based at Brighton and Hove Albion Football Club, an assessment of the most suitable research method had to be established. In addition, any issues that are associated with that method need to be considered. This chapter seeks to explain why the chosen method of participant observation was used and what research of this nature entails.

6.1 Critical Investigations

When embarking upon this research, the original intention was to base the technique upon a similar style used by Sugden and Tomlinson. Giulianotti (1999:184) sees the "Brighton-based researchers" as having made a distinct contribution to the study of football cultures. Sugden and Tomlinson (2002:10) describe their style of social research as being "based upon six overlapping elements: historiography; comparative methods; critical sociology; ethnography; investigative research; and gonzo".

Sugden and Tomlinson (ibid.) see it as "vital to give research into contemporary phenomena a dynamic historical dimension", and further, any account of the present that does not account for the past is "seriously weakened". (For this research, an historical perspective has been discussed in Chapters 1 and 4).

In order to gain a wider knowledge of a field of study they suggest that comparisons are made, either through research or case studies. For any particular piece of research it is clearly beneficial to use a variety of methods in order to try to validate the results (as discussed in 6.6)

For the element, critical sociology, Sugden and Tomlinson use phrases (2002:11) such as "never take things at face value", "question authority" and "get under the skin of daily life" in order to gain an understanding of the field of research. One of the strengths of participant observation is to sample daily life from first hand (see 6.5) and so this would be very suitable for this particular element. It is also a strength when considering the fourth element listed by Sugden and Tomlinson; ethnography. For this, they state the virtues of spending time in the research environment in order to formulate questions enhance interpretation.

The final elements, investigative research and gonzo, are similar to each other in that they are both methods that go beyond secondary sources of research in order to gain a truer picture. Investigative research ignores the publicity machine of the organisation in question (see 6.5) and the gonzo approach is linked to journalism that allows the reporter to infiltrate into an organisation, without necessarily being invited.

Sugden and Tomlinson (2002) summarise their overall approach by describing the researcher as someone who is attempting to gain a social impression of the field of study in the same way that an artist displays his interpretation of a subject. They also stress the need for a strong moral commitment for the quest for the truth.

6.2 Ethics

May (2001: 59) states that "ethics is concerned with the attempt to formulate codes and principles of moral behaviour." So closely are the words 'ethics' and 'morals' linked in research that Kimmel (1988) believes they may be used inter-changeably when referring to the rules of proper conduct. However, he goes on to explain that there is a difference between the two in terms of the context of codified principles. For example, a teacher or a coach of a team knows that ethically he should treat everyone equally, but morally he sees some people's needs as greater than others and therefore he feels unable to do this. When comparing the professions of medicine and social research, Homan (1991) argues that both have ethical codes that attempt to foster and guarantee professional ethos and standards. However, when dealing with morality, medicine has historically openly shared issues with the public whereas in the context of social research, morality is often seen as exogenous, due to the fact that each piece of research must be judged individually upon its merits. A natural assumption is that there is no reason why, as with the medical profession, the public, particularly the subjects, should not be made more fully aware of the issues involved with specific social research. The Market Research Society states in its *Code of Conduct* (1986) (cited in Homan 1991) that public and business confidence is dependent upon, amongst other factors, honest and objective reporting without unwelcome intrusion. Indeed, any perceptions held by the public that are contrary to this

78

might harm future research. In addition, others may argue that the public has a right to know what is going on. Baumrind (1971) insists that if the method of research conflicts with the rights of the subjects, then the method must be changed. May (2001) highlights the issue of informed consent, and in particular with regard to children under eighteen, where it could be seen as the moral duty of a researcher to inform parents of the fact that their children are the subjects of a study.

In contrast, there are those who believe that in order to produce meaningful research, total honesty and openness may have to be compromised. Kimmel (1988) believes that although deception is not a defence for lying, cheating and stealing, milder forms should not be ruled out. And in direct contrast to the subject's right to know, Homan (1991) balances the argument by stating that although it may be in the interests of the public to have a 'true' picture – if the subjects have intimate knowledge of the purposes of research, they may advertently or inadvertently change their pattern of behaviour and this in turn may distort the research.

It seems that rigid sets of rules or ethics do not bode well for the research scientist, and Bronfenbrenner (quoted in Barnes 1979: preface) states that, "the only safe way to avoid violating principles of professional ethics is to refrain from doing social research altogether".

It is clear that both sides of the argument have their merits and weaknesses and it is difficult to foresee a compromise. However, May (2001:62) attempts to do just that when he states: "If research is to be viewed as a credible endeavour, then perhaps the relations which are established with all those party to the research must utilise some ethical basis which provides guidelines for, but not constraints on, the researcher".

Conversely, research that is unethical should clearly be avoided. Homan (1991:7) also emphasises the importance of getting accurate information: "What the public and profession is entitled to expect of social researchers is that they are open to the range possible findings and that their methods are not loaded to produce the results they want to achieve."

There can be no dispute concerning the importance of recording information accurately. However, telling the 'truth' can be a contentious issue within social research as often 'truth' can range from fact, to multiple accounts of interpretation and even to the extreme of an individual's opinion. For example, Dean, Eichhorn and Dean (1969) state that the likelihood of bias can occur due to the relationships that the researcher establishes in the field. Also, the information recorded may be factual, but the way the researcher portrays that information could be open to interpretation.

6.3 Values

May suggests (2001) that for every piece of social research that is conducted, certain questions ought to be answered by the researcher as a matter of routine. For example, is it being funded and if so by whom? Also, what is the overall intention of the study? Answers to these questions may jeopardise the researcher's intended position of neutrality and his ability to make value judgements. Nagel (cited in May 2001:55) was aware of the problems faced by a researcher trying to maintain a neutral stance. In order to clarify their position, he made a distinction between two types of value judgements: *characterising* and *appraising*. An example of a characterising value judgement would be when the researcher estimates the degree of feeling towards a certain issue by a number of people. An example of an appraising value judgement would be if the researcher attempted to cast his opinion in terms of approval or disapproval concerning the feelings of that number of people. It is therefore the researcher that uses appraising value judgements who is moving away from objectivity. May (2001:55) argues that role of the scientist is not to thrust values upon people, but "to demonstrate the pros and cons involved of different means and perhaps the social, economic and political costs involved, but not tell people what they should desire as ends".

Indeed, one of the problems faced by an ethnographer (an individual who studies human societies) is to use a method of research that will not impose values or opinions upon the subjects. Lee (2000:2) claims that one of the major weaknesses of questionnaires and interviews, is they can encourage precisely that. This is because the respondents will often try to "manage impressions of themselves in order to maintain their standing in the eyes of the interviewer". He concludes that unobtrusive methods can solve this problem, as the researcher should go to great lengths to ensure that his mere presence does not affect the outcome of the research.

6.4 Types of Observation

Gold (1969, cited in Denzin 1989), identified four techniques a researcher may undertake in order obtain information in the field that come under the umbrella of observation. He states that there is a mixture of obtrusive and unobtrusive methods. Firstly, the *complete participant*, whereby the researcher does not fully identify the purpose of the investigation, and attempts to fully integrate within the group. Secondly, *participant as observer*, from where the researcher acquaints the subjects with his aims. In this position he attempts to establish a rapport with the subjects in order to acquire relevant information. Thirdly, *observer as participant,* where the researcher only visits the field on one occasion in order to make formal interviews with the subjects, and finally *complete observer* in which the researcher does not have any contact with the subjects whatsoever and may view the field through, for example, one way mirrors.

Clearly, there are advantages and disadvantages for all methods and the one that is chosen will normally depend upon the type of research being done. For example, the role of *complete observer* may best suit someone who was researching the behavioural aspects of animals.

However, the method that would perhaps best suit research based upon a youth system at a professional football club would be that of *participant as observer,* and this can be justified purely by a process of elimination. The role of *complete participant* as the researcher would either have to be someone of the same age and similar ability, or an official at the club, and this in itself would not work, as he would then be in a position of responsibility and this could hinder the gathering of information. The role of *observer as participant* would not be suitable as one visit is not sufficient to gather enough information and a *complete observer* would not be appropriate either as it would be totally unrealistic to spend long periods of time observing a youth team without them knowing you are there.

However, it is possible to almost play the role of *complete observer*, and yet actually be a participant. For example, when Yorganci (1997) studied the sensitive issue of sexual harassment in sport, she did not tell the subjects of her research or that she was a researcher. For her, this was quite easy to do as the setting was an athletics track, and she herself was an athlete. If she had made the purposes of her research publicly known, it is extremely likely that the harassers she was observing would have adapted their behaviour accordingly. She therefore played a covert role – that is gathering data without the knowledge of those being involved. In reality she could not be considered a *complete observer* as she was actually physically interacting with her subjects.

As a participant observer, the researcher must carefully decide how much he is going to let his subjects know about the purposes of his presence, and in the example used, Yorganci did not need to divulge anything. However, being in such an advantageous position is not always possible and a researcher may find that it is better to let his subjects be fully acquainted with what he is doing from the start. Therefore, the role of participant observer may change according to the research that is being done and furthermore could change during the same study.

McCall and Simmons (1969:1) see participant observation as a wide area of research: "As a number of commentators have observed, it is probably misleading to regard participant observation as a single method. Rather in common parlance, it refers to a characteristic blend or combination of methods and techniques that is employed in certain types of subject matter…"

They go on to say that it "does not lend itself to the standardization of procedure that social scientists come to expect of their methods" (1969:2). If this is the case, does the researcher using this type of approach leave himself open to criticism that it cannot be considered valid due to the lack of procedure standardisation? For if there is no real form of standardisation then the results of the research may be seen as observer biased and generally unreliable. Dean, Eichhorn and Dean (1969) also see potential bias as a weakness in this procedure. They give the example of when in the early stages of the fieldwork, the researcher may begin to form a hunch or hypothesis and without necessarily meaning to, will present the data he has collected to match it. However, it is acceptable to test or explore a hypothesis.

Another weakness highlighted by Dean, Eichhorn and Dean (ibid) is that the data collected from this type of research cannot be easily represented statistically. Although there is no intention to formulate statistics, this in itself can cause a problem as the validity of conclusions is subjective and a hypothesis, if there is one, cannot be easily tested.

82

To counter this type of criticism, May (2001) states that it is the job of the researcher to communicate his work persuasively and in a well-argued manner in order convince the public of its authenticity. Even if this counter argument does not solely give a watertight explanation as to why participant observation should be seen as a totally valid form of research, the advantages for using it are perhaps more persuasive.

Dean, Eichhorn and Dean (1969) list a whole host of these advantages, most of which would apply in researching the youth system at a professional football club. To begin with they state that the researcher of unstructured observation (for example, with participant observation, non-standardization of procedure) does not need to formulate a hypothesis at the start of his research and even when he does manage to do so, can change as his research progresses. In a similar manner, what the researcher sees as irrelevant at the time may prove to be valuable at a later stage. He will also be in the position of being able to follow up leads from small pieces of information so that he can go into more detail where he sees fit. It is not possible to do this by just using a questionnaire – one would have to use a follow up interview in order to gain more information into a particular area.

The participant observer is also able to modify his approach as he sees fit during his research. This is often referred to as flexibility and according to May (2001:159) is one of the main strengths of this method. He states: "There are just a small number of possible questions that ethnographers would routinely ask themselves during the course of fieldwork. It is then possible to focus the next series of observations on answering these questions and thereby utilizing the flexibility of the method".

Other advantages of this method according to Dean, Eichhorn and Dean (1969), include the fact that it is often easier for the researcher to investigate delicate situations in this way than with others. For example, the subjects are more likely to give valuable information to the researcher in an informal setting than they would in a formal situation like a formal interview. Of course this type of approach may mean undertaking covert research that in some cases (Sugden 1996) can lead to potentially dangerous situations. However, sometimes this is the only way that social phenomena or social relations can be properly investigated.

In dealing with subjects, often on a daily basis, not only are they more likely to confide in the researcher, they are also able to give their own valuable insights and can talk about what they want to. In contrast, a survey researcher will base his work on what he initially thought he wanted to discuss, and therefore this may be fairly limiting as important information (found by the participant observer) that he would have found of relevance, interest and importance, may be omitted.

A final point worth mentioning concerning the advantages with unstructured methods over others is that in any research, according to Dean, Eichhorn and Dean (1969), there will be certain variables within the results that are difficult to quantify. For the participant observer there is no reason for him to make these results quantifiable, and yet a survey researcher may try to do this in line with the rest of his research, thus giving misleading information and drawing invalid conclusions.

Overall, when determining which method would best suit the researching of a youth system at a professional football club, it is worth considering the views of Webb *et al* (1966 as cited in Lee 2000) which pour scorn on any study that uses just one single method of data collection. They regard this type of study as far inferior to any that use multiple methods because every method is fallible in one form or another, and it is unwise to base too much reliance on one. Bryman (1988:131) explores this theme further when he discusses the strategy referred to as 'triangulation of measurement'. He states that (ibid.): "By and large, researchers have viewed the main message of the idea of triangulation as entailing a need to employ more than one method of investigation and hence more than one type of data. Within this context, quantitative and qualitative research may be perceived as different ways of examining the same research problem." With this in mind, it would seem wise to ensure that whilst participant observation seems eminently suitable, the possibility of interviews, either informal or formal, and collection of numerical data should not be ruled out.

6.5 Examples of Research in Participant Observation
Now that the theoretical aspects of the type of research most suited to this study have been discussed, it is worth noting some of the key points that have arisen from a small

selection of previous studies in participant observation (with particular emphasis on research with children), as it is this method that will feature most heavily in the research. One of the problems that participant observers often face is the ability to find a way into the field. The initial difficulty for the researcher is making contact with someone who can allow them access to the field – this person is usually referred to as the gatekeeper. According to Homan (1991), there are four types of gatekeeper. Firstly, there is the person who has some kind of right or legal obligation to look after another's welfare, for example a head teacher or a hospital administrator. Secondly, the person who has access to raw data is related to the subject. Thirdly, someone whom is acting *in loco parentis,* and fourthly, a person who acts as an intermediary between the researcher and the subjects who makes that sure the subjects are happy to be party to the research. If one were to take a teacher as an example, then all four types may apply to the same person. For the researcher, it is then a case of persuading the gatekeeper that they are doing something that is worthwhile and perhaps more importantly, that is also ethically acceptable. Cox (1997), although referring to the role of questionnaires, argues strongly that children should have the right to say no if they do not want to be party to the research and therefore the researcher is faced with a moral dilemma of whether or not to go ahead in the first place.

Fleming (1997) found that there were other difficulties when researching the behaviour of children, notably in how to gain access into their world. Purely as an adult researcher trying to gain a child's confidence is problem enough, but this can also be exacerbated when the child also considers the researcher to be a stranger.

Once the researcher has access to the knowledge he is seeking, there are further issues that can cause moral dilemmas. For example, the issue touched upon when discussing the arguments presented by Cox (1997), was based upon privacy and intrusion. When can information become public knowledge? Homan (1991) argues that in our society, there are some conceptions of privacy within public places. He gives an example whereby it may be taboo to stare at somebody on a beach who is having difficulty changing his (or her) clothes, and one would be expected to look in the other direction until the embarrassment has passed. However, he goes on to say (1991:45) that that "does not stop their being observed by assiduous students of human behaviour", and this would seem a reasonable conclusion. Wheaton (1997) expressed the difficulties she faced in her research on windsurfing and surfing cultures with regard to informal conversations she had, particularly when these conversations were based with people who lived in the same house as her. Here there is a link between confidentiality and the betrayal of trust, an issue made even more difficult by the fact that some of her subjects were her friends. In contrast, Yorganci (1997:154) felt totally at ease with divulging information with regard to her study of an athletics club that "concluded that some women and girls are sexually harassed by their coaches". Her methods for this research involved covert participant observation, informal interviews and questionnaires and she concludes (ibid: 160) that "ethical issues must be recognised, and thought through, but do not preclude the use of such methods". Although, to different levels of morality, (Wheaton's dilemma was concerned with whether to reveal the gossip amongst friends whilst Yorganci's was related to sexual harassment between the coaches and the athletes), both had to make decisions concerning, in the interests of research, what could be revealed.

When Smith (1975) researched the role and impact of collective violence in sport, he found that the problems he faced included the necessity to be ready for explosive reactions from various individuals at any time. Without being in a state of perpetual readiness, he risked the pitfall of missing crucial pieces of information. It also became clear to him that the accounts of crowd members to whom he spoke after the events, were vulnerable to conscious or unconscious distortions of the truth in order maintain their status within the group.

Of course, distortion of the truth is not only confined to individuals for this reason. Sugden and Tomlinson (1999:395), in their research of the world football governing body FIFA, found that their version of the 'facts' differed somewhat from FIFA's. In a letter to the authors Keith Cooper (FIFA Director of Communications) stated that he felt the people best placed to represent FIFA's opinions are those who officially represent the organisation. It is not entirely surprising that those employed by an organisation may wish their employers to be shown in the best possible light, but this does not necessarily mean they come to the same conclusions about the way it is run as the researchers. Obviously, the researcher needs to be aware that official accounts are not always valid.

Finally, there are two crucial aspects of participant observation that must be considered before entering into the field and both are aptly discussed by Dandelion (1997:187). Firstly, he considers the problem of 'knowing too much'. This has already been discussed with relation to bias, but it should also be realised that this bias may be purely unintentional. Often, a researcher will be knowledgeable about the field he is entering, but he must make sure that this prior knowledge is not used to produce inaccurate or inappropriate conclusions. Secondly, Dandelion (ibid: 188) highlights the perils of 'saying too much'. He describes his own experiences when researching the behaviour of a Quaker group in which he found that he was manipulating them by inadvertently playing a lead role in group discussion. More pertinently to this work, Bryman cites an example, of when journalist Hunter Davis was given permission to be a participant observer at Tottenham Hotspur Football Club. The manager, Bill Nicholson, stated that he regretted this (cited in Bryman 1988:112-3): "Permission was not given by me but by someone else at the Club. In hindsight I should have over-ruled the decision. I know Davies' work was highly acclaimed, but after this particular match I was forced to keep quiet when I wanted to say a lot of things straight away."

In this case Davies was having an effect upon the people he was observing and a researcher should try to go to lengths to ensure that this does not happen. These two key points clearly show the need to carefully consider the role one plays during this research method.

6.6 Case Studies

The main aim of this research is to analyse the vocational socialisation of a young person into professional football. In order to do that, a detailed case study of a football club would need to be undertaken. Holloway (1997:30) defines a case study as, "an entity which is researched as a single unit and has clear boundaries; it is an investigation of an organisation, an event, a process or a programme".

According to Yin (1994) and Murray and Lawrence (2000), a case study does not just require a single data-gathering technique, but could involve several. Murray and Lawrence (2000:113) state that: "A key feature of case studies is observation. This may mean active deployment of techniques such as participant observation and direct observation. It also means the use and application of other data-gathering techniques such as interviews, content analysis of documents, anecdotal data- gathering, discourse analysis and ethnography...".

Therefore, a case study describes the general methodology, where participant observation can be a major feature of it. Murray and Lawrence (ibid) highlight the fact that case studies are good for uncovering social interaction within small groups, but as with the more specific method of participant observation, one must be aware of the danger of showing bias within the research.

When doing research based upon a case study, Yin (1994:35) states that the researcher must be aware of the issue of validity. This involves "knowing whether a study's findings are generalized beyond the immediate case study". In order to find the answer to this, he explains that the study must be able to be replicated. Thus, the procedures used must be clear and well documented in order to make it possible to ensure that this can happen.

Yin also discusses the issue of reliability. He states (1994:36) that "the goal of reliability is to minimize the errors and biases in a study". In order to prove that the results are reliable he claims that it should be possible to do the same case study again (at the same place) and arrive at the same findings. One could argue here that although ideally this is true, one should also be aware that situations change over time. The findings may not be the same in a later study, but this does not mean that they were unreliable at the time the initial case study was undertaken.

6.7 Method and Data Analysis

This research is based upon an in-depth case study of a youth system at Brighton and Hove Football Club between 2000 and 2003. The technique I used in order to gain information within this case study is participant observation. It took the form of me taking the role as participant observer, whereby I was a regular visitor to the club. In so doing, I was happy to explain the purpose of my research to any interested party.

For all three seasons, (2000/1, 2001/2, 2002/3) my visits on Monday evenings to the Worthing Sports Centre (where the Centre of Excellence was based) enabled me to mix with parents, who stood watching the coaching sessions on the sidelines, and with the coaches when they were available. There were occasions when I was able to talk to the boys, but this proved quite difficult, because as soon as they arrived they got changed and then went straight into the coaching session. At the end of the session, their parents would often whisk them away in the car in order to get home quickly. However, as a teacher involved in sport who took charge of district football teams, I was able to talk to boys on other occasions. I also attended a few matches against other clubs that occurred on Sundays at a local public school. As a teacher I also had easy access to those boys who were rejected by the club at some stage between nine and sixteen.

My research initially involved me visiting the Club's training ground on a weekly basis in order to watch and talk to all of those (staff and players) who were involved with the Scholarship Scheme. For the 2000/01 season, I began my visits from July 1st onwards purely as a research student. However, in September of that year I was asked by the Director of Youth, if it would be possible to find educational courses that would be appropriate for part-time study for five third years, two first years and an eighteen year old player who had signed for the Club but was not part of the Scholarship Scheme. As a Head of Physical Education at a local sixth form college, I said that I could help by offering courses at my place of work. I saw this not only as an opportunity to help the club but also as a way of allowing me greater access to the youth players I was researching.

I arranged for the third years to study for General Studies 'A' level and the 'European Computer Driving Course' (ECDL) and to be taught by my colleagues. For the two first years I, along with another colleague, taught them Physical Education 'AS' level. In addition I arranged for one of them to have private tuition in Mathematics 'AS' level and for the other in English Literature 'AS' level. For the eighteen year old, I taught, again with a colleague, the second year of Physical Education 'A' level. (He had already completed the first at his previous school.)

For the 2001/2 season, I was again approached by the Director of Youth, and asked if I would consider taking up a part-time post with the football club as Educational Liaison Officer. This post would initially mean that I had responsibility to find educational courses for all Scholars, which I did not see as too much of a problem. However, it transpired that it also meant being responsible for delivering a 'Core Skills' programme. This course was devised by the Professional Football Association, and it is a requirement for all football clubs to provide for their scholars in order to qualify for funding for the scheme. The course involves teaching all three age groups how to deal with life as a professional footballer. (For example, topics such as media attention and financial awareness). I was in fact undertaking the role of a pastoral tutor. At this point, I felt I had some issues to address with regard to the effect this might have on my research.

On the positive side, I knew I would get to know the youth team players much better and as a member of staff, I would now had much greater access within the club and would be able to freely mix with the players, parents and other staff. In addition, I knew I would become party to conversations about life at the club, which would not be possible without this new post.

However, a formal post within the organisation I was researching could lead to bias in my reporting (more likely in a positive form in order not to antagonise my employers). It could also mean players (and parents) feeling constrained in their conversations with me in case I reported anything that could have a negative affect on them, back to the coaches. I therefore risked losing their trust, and this would make any valuable fieldwork almost impossible.

Having carefully considered the problems created by such a development, I decided to accept the post offered, as the advantage of having virtual free access within the club, particularly at the training ground and regular meetings with the youth team players seemed to clearly outweigh any problems anticipated. I made every attempt to gain and keep the trust of players and parents in order to limit any adverse preconceptions on their part. I did this by making sure that I was not seen publicly in the company of the coaches on a regular basis and by ensuring that every conversation they had with me remained private unless I informed them otherwise.

For the final season of my research this whole issue became more acute as my involvement with the club deepened on two levels. Firstly, in July 2002 I was asked by the Club's Community Affairs Manager to apply for a new full time post at the club entitled 'Manager of Study Support'. Although this post did not have anything to do with the football side of the club (it involved being head of an educational centre at the Withdean Stadium where the first team play their matches and is more to do with links with schools and adult education), it was nevertheless a full time job at the club. I was eventually offered the post but I knew that this could make objective research more problematical.

Secondly, a part of my new job was to act as a link between the club and the schools of those boys who play for the Centre of Excellence teams. My job title at the club was now, 'Manager of the Study Support Centre and Educational and Welfare'. Clearly, the impression this would give to the boys and their parents was that I was someone they had to talk to, but that I was seen as part of the coaching staff and could therefore have a say in their future at the club. Ultimately, this could result in my research being severely flawed.

The conclusions that I made before I took up the full-time post were exactly the same as I had made the previous year with regard to the part-time post. It did make me re-evaluate the need to ensure the objectivity of my research at the club and the people who work there. I went to even more extremes to convince players and parents of confidentiality when informing me of their views about the club. One way I was able to do this was to assure all that I would give all players (both those at the Centre of Excellence and also those involved with the Scholarship Scheme) different names in order to protect their anonymity and therefore their chances of success. I did not feel it necessary to do the same for the coaching staff as I did not expect their position at the club to be compromised and also that I would stand by anything I wrote.

My method for collecting data changed fairly significantly as my research progressed. I began by basing my research upon secondary sources in order to gain a detailed understanding of the professional football industry. Once I felt I had a good background of knowledge, I embarked upon research that was mainly based on primary sources – in other words fieldwork.

These primary sources included semi-structured interviews with players, parents and coaches from the Centre of Excellence at Brighton and Hove Albion as well as with players and coaches at the Club's Training Ground. Throughout the three years of fieldwork, I undertook the role of participant observer at both.

Initially, during the time that I was at the Centre of Excellence I used a Dictaphone to record interviews that were done on a semi-structured basis. However, by the second year and even more so by the third year of research, I was spending so much time in the company of the people I was researching that I often wrote down what they said in my notebook which I carried with me. On most occasions I did this whilst in the presence of my subjects. It would not have been feasible to have carried a Dictaphone with me at all times and pressing the record button at the time when an individual was about to say something of relevance would have been extremely difficult.

In addition, when I became teacher of the Core Skills programme to the Scholars, every two or three months I asked them to write down answers to some set questions which would help them to evaluate how they were progressing. Sometimes I would ask the boys not to put their names on the returned papers, although this would depend upon the nature of the questions.

To add to my knowledge about the club, I also had access to the Club information about past youth team players (for example, the year they joined the Club and the school(s) they attended) which I was able to draw upon.

Fortunately, I was able to visit and expand my research at Bristol City and Charlton Athletic as I knew the Academy Directors at both Clubs. It would not have been possible to have done in-depth research with these Clubs that could be considered comparable to the research undertaken at Brighton and Hove Albion due to time constraints. I therefore chose to restrict my primary research to semi-structured interviews with the Academy Directors. I knew that this could only ever give me limited information about life s a prospective footballer at both clubs.

Finally, I was able to add to my own findings with secondary research through Owsley (2000) for Bristol City and Garland and Chakraborti for Charlton Athletic (2001).

CHAPTER 7
ACQUIRING THE HABITUS OF A PROFESSIONAL FOOTBALLER AT BRIGHTON & HOVE ALBION FOOTBALL CLUB

7.1. Introduction

The main purpose of the field work related within this book is to provide a case study that will aptly illustrate the vocational socialisation processes that a young aspiring footballer has to go through in order to become a professional. Ingrained within these processes is the acquiring of a habitus that is an essential part of being a successful player. The challenge of undertaking such field work is to observe and identify the significant elements of a professional footballer's habitus and evaluate how this is acquired. Brighton and Hove Albion Football Club provided me with the perfect opportunity for such a case study, not only because of its location (I live in the city of Brighton), but also because of the access I was able gain within it. What follows is a descriptive account of the field work combined with an interpretive discussion of the key issues.

7.2. A recent history of the club

Since 1999, Brighton & Hove Albion has been through a complete transformation from the difficult times the club suffered during the mid-1990's. The Club had been in acute financial trouble and the problems were compounded by the fact that the Goldstone Ground, (where home matches were once played) with its decaying structure, was seen by many to be unfit for modern professional football. In order to try to rectify the situation the Club's board of directors elected to sell the ground without having been able to build another or even to find a suitable site for a new one. The solution as the directors saw it, was to ground share with Gillingham Football Club in Kent (about 75 miles away), until a permanent home could be found in the Brighton area. The plight of the Club became national news (Chuter et al. 2001(b)). This caused much indignation from the fans, and many local politicians and the local newspaper shared their views. Demonstrations were held and the directors were accused of asset stripping the Football Club for their own gain. The Club had also slipped down the divisions and had spent two seasons languishing towards the bottom of Division 3, facing the prospect of semi-professional football if they were relegated to the Conference League (ibid).

As the only professional football club in Sussex, Brighton & Hove Albion has a potentially very high fan base. The nearest clubs to it are, to the west Portsmouth (40 miles away), to the north Crystal Palace (35 miles away) and to the north-east, Gillingham. However, with a tarnished reputation, a low league position, poor performances and playing home games 75 miles from the town meant that at best the fan base lay dormant and at worst, the Club was seen as a disaster. On average, only two thousand Brighton fans were making the journey to Gillingham for the home games: prior to moving, an average of six thousand home supporters had attended matches at the Goldstone Ground. A potential knock-on effect meant that the Club ran the risk of young local players who had a chance of becoming professionals turning their back on the club and looking to play for others instead. This problem was exacerbated by the fact that the Club had a bad reputation for nurturing young local players through to their first team, sometimes bringing in young players from areas outside Sussex.

However, in 1999 after two years at Gillingham, the club returned to Brighton and used the local athletics stadium (Withdean) as its temporary home base (Chuter et al. 2001(b)). The Club also had a new chairman and set of directors, and they had appointed a new manager, Mickey Adams, who had an excellent reputation for managing lower division clubs. This marked a new dawn for the club. In addition, Martin Hinshelwood, who was appointed Director of Youth in 1997, was beginning to improve the reputation of the Club's youth policy and was using a higher percentage of local players for the youth teams. In the same year that Hinshelwood was appointed, the F.A. had produced the 'Charter for Quality'. In response to this, Brighton & Hove Albion set up a Centre of Excellence. (Academies were essentially only to be set up by Premiership clubs due to the financial implications).

This was funded in the following way;

Sport England	£69,000
Premier League	£69,000
Total	£138,000

By the third year of my research, this had changed to:

FA	£34,500	(25%)
Premier League	£34,500	(25%)

The Government	£20,700	(15%)
PFA	£17,250	(12.5%)
The Football Foundation	£17,250	(12.5%)
Sport England	£13,800	(10 %)
Total	£138,000	

In addition, the Club contributed £62,500 towards the Scheme and had secured £7,500 worth of sponsorship to reach a total of £208,000. From this, the main expenses to be paid were the salary of the Director of Youth, the Youth Team Manager and all part time coaches used for the Centre of Excellence.

During the third season of research (2000-2003), there was cause for concern at the Club as the contributions promised by the Government and Sport England had not been forthcoming.

In the Club's first season at Withdean (1999-2000), the first team began to improve, finishing eighth in Division 3. The future for the club now looked a lot brighter and the youth teams were performing well against other clubs. When Adams was originally given the job of first team manager, he had asked the Chairman of the Club (Dick Knight) if he could bring in his own staff to run the youth programme and by doing, relinquish the services of Martin Hinshelwood and Dean Wilkins (Youth Team Coach). Knight had refused this request, although Hinshelwood knew that if he was seen by Adams after a period of time not to be doing the job to Adam's satisfaction, his position might well become untenable (Field Notes 30/8/00). In terms of continuity, this type of situation has long been a problem with regard to professional football clubs and their youth set up. New first team managers often like to bring in people they know and trust, but because of the high turnover rate that is customary for managers at football clubs, the youth system can be adversely affected in the process. Also, the youth team coaches may lose their jobs as a knock-on effect of the failure of the first team manager who was sacked.

7.3. The Centre of Excellence

7.3. a) Structure

At the start of my research, during the season of 2000/1, the Centre of Excellence consisted of players from six different age groups, ranging from the Under 11's to the

Under 16's. By the beginning of the 2002/3 season, an Under 9 and an Under 10 team had been added. Each team had been designated a coach/manager who took charge of the team throughout the season.

The players attended training on Monday evenings at either Worthing Leisure Centre or Park College Eastbourne, depending on which of the two sites was closest to their home. The players from the Under 13's up to the Under 16's also attended training altogether on Thursday evenings at Sussex University (the Club's Training Ground). Matches for all age groups were played on Sunday mornings, the home pitch for the Brighton teams being one of two local public schools.

Each site had a Centre Director, Vic Bragg at Worthing and John Lambert at Eastbourne, both of whom were local teachers. Vic Bragg is also current England Under 18 Schools Manager. The person with overall responsibility for both sites was Director of Youth, Martin Hinshelwood. The 'Charter for Quality' stated that Centre Directors must have a UEFA 'A' Coaching Licence (which Bragg and Lambert both had) and the team coaches must have or be working towards a UEFA 'B' Licence, as was the case at Brighton. Many of the coaches, of which there are nineteen altogether, were local teachers or people who had played or were playing semi-professional football themselves. However, some of the coaches were people who had little playing experience, but had a desire to coach at the Club and had taken the appropriate coaching qualifications.

The aims of the Centre of Excellence (see below), which were devised by Martin Hinshelwood and Vic Bragg, focussed on assisting the boys in their football and social development although it was not clear from this how the Club helped the boys to cope with failure.

Centre of Excellence – Aims

1. To develop boys' social skills and football education in a safe, disciplined, working environment.
2. To create an enjoyable atmosphere using a structured learning programme.
3. To develop boys' football techniques and skills.
4. To enhance boys' understanding of football.
5. To ultimately, produce boys who are capable of becoming professional Footballers.

This is particularly poignant, as typically each age group will have a squad average of fifteen players. The number that the PFA fund to go on the Scholarship Scheme each year is eighteen, therefore averaging six for each age group. It follows that on average, nine of the fifteen will be disappointed at the end of their season with the Under 16's. In addition, from Under 9's through to Under 16's, the Club will normally sign boys on for a one or two-year period and at the end of that time, the Club may well wish to releases them, thus increasing the number of disappointed youngsters.

Coaches for each age group received a 'Programme of Work' and a job description (see below).

Centre of Excellence

Programme of Work (2000/1)

Each session will start with 20 minutes Passing and Movement.

September 7th – October 26th

    1. Receiving/Control

       Passing and Movement (all age groups)

November 2nd – December 7th

    2. Defending: Individually and as a team

       (13/14/15/16)

    2. Turning/Dribbling/Running with the ball

       (10/11/12)

December 14th – January 18th

    3. Shooting (10/11/12/13/14)

    3. Crossing/Finishing from crosses

       (15/16)

January 25th – February – 22nd

    4. Heading (10/11/12/13)

    4. Crossing (14)

    4. Shooting (15/16)

March 1st – March 22nd

    5. Defending: Individually and basic team defending

       (10/11/12)

    5. Turning, Dribbling, Running with the ball

       (13/14/15/16)

March 29th – End of Season

    6. Receiving/Control Passing and Movement (All age groups)

Job Descriptions for Coaches

1. Prepare and organise coaching sessions at the centre of Excellence in line with the Syllabus of work laid down by the Centre of Excellence Director and Director of Youth.
2. Ensure that the safety of players in their charge is of paramount importance.
3. Assess the progress of players so as to be able to make decisions about each boy's future development.
4. Work with triallists and help make decisions about their future within the time laid down by league rules.
5. Keep a register of attendance of players. Registers to be given to Director of Youth at the end of each season.
6. To take opportunities to develop their own coaching knowledge.
7. Attend staff in-service training days as designated by the club.
8. Liaise with parents in conjunction with the Centre Director and/or Director of Youth.
9. Report any emotional or developmental problems to the Club's Child Protection Officer.
10. Liaise with the Club's medical advisors regarding injuries, treatment and rehabilitation of players.

Vic Bragg and Martin Hinshelwood devised both of these documents. Other staff at the Centre included a physiotherapist, Kim Eaton who was a full time member of staff and a Child Protection Officer, Les Rogers, who was also one of the coaches.

As with any football club that run a Centre of Excellence, the players sign contracts for varying lengths of time according to what age group they are in. The under 9's, under10's, under11's and under 12's are all given one year contracts. At the end of that year, if they are to be kept on they must be offered two-year contract (for when they are under 13 and under 14). However, the player is allowed to leave at the end of his year at under 13 if he wishes, although the Club is not allowed to release the player unless requested to do so by the player and his parents. Upon entering the under 13 age group, the Club is also able to offer players a YD6 contract. This means that the player is given the opportunity of signing a four-year contract. Finally, upon entering the under 15 age group, the player is either offered a two year contract or released. It is at the end of the season, as an Under 16, that the player is informed about whether he is to be taken on the Scholarship Scheme or be released. In theory, at this age he could be taken on as a full professional.

During the time when a player is out of contract with another Club, a player is able to sign for another professional club, providing it is within an hour and a half travelling distance of the player's home. Any player, who attends a Centre of Excellence, is still allowed to play for his school and schools representative teams, but he is not allowed to play for any other club, be it professional or non-professional.

At Brighton and Hove Albion, as with all other professional clubs, a player must be invited to the Centre of Excellence in order to play for the Club at the younger age groups. Players are watched playing for the school, club or representative sides by coaches or specially appointed scouts from the Club (currently there are three), although Martin Hinshelwood does do the large percentage of this work. He reports (Field Notes 5/10/03) that he regularly watches up to ten games a week during the football season, and during one week watched seventeen. He is keen to point out that this rarely involves watching the whole game, due partly to time restraints, and also because he would rather watch a large number of players over a short period of time as opposed to few for a whole game.

Both Hinshelwood and Wilkins have letters sent to them from boys or teachers and coaches representing the boys asking for trials. They normally average between thirty and forty letters a week between them. All letters received a reply. If upon reading the letter it is decided that the player may be worth watching, Hinshelwood will ask for a fixture list of the teams the boy plays for so that he can be seen. Generally though, any player Under 16 will not be watched if he lives outside Sussex due to the FA ruling regarding a player having to live within an hour and a half's travel of the Club he plays for. Letters are not only sent from the south east of England, but are also received from as far away as Africa and Australia.

Hinshelwood and Wilkins also have to make value judgements without seeing the player. He said (Field Notes 4/3/03):

> "Let me give an example of one I received today. I've been sent

a newspaper cutting from a boy who is seventeen. The article
says that he scored two goals for his village team, Buxted. It
also says that one of the players he was playing against was 53
and another 64. On the strength of this he asks if there
is any chance of him getting a scholarship with the Club. What
do you reckon? Do you think I should be tempted? I have
to say that on the other hand some letters may tempt me a little
more."

It became clear to me during the first season of fieldwork that Hinshelwood was selective
when deciding which players to watch. This was due to the fact that he did most of the
scouting and time did not allow him to see all the boys who wrote to the club or were
identified as being worth seeing. However, by the third season of fieldwork, Hinshelwood
had begun to ask people whose opinion he trusted, mainly the Centre of Excellence
coaching staff, to watch players for him and to report back. This delegation meant that the
number of players watched increased quite significantly.

7.3. b) My relationship with those attending the Centre of Excellence

During my first visit to the Worthing Leisure Centre, it became clear to me that
accessibility to the players in this situation was going to be quite difficult. Three age
groups train at any one time and as soon as the session was finished, their parents took
the boys straight home. Some of the parents waited at the side of the training area until
the end, whilst others went home and returned to collect their sons when the session was
finished. The parents who waited chatted amongst themselves and I felt that to interrupt
them would appear to be intrusive.

However, I was very familiar with the boys and parents from one of the age groups
(Under 15's) as I had been Brighton Schools District Manager to many of them for two
years at a younger age (Under 12 and 13). I decided to concentrate on this group and
chart their progress as I did have a good deal of prior knowledge and in addition,
accessibility to them and their parents was not a problem. This did not limit me to
concentrate solely upon this group, as a few had brothers who played with other age

groups. Also, I did know some parents of boys from other age groups either from my own playing days or on a social basis.

My first visit was mainly spent talking to people I already knew, (Martin Hinshelwood, Vic Bragg and two of the coaches, Bob Bantock and Kevin Keehan), about the way the Centre was run. All discussions were extremely helpful and the information they gave me allowed me to quickly gain a grasp of the processes involved at a Centre of Excellence.

7.3. c) The players

When I started my research, my focus age group, the under 15's, had fifteen players signed on for two years. One of the players, Conor, who had been with this age group left the previous summer to join Crystal Palace. He was one of two goalkeepers at Brighton and both had long been considered by the coaches at the Club and by schoolteachers of representative teams (including myself) to be of similar overall ability and potential, suffice to say that they had their own strengths and weaknesses. As only one goalkeeper can be played at any one time, both players only played fifty per cent of the matches. Conor's parents felt that he was the better of the two and that he should be playing all of the games. When Crystal Palace offered him the opportunity to go there, he and his parents decided to take it. At this time Brighton were in Division 3 and Crystal Palace in Division 1 and therefore this decision was not difficult to understand, despite Martin Hinshelwood's efforts to persuade him to stay. Since that time, he has been offered a Scholarship with Crystal Palace, been substitute for the first team and represented England under 18's.

One other player, Don left at the beginning of his final year (under 16), as he felt he wasn't going to be selected at the end of the season for the Scholarship Scheme and that he would be wasting his time if he stayed.

I was intrigued by the fact that a player in this age group who had played for the schools district team when I was manager never attended the Centre of Excellence. He was considered by many of his peers to be one of the best players for that age group. When I asked some of the players why they thought he had not been asked to attend, Liam replied (Field Notes 5/2/03):

"It's because of his Dad. He is a bit mouthy. I don't think the Club

102

would have wanted all the hassle he would have brought with him.

The Club don't like parents getting involved – if they do, it only
works against you."

However, when I asked Hinshelwood why he was never asked to attend he said that
(Field Notes 9/2/03) "he just wasn't good enough". The player's peers did not share this
view.

7.3. d) The players' families

For obvious reasons, parents of aspiring players often take enough interest in their son's
progress to want to watch them play whenever they can. From my experience as a
district/county schools football manager, I was aware just how much some of the parents
wanted to be involved, particularly from the under 11 to the under 14 age groups. Most of
the parents of the boys who played for these teams would drive to away games and many
would offer to provide refreshments for both teams for the home games. As the children
got older, from the under 15's through to the under 19's, the number of parents attending
the matches tended to dwindle. This, according to many of the players I taught, was
because they were embarrassed to have the parents watching them.

However, this did not tend to happen with parents of my focus year group who attended
the Centre of Excellence, as virtually all parents attended the matches throughout their
association with Brighton and Hove Albion. Clearly, the parents of this group got to
know each other very well over the years and formed friendships. Within this group of
friends were sub-groups, although these could change according to the friendship groups
of the boys themselves. Players could fall out over positional rivalry or an issue not
associated with football.

The Club gives all parents a code of conduct, which aims to ensure amongst other issues,
that parents behave themselves at matches. The Club is insistent that parents do not shout
anything (including advice) from the sidelines. The only problems that have occurred
with parents during actual matches according to one of the coaches (Field Notes 3/3/03)
have been those from other clubs.

The coaches' response to my questions about whether parents ever caused problems other
than during matches was that most said that it did not happen whilst others could only

remember isolated incidents. One coach, Les Rogers, told me (Field Notes 7/2/03) that he had his own rule, never to become too familiar with the parents. He always insisted on avoiding use of Christian names. Another coach told me (Field Notes 7/2/03) that a parent wrote an eight page letter to the first team manager saying that his son's Centre of Excellence coach knew nothing about football or how to deal with young players. This letter was never replied to. The boy continued to play for the team but was not one of those who were offered a Scholarship place. The coach said (Field Notes 7/2/03) that the parents' 'bad' attitude was one of the reasons why he was not chosen.

For the age group (the under 15's) I was focussing the majority of my fieldwork upon, the parent with the most influence on the players was Kevin Keehan. He was well known in local football circles, both as an outstanding player and as a manager in the men's County League. His eldest son showed signs of potential as a footballer at an early age and began to form close friendships with other boys in the area of a similar ability. Kevin Keehan set up an under 9 team for his son and his friends to play in a local league and they performed particularly well in this competition, especially as it was for the under 10 age group year. Many of the team joined the Brighton and Hove Albion Centre of Excellence, which is done by invitation only. Keehan then went on to take his UEFA 'B' coaching qualification and was then asked to be a coach at the Club himself. The team he was asked to coach was his son's age group as it was felt that he knew the boys better than anyone else.

Most of the parents got on very well with Keehan, as he had spent a lot of time coaching their sons and throughout the time he was manager, I was unaware of any animosity towards him being the manager of his son's team from any other parents or players of the team. There were differences of opinion over team selection, particularly if a parent's own son was made substitute, but to my knowledge, no parent accused Kevin Keehan of being biased towards his own son, who was occasionally dropped himself. However, when I asked Liam and Gordon of their thoughts a couple of years later, they said (Field Notes 5/2/03) that although Stuart was undoubtedly one of the better players they did not think that his Dad should have made him captain and that doing this merely invited criticism.

The Club was leaving itself open to criticism from parents of boys not selected for the Centre of Excellence who had not been in Keehan's original team. In all, of the sixteen at the Club, eleven had been in Keehan's team.

However, to balance the argument that the best players in the area were at the Centre of Excellence, ten of these boys represented Sussex Schools at football, and this was selected and managed by a schoolteacher from mid-Sussex who had no links with the Club. This argument was weak as far as some of the boys were concerned.

Both Gordon and Liam agreed that Hinshelwood heavily influenced all Sussex Schools managers in their selection of players. They agreed that he did not set out to do this deliberately, but the mere fact that any player he saw as being good enough to be invited to represent the Centre of Excellence, should inevitably be carefully considered for the school's county team.

I was particularly interested to see that of this year group at the Centre of Excellence, ten of the sixteen (60%) lived in Brighton. This is disproportionate to the to the number of people living in Brighton compared to the catchment area of the Centre of Excellence, in other words, anywhere within one hour's drive of the Centre, which in general terms means residing in Sussex or just beyond its borders. One of the parents of a boy from an older age group, who had been rejected, complained to me (Field Notes 12/8/00) that his son had never had a chance as he lived in Crawley (a town situated in the north of Sussex and to the south of London). He felt that there was a strong bias towards the boys who lived in Brighton, and there was a feeling of an 'us and them' situation.

Joe, a player who also lived in Crawley, was offered a place on the Scholarship despite not ever having attended the Centre of Excellence. He was only seen by Martin Hinshelwood playing for the Sussex County Under 16 towards the end of the season. I asked him why he thought he had not been asked to join the Centre of Excellence when he was younger. He replied (Field Notes 22/1/02):

> "I just was never noticed by anyone at the Albion. You feel
> an outsider not living in Brighton. Living in Crawley is bad
> news as far as playing for the Albion is concerned – it's a
> a real disadvantage. If you're lucky, you can get spotted by
> one of the London clubs, but they don't seem come into

Sussex that much."

For Joe, attracting the attention of the London clubs did not seem to be a major problem. He had been at the Crystal Palace Centre of Excellence for two years as an Under 11 and under 12, with Fulham for six weeks when he was under 13 and with Charlton when he was under 14.

The issue of the effects an area of residence can have on an individual's chances of success is discussed in more detail (see 7.2.e).

When the team reached the under 15 stage, Martin Hinshelwood decided to ask Kevin Keehan to take another age group and hand over this team to one of his other coaches. At this point Keehan decided not to coach at the Club any more. There was another twist to the tale. Dick Knight, the Club's Chairman, was in fact Keehan's uncle. Had Keehan remained the coach of that team, he would have been instrumental in advising Martin Hinshelwood who from that age group should be offered a scholarship at the Club when the team reached the end of their time as under 16's. Added to this was the fact that Keehan had just been appointed as Brighton and Hove Albion's Commercial Manager. His position as a coach at the Centre of Excellence at the Club had become untenable as far as he was concerned.

Overall, the parent's attitude towards the Club was very supportive, particularly towards Hinshelwood, who with Wilkins was generally seen as the main catalyst behind the success of the Club's youth programme. However, the parents of the some of the boys who were not to be selected for the Scholarship Scheme did tend to show signs of discontent when it began to dawn on them that their son might not be chosen. For example, Phil's father complained that his son "is never allowed to play in his best position" (Field Notes 13/1/02).

7.3. e) Location of residence

As part of the responsibilities within my job as Manager of Education and Welfare, I was given the task of compiling a list of all the schools attended by those who were to attend the Centre of Excellence for the season 2003/4. In all there were ninety-five boys who between them attended fifty-seven schools. These schools comprised of thirty-eight secondary schools and nineteen primary or middle schools. Overall, fifty-four of the schools were state schools, with only three boys attending public or private schools. Two of the schools attended were outside Sussex (one in Tunbridge Wells, Kent and the other in Southampton, Hampshire).

The most startling fact was the fact that all of the schools based in Sussex were located on the coast or within a few miles of the A23/M23 corridor that runs through the centre of Sussex from Brighton to London. The majority of players (over 70%) went to schools within half an hour's drive of Brighton. This means that there were large towns in Sussex, for example Horsham and East Grinstead, which did not have Brighton and Hove Albion players attending one of their schools. Also, no players at the Centre of Excellence attended a rural school.

Within the conurbation of Brighton and Hove are ten secondary state schools. Eight of these schools are represented at the Centre – the two that are not represented are situated in the most deprived areas of the city. Both of these schools have had significant problems over recent years, with one labelled by the Government as a failing school. This school is due to close by 2005. Although when asked, Hinshelwood stated (Field Notes 2/6/03) that the omission of representatives of these two schools was pure chance, it did seem likely that boys from them may not be seen as the type who would respond to the fairly strict lifestyle required for professional football.

7.3. f) Place of birth

Although it had already been established that all the of players bar two who were attending the Centre of Excellence during this research were resident in East and West Sussex, one way of extending this line of research was to find out how many professionals who were born in Sussex were playing in the Premiership or the Football League. By doing this it would give an indication as to how successful the counties of East and West Sussex are at producing professional footballers. As Brighton and Hove Albion are the only professional football club in either county and generally have the pick of the players, it could also be seen as a measure for assessing the success of the Club's youth system.

According to Rollin and Rollin (2003) there were 21 born in either East or West Sussex from a total of 2172 that were born in England. Of the 21, at the stage of this research, 8 were full-time professionals at the Club.

However, it is difficult to use these figures to accurately assess the youth system at the Club, as one of the players listed, left the Club and professional football four years beforehand, therefore making the figures inaccurate. In addition, three more players who were at the Club had attended Sussex schools but were not actually born in Sussex. Furthermore, it is possible that as many as five of the 21 listed did not actually reside in Sussex after the age of five.

It is therefore difficult to accurately assess the Club's ability to produce professional footballers when there appear to be both inconsistencies within the data and a lack of accuracy concerning who went to school for a significant amount of time within either East or West Sussex. However, on the simple calculation that on average if the 2172 were evenly distributed throughout the 46 English county or unitary authorities, there would be 47 professional players per authority. By this alone, the number of professional players born in Brighton, East or West Sussex (20 in total for all three) is very low – the average expected for three authorities being 141.

7.3. g) Family background

As a sport that has a history since the late nineteenth century of being a working class game, I was keen to find out if the current players that are coming through football clubs' youth systems are predominantly from families whose main earner is from the lower occupational groups.

Table 5 shows the Registrar General's scale of social class based upon typical occupations. This forms the basis for Table 6, which compares the fathers' occupation of players at the Centre of Excellence with those of the male population in Great Britain.

CLASS	DESCRIPTION
I	**Professional** – Accountant, barrister, doctor, lawyer, scientist, university lecturer.
II	**Intermediate/managerial and technical** – Author, farmer, fire service officer, journalist, manager, nurse, police officer (inspector or above), school teacher.
III N	**Skilled non-manual** – Cashier, clerk, computer operator, fire officer, playgroup leader, police officer (sergeant and below) sales representative, secretary.
III M	**Skilled manual** – Bus driver, bricklayer, cook, motor mechanic, van sales person.
IV	**Partly skilled/semi skilled** – Farm worker, bar staff, gardener, street trader, postman, shelf filler, traffic warden, tyre and exhaust fitter
V	**Unskilled** – Cleaners, labourer, refuse collector, road construction, road sweeper, window cleaner

Typical occupations based upon the registrar general's scale of social class

Table 5

Registrar General's Scale of Social Class	Father's Occupation Centre of Excellence Under 13-16 (2002/3)	Distribution of male population by social class in Great Britain (1991)[†]
I	3 (4.5%)	7 %
II	11* (18%)	28%
III (N)	18 (27%)	11%
III (M)	19 (28.5%)	33%
IV	10 (15%)	16%
V	4 (6%)	6%
Total	66 (100%)	100%

* One player's mother was the only earner
† Based upon 1991 Census Economic Activity (cited in Reid (1998)
Father's occupation of players at the Centre of Excellence (under 13-16) (2002/3) and the distribution of the male population by social class in Great Britain (1991)
Table 6

Table 6 is based upon the distribution of the fathers' occupation at the Centre of Excellence (Under 13's-Under 16's 2002-3) by social class compared to the distribution of the British working male population in 1991. The data was gathered by interviewing the players on a one to one basis and asking them what their father's occupation was. It should be noted that three boys did not know exactly at what level their father worked (for example, manager or shop floor worker) but from the information they gave calculated guesses were made. The younger age groups (Under 9 – 12) were not asked this question, as I felt it likely (although I had no actual evidence) that their knowledge of what their father did may be less accurate than the older groups.

Table 6 clearly shows that for this group of players, the main family earners are represented in a complete range of occupational classes. It also shows that the percentages for each of the categories for the father's occupation compare quite significantly with Great Britain's male population. The only major difference is between the percentages of the Social Class II and III – all others being fairly similar.

For the Under 16's, the major focus group, other important issues concerning the families of these boys include the fact that five of the seventeen have brothers (two older and three younger) playing for the Club's Centre of Excellence teams in other age groups. Also, that three have fathers who were professional footballers and another three have fathers who had played at semi-professional level.

Sussex is not a county that has a large percentage of non-white ethnic minority groups within the whole population (2.24% according to the Office of National Statistics (2001)), and therefore it was not surprising that very few boys at the Centre of Excellence were anything other than white Caucasian. In this target group only one was of mixed race. For the all the boys who were playing for the Centre of Excellence teams during the season of 2001/2, 7 of the 145 boys (5%) were non-Caucasian. Of the 7, only 2 were black and just as significantly, none were Asian – the others all being of mixed race. However, as the percentage of ethnic minorities within the population in Sussex is proportionally slightly lower than the percentage of ethnic minority footballers at the Centre of Excellence, it would seem to suggest being non-Caucasian does not disadvantage a boy's chances of success at this Club.

7.3. h) Other influences

As a year group the class of 2002 were an exception. During my research, very few other boys I came across had a father who had played professional football, although quite a number had played to a semi-professional level. It was not difficult to predict the response of the boys who had fathers who had played professional football, who had been their biggest influence in choice of career. However, I did ask many of the boys who were not successful from a variety of age groups who or what their biggest influence was, and the overwhelming response was that it was their parents, and more usually, their father. The reasons for this were because of the support they had given them, for example, driving to matches and watching them play. No player felt their school or any specific teacher had the most influence, in fact many of the boys felt that the teachers at school had no influence whatsoever. As a schoolteacher who had spent many hours managing school teams, this came as quite a shock. A large proportion of the players confirmed that many of their teachers did actually take an interest in their football development, but it went no further than that.

It became clear to me at an early stage of my fieldwork, that the boys who attended the Centre of Excellence had very few complaints about the Club – in fact the general feeling was one that was very positive. I was mindful of the fact that whilst their responses and overall attitude seemed to be very genuine, they may have seen it within their interests to show nothing other than happiness. It may not be helpful to his chances overall if their manager felt the boy or his parents had a problem with the Club. Equally, they may have felt that if they had complained to me, I would have passed on their feelings to others at the Club. My overall opinion was that some players and parents appeared to be very careful about what they said and this was a barrier for me, which at times I felt would seriously affect the quality and value of this case study.

The times when I got most response was when the players had left the Centre of Excellence, either to go on to the Scholarship Scheme or as a player who had been rejected. According to the boys, the coaches at the Club varied greatly in their knowledge and their approach. Some of the coaches were heavily criticised. Dick, one of the scholars said (Field Notes 14/1/03): "I don't think the coach I had when I was fourteen related very well to the players. He had difficulty putting his ideas across. I don't think he had much idea. The one we got for the last two years was really good though – what he said was the same as Deano. (Dean Wilkins)".

Another criticism that was regularly made about some of the coaches was that they tried to make things too complicated, so much so that the players did not understand what they were being asked to do.

Perhaps not surprisingly, most of the criticism about the coaches came from the players who had been rejected. Liam and Gordon, two players who had been in my focus group at the Centre of Excellence, both thought that as neither of their fathers had played professional football, they never really had any chance of being chosen for the Scholarship Scheme. Liam also said of one of the players that were chosen (Field Notes 7/2/03): "I think they must have only seen Joe play a couple of times. He never attended the Centre of Excellence. As soon as they found out that his Dad was an ex-pro' – they signed him. It makes you sick."

Gordon felt that fitting in and getting on with the coach were the main keys to success. He said (Field Notes 7/2/03) he was under no illusion that all coaches had favourites and that: "I know you are not going to believe this but the most I ever got to play in my last year during one game was forty five minutes. He (the coach) just didn't like me. I never had a chance. If they didn't rate me, why did they let me stay at the Club for so long? I just feel as if they wasted my time. I think I was used."

Clearly, the fact Gordon was upset by having to be substitute most weeks and felt that he was only kept on to make up the numbers.

Stuart was very upset by the lack of motivation he received from the coaches during his final two years at the Centre of Excellence. He said that (Field Notes 22/2/03):

> "It is so obvious that they have favourites. They just don't
> make you feel wanted if you are not one of them and as a
> result your confidence suffers. This can have a bad effect
> on your game and you have to work really hard to make
> sure it doesn't get to you."

The perception amongst some of the local football fraternity not associated with Brighton & Hove Albion was that some of the Club's coaches could not be fully respected, as they had not played to a high standard themselves. It was felt that although they had read the right textbooks and achieved the required coaching badges, it didn't make them great coaches as nothing can replace the experience of playing.

Interestingly, I was also told by a UEFA 'A' License coach (not associated with Brighton & Hove Albion) that he had stopped being an assessor of coaching courses for the FA as he was fed up with being told before his courses had even started which people had to pass the course – these people always being ex-professional footballers. He insisted that being an ex-professional was not a pre-requisite to being a good coach. In contrast, when I broached Dean Wilkins (himself a UEFA 'A' Licence coach) on the matter that there were accusations that gaining a UEFA 'A' Licence was biased towards ex-footballers and was fixed, his reply (Field Notes 10/7/03) was that in his experience, in general those people who made such accusations were those who had failed the course.

On topic of the standard of coaches at the Brighton and Hove Albion's Centre of Excellence, Martin Hinshelwood stated (Field Notes 10/9/02):

> "I think the coaches we've got do quite a good job. They've
> all got their 'B' Licence, or at least working towards it. I
> suppose ideally I would want people with more experience,
> but I've only got so much in my budget."

When I asked the players about the influence friends had on their football development, many stated than their best friends were also footballers at the Club. It was strongly apparent that once a boy had been signed on by the Club, he then became part of a social as well as a football group, particularly if he lived in Brighton. A typical response was given by Graham, a fifteen year old at the Centre of Excellence, who said (Field Notes 23/1/01):

> "My best friends are those I made when I played for Brighton
> Boys (the local district side) when I was an under 12. Most
> of them are still at the Club now. I tend to hang around with
> other footballers anyway, after all, it is my main interest."

It also became apparent that all of the boys had strong thoughts about becoming a professional footballer at an early age. Some of them had these feelings as long as they could remember, mainly because their fathers had played professional football and their upbringing had intertwined with the game. Others remembered watching football on television when they were aged seven or eight and had dreamed of emulating the players they were watching. Clearly, this is an example of the way the media can influence a child about his perceived future and is what Kidd (1981) describes as an "incidental factor".

Not surprisingly they felt this dream started to stand every chance of becoming a reality when the Club signed them on as members of the Centre of Excellence at the age of ten. Now that the Club has added an under 9 team, the period when boys start to think they could well become a professional footballer becomes that much lower. Children are therefore making decisions about vocational choice that are well within the "fantasy period" as labelled by Ginsberg (1951).

Most of the players had role models they looked up to, and in all cases these were professional footballers that had or were playing in the Premiership. It was clear after speaking to the boys (Field Notes 21/3/03) that most thought that role models had more of an effect on their development (in an indirect way) than their teachers at school. The influence of role models for these players should not be underestimated.

In addition, the majority of these role models were playing in the same position as themselves. There was however one player who was mentioned a few times by different players and that was ex-Arsenal and England international, Tony Adams. He was a popular choice because of his ability to triumph over adversity (he had served a three month jail sentence and overcome an addiction to alcohol) and had been a 'model professional' (Field Notes 21/1/03). Interestingly, none of the young players chose any of the professionals at Brighton and Hove Albion.

7.3. i) Psychological make-up

Although the main theme of this work is to analyse the vocational socialisation processes that one has to go through in order to become a professional footballer, I was keen to see if I could determine in a broad sense, what sort of psychological profile a potential player would need in order to become successful. For this, I decided to try and determine the personality types from an observational capacity only, as in-depth psychological testing would have changed the emphasis of this work.

I found at an early stage of my research, that although this method gave me flexibility in allowing me to make my own judgements it did present its own problems. I certainly had a distinct advantage in assessing personality types, as I knew most of the boys from the target age group since they were ten as I was their schools' district football manager. The difficulty I had was the way they viewed me, and consequently this affected their behaviour in my presence. I had only ever known them in an official capacity - as a teacher who ran their football team. I felt that I always got on well with them, but I did not really know how they behaved outside this football circle. I did not know how they related to other people, including their own families and therefore I did not feel confident in drawing up an accurate picture about what they were really like. My assessment of them during my fieldwork must therefore be taken into context, as with this method of research I could only ever make analytical judgements about the personality of the players in a football environment. In addition, this environment at the Centre of Excellence was different from one found at a standard boys' team. Failure to impress here could mean the end of any hope of becoming a professional footballer.

It therefore may come as no surprise that whilst accepting the subjectivity of my judgements, perhaps the most significant factor regarding personality, was that generally they all behaved in a similar manner. Virtually all could be described as reasonably confident off the pitch, but none behaved in an extrovert manner. There was no doubt that some would talk more than others, but no individual appeared to dominate. All were keen to learn and would try to follow any advice given by the coaches. During matches, some players were more vocal than others and would try to drive the team on, but rarely did I ever hear any moaning or arguments develop from the players. The clear message that came across throughout my fieldwork at the Centre of Excellence was that the players realised that in order to succeed they had to conform both on and off the pitch.

The issue of players developing similar behavioural patterns also stretched to physical appearance. Off the pitch, all the boys had similar haircuts and wore similar clothes. As with any professional football club this approach is encouraged. Brighton & Hove Albion provided the players with Club tracksuits and other clothing items for training and match days.

Martin Hinshelwood stressed the importance of matching clothes and equipment when he said (Field Notes 27/1/02):

> "Honestly, before I came here, the boys looked a right mess. They
> all had to bring their own stuff. I want to give them a sense of
> belonging. I bought loads of gear for the players, so that felt
> proud about playing for the Club."

However, there were differences amongst the boys that did stand out. It was noticeable that some had lost confidence more easily than others and when this happened, they would often either continue to make mistakes or try not to get too involved in case they made more. From a theoretical viewpoint, this outcome is part of 'achievement motivation' whereby these boys would fall into a category that Atkinson (1974) described as people that "needed to avoid failure". According to my observations during matches, few players seemed to have the ability to not let their own bad performance affect them. The only player who seemed to be able to overcome a bad performance during a game to the effect that he would carry on regardless was Graham. Perhaps it was this ability that helped him to be one of those who were offered a Scholarship.

During my fieldwork, it was very noticeable how being chosen to play for the Club's Centre of Excellence teams was itself seen as a great honour. Players appeared to be genuinely proud to be part of the Club. Many would wear Club kit, for example tracksuits, as casual wear, and a lot of young players bought their own Albion kit even though they were not required to do so. It was difficult to assess whether the boys who were at the Centre of Excellence generally appeared confident because of their association with the Club, because they happened to be good at football or whether it was this type of personality that was required in order to be a good player.

As my work in the field progressed, the importance to which the Club's coaches gave to player psychology seemed to increase. This was particularly apparent when the player progressed to the Scholarship Scheme and to the full-time professionals, and it will be discussed in due course. However, the key issue that arose from this area of research, was not what psychological profile the players needed to have (which I never actually discovered), but rather the aspects of character that were to the liking of the coaches. (These are discussed in 7.3.m).

7.3. j) Special treatment

For a minority of players, predictions about their chances of being offered a scholarship was made easier from the time that they were singled out for special treatment by the senior coaches. This could include extra amounts of time spent persuading the parents that Brighton and Hove Albion was the best club for their son to be at, and the player being offered a Scholarship months or even years before others in the same year group were told of their fate.

Hinshelwood claimed (Field Notes 21/1/03) that any player who received special attention on the whole did not tell the other boys and they would not have been aware of it anyway. However, I was not convinced that the players would be able keep quiet about such things, and if that were the case I could begin to understand some of the players' views about favouritism within the Club.

Although during my research I was only aware of a few boys receiving special attention, I was drawn into a situation where I was the one trying to persuade the parents of a player to accept a place on the Brighton & Hove Albion Scholarship Scheme when the boy was in Year 10 at school. (Decisions do not have to be made until 1st March of Year 11). The parents were keen to know how the Club could guarantee that their son would receive a good education at the Club as part of the Scheme. Both the parents and the player agreed that he should expect to achieve nine grade 'C's or above, with the majority being 'A's or 'A*'s at GCSE, and that he would ideally like to study for four AS levels. This would hopefully be done within a scholarship scheme at a professional football club, wherever that may be. The player and his parents had still not made up their minds whether or not to accept the Club's offer at the time of writing.

I was informed by a very senior member of the coaching staff (Field Notes 7/3/03) that it is commonplace for Premiership clubs to offer financial inducements that could be counted in tens of thousands to boys and their parents. He said that although he was very much against it, he knew of occasions when families had been offered between £30,000 and £40,000 for the boy to sign on as a scholar when the player was sixteen. In these situations, the families of talented boys are approached when they are attending another club's academy or usually, centre of excellence and told to continue to train there. However, they are also invited to train at a satellite centre of the club making the

117

approach in the boy's geographical region during the school holidays. In this way the club making the illegal approach is able to keep in close contact with the player even though he is not attending their academy or centre of excellence.

Since the introduction of the academy and centre of excellence system, there is no doubt that Brighton & Hove Albion has never made such an illegal approach, if not for moral reasons, certainly for financial ones.

Towards the end of my research, I was informed (Field Notes 10/7/03) that one of the eighteen year olds was no longer a scholar and had become a full time professional with a one year contract. This was because when he was sixteen, there was a lot of interest from other clubs and as a way of enticing him to sign for Brighton was guaranteed a professional contract at the end of his second year as a scholar. When I broached the player about this he was extremely embarrassed and only began to relax when I assured him that I would not inform his team mates.

7.3. k) The player's date of birth

When collating all of the dates of births of the players who were to attend Centre of Excellence for the 2003-4 season I found the following results:

Month	Sept	Oct	Nov	Dec	Jan	Feb	Mar	April	May	June	July	Aug
Number of players born in this month	24	13	18	11	9	6	5	11	5	5	1	4

Birth dates of players attending the Centre of Excellence (2003-4)
Table 7

This shows that there are a significant number of boys whose birth dates are in the first six months (September-February) of the academic year (total: 81) as opposed to the second six months (March-August) (total: 31). In order to extend this line of research, I collated the total number of professional players registered in the 'Rothmans Yearbook 2003/4' as British. The results for British born Premiership players are shown in Table 8 and all British born Football League players in Table 9.

Month	Sept	Oct	Nov	Dec	Jan	Feb	Mar	April	May	June	July	Aug
Number of players born in this month	83	67	63	60	66	57	40	39	30	24	26	31

Birth dates of English born Premiership players 2003/4
Table 8

Month	Sept	Oct	Nov	Dec	Jan	Feb	Mar	April	May	June	July	Aug
Number of players born in this month	295	256	222	198	173	144	152	122	155	118	108	171

Birth dates of English born English Football League players 2003/4
Table 9

Therefore, research into the birth dates of youth players at Brighton and Hove Albion and English players in this country's professional leagues for the 2002-3 season concludes that those born in the first half of the academic year have a distinct advantage over those born in the latter half. This supports research carried out by Helsen, Williams, Van Winckel and Ward (2003) and Simmons (2002).

7.3. l) Birth Order

All players who attend the Centre of Excellence are invited to the Club's training ground for a one off pre-season training get-together. I took this opportunity to speak to each player individually to confirm their addresses (for Club use) and also to ask them their position in birth order in relation to their siblings. Of the 102 that were signed on by the Club for 2003/4, 84 boys were present. The data (see Table 10) showed that there was a significant number (44) who were the youngest in the family compared to the oldest (22). (These figures did not include the two boys who were from one-child families).

Number in Family/Position in Family	Number of Boys
1/1 (Only child)	2
1/2 (Oldest of two)	18
2/2 (Youngest of two)	24
1/3	3
2/3	9
3/3	15
1/4	1
2/4	2
3/4	2*
4/4	5
1/5	0
2/5	1
3/5	1
4/5	0
5/5	0
1/6	0
2/6	0
3/6	0
4/6	0
5/6	1
6/6	0
TOTAL	84

* The two eldest siblings are stepsisters
Family order for players attending the Centre of Excellence (Under 9 –Under 16 (2003/4)
Table 10

7.3. m) What it takes to be kept on – the coaches' opinions

From the Under 9's to the Under 16's, the coaches, ranging from those in charge of specific age groups to the Centre Directors and the Director of Youth, are constantly judging the young charges that represent the Centre of Excellence teams. Initially, any player who is invited to join the Centre is given a six-week trial. After that he is offered a one or two year part time contract, depending upon his age group. At the end of the contract period, the coaches make a decision on the player's future. Ultimately, in all cases for those who attend the Centre of Excellence, it is Martin Hinshelwood, as Director of Youth, who has the final say. However, there are many others who will be asked their opinion. These include Vic Bragg and John Lambert as Centre Directors (for the Worthing and Eastbourne sites respectively), the coach/manager for each individual age group, and in the case of a player being a goalkeeper, the goalkeeping coaches (John

Keeley and Bob Bantock). When at Under 16 level, the decisions about who will be offered a place on the Scholarship Scheme are being made, Dean Wilkins as Youth Team Coach, is asked to contribute. It should be added that Wilkins will also coach various age groups from time to time, and so his opinion can be called upon at any time. The overall feeling then was that although Hinshelwood had the final say, it is very much a team decision.

I was keen to establish upon what criteria were they basing their judgements? Hinshelwood claims (Field Notes 15/11/02) that they must have the right attitude and the ability to go on to the next level at what ever stage that may be. Wilkins whilst in agreement (Field Notes 15/11/02) emphasised the need for the player to 'want it enough'. (An expansion of their views can be found in 7.4.m). Lambert stated (Field Notes 6/3/03) that:

> "They must have good coachability. They must have a good understanding of the game so that they are able to make the right decisions when they are playing. Also they have got to have a good attitude.

When he spoke about the need for a good attitude, I asked if he had ever not recommended a player because of a bad attitude even though he had the ability to go on. He added that this had happened many times.

In general, the coaches I interviewed had similar views to those already mentioned. One spoke (Field Notes 28/1/03) of the "willingness to listen and the ability to act upon the advice" whilst another said (Field Notes 3/10/02) that self discipline was an "essential ingredient" to becoming a professional player. However, the key words that re-occurred time after time were good 'attitude' and 'ability', and I was able to conclude that the older a player became the more emphasis there was placed upon his attitude. In many ways it seemed that the psychology profile of the player that was being applied to the decision making process by the coaches was central to the final outcome of whether or not the player was to be successful, and that this was totally akin to the ideas set out by Colin Murphy, the FA's Chief Scout as previously discussed.

7.3. n) Making the grade and coping with failure

When the day of judgement came for this age group, the atmosphere at the Centre in Worthing was tense. This was the time when they would be told whether they were to be offered a Football Scholarship at the Club or whether they were to be released. Each age group on average has six accepted. All the boys, who had to be accompanied by a parent/guardian, were given an appointment for a formal meeting with Martin Hinshelwood, Dean Wilkins and team coach Colin Smart.

As all had appointments, there were never many waiting outside in the bar area of the Centre at any one time. Those that were waiting chatted nervously and often offered words of encouragement to each other. Many would guess about who would be chosen – the boys who were listening always being told they would make it by other parents.

I had been asked to attend so that I could offer words of comfort to those who were rejected and give educational advice concerning courses they could take as part of the Scholarship Scheme to those who were accepted. In reality, those who were rejected went straight home with their parents and many of these boys were in tears. It was for them the end of a dream. For the boys who were chosen, it was a time for them and their parents to rejoice. Once they were told, they came out of the room smiling and mingled with other successful players and those waiting to go in. One by one they came over to me for advice. The decisions were as follows:

Harry	Accepted place on Scholarship Scheme
Sean	Accepted place on Scholarship Scheme
Derek	Accepted place on Scholarship Scheme
Graham	Accepted place on Scholarship Scheme
Liam	Rejected
Joe	Accepted place on Scholarship Scheme
Carl	Accepted place on Scholarship Scheme
Gordon	Rejected
Conor	Rejected
Phil	Rejected
Stuart	Rejected
Don	Rejected

The five that were successful were Harry, Sean, Graham, Carl and Derek. Both Harry and Sean's fathers had played for the Albion and Graham's had played for Stoke City. Derek's father and more particularly his uncle were well known in local football circles as they had both played at semi-professional in the Sussex County League. Carl was the only successful player whose father had not played football to at least semi-professional level.

All the parents knew that six players were funded for each age group and so it was somewhat of a surprise that only five had been selected. This in itself was not received well by all of the parents as I subsequently found out. For example, Stuart who had spent most of the season injured had hoped he may be given the benefit of the doubt, but this was not the case. However, he was told that he could still train and play for the team although he would not be asked to join the Scholarship Scheme on a full-time basis. Joe, who had not been at the Club's Centre of Excellence but had been rejected by Chelsea where his father had been a professional footballer, filled the sixth place two months later.

It must be stated here that although in total four of the six players chosen had fathers who had played professional football, this situation was exceptional to every other age group. No player from any of the four other age groups I researched who participated in the Scholarship Scheme had fathers who had been involved in football at this level.

Most of those who were rejected took up their places at local sixth form colleges where they had already reserved places in case they were not chosen. Only Stuart was asked to continue playing without becoming part of the Scholarship Scheme. Here was a very delicate situation. On the one hand, it may be that Hinshelwood and Wilkins would not let Stuart go entirely solely because he was the Chairman's nephew and the Commercial Manager's son or on the other hand it may have been because it was due to the fact that he had been injured for most of the season and could go on to make the progress required in order to make the grade.

Of course, this difficult situation was one that could be predicted months before it actually came about. I asked Hinshelwood the previous season if he felt any extra pressure. He replied that 'the day I have to pick a player because of who their Dad or

Uncle is, is the day I pack up the game'. (Field Notes 14/4/01). He did go on to say that he felt the Chairman respected him and understood his position.

Stuart continued to play for the club until December of the following season. He finally left the Club after being made substitute for an important FA Youth Cup game. He was not asked to go on during that game, Wilkins choosing instead to bring on a player from a younger age group who played in the same position. Stuart went to Bradford City for a two week trial where his cousin was at the time playing in the first team. This trial was extended to two months as the Club felt that he was playing well. In February 2003, Bradford decided to offer Stuart a three and a half year Scholarship, whereby the Club would pay him until the end of that season as all of the Club's quota for funded players had been used up (there were already eighteen players on the Scheme) and he would then join the new first years for the remaining three years. The Club were happy to offer Stuart this deal as he was seen as being a late developer.

I asked Stuart why he thought Brighton had rejected him and Bradford had been so keen to take him on. He replied (Field Notes 22/2/03):

"Either your face fits or it doesn't. The Clubs don't do anything differently, it's just that they rate me there. I know I'm as good as those who were chosen by Brighton, but what could I do?"

The following season Hinshelwood had decided to approach the problem of releasing players slightly differently. He told me (Field Notes 10/1/03) that he felt it was unfair to keep the players waiting until February of their final year at the Centre of Excellence before telling them that they were not going to be offered a Scholarship. He therefore began to release players from as early as the beginning of January. Subsequently, when the time arrived for final decisions to be made about who was to be offered a Scholarship, only eight players were still to be told of their fate.

For most years, the number of places available for the new age group was six, as there is a maximum of eighteen players for three age groups. However, this year, as there were currently only three second year boys still at the Club, the number coming in to the Scheme could be as many as nine. Therefore, the eight players left could all effectively be offered a place. Once again I was invited to the evening to talk to the parents and their sons once they knew of the outcome. The first two families that went in to the office to meet Martin Hinshelwood, Dean Wilkins and Colin Smart (Under 16 and Under 17 Manager) were told that the boys were not being offered a scholarship. Neither chose to speak to me as I waited in the adjoining office and one of the families left very upset with the mother shouting that it was a waste of time trying to talk to them. The remaining six were all offered scholarships.

I asked Hinshelwood a week later what he felt about the reaction of the mother and he said (Field Notes 24/4/03) that he was disappointed in the reaction. He also said that he had taken the trouble to telephone some of his contacts at other clubs and had been successful in arranging a trial for the player at Southend United. He remarked that firstly, he had not been thanked by the parents for his troubles and secondly that he normally approached other clubs if he felt that the boys had a chance of raising some interest. He had not done this because he felt in any way guilty for upsetting the family.

7.4. The Youth Team and the Apprenticeship Scheme

7.4. a) Background

At the beginning of the 2000/01 season, when the fieldwork for this work commenced, Brighton had six first year, six-second year and five third year players in their youth team squad. One player had left the club at the end of his second year as the club felt he had not progressed to the required standard and as result he had decided to take up a football scholarship at a university in the United States. Hence, the club had only seventeen full-time youth team players on the Apprenticeship Scheme as opposed to the eighteen that they would be entitled to under the PFA funding scheme. In the second year of my research, the Club decided to take on only five players, and having had five in the third year the numbers initially remained the same. However, within a month of the start of this second year, one player dropped out leaving sixteen. In my final year, another six replaced six players and therefore no change in number was made.

The Scheme does give the club the right to discard any player after two years from the football element, but it must provide all players with three years of education.

The Club enters an Under 17 and an Under 19 team in the Football League Youth Alliance (South East) and an Under 18 team in the F.A. Youth Cup. As there were only six full-time apprenticeship players who are under 17, many of the players who were rejected for this Scheme and who played for the Under 16's, made up the rest of the side. Only two or three players who were not on a full-time contract were required for the Under 19 team. Some of the full time players were required to play for the Club's reserve team.

7.4. b) The situation and site of the Training Ground

During the two years that the football club had played all of their first team football matches at Gillingham, the Club had meanwhile moved its offices to the centre of Brighton. The youth team and the full time professionals continued to train at the University of Sussex, where they had been for the previous 10 years. The University is based along the A27, approximately four miles from the centre of Brighton, and the Training Ground itself is behind the main campus. The Club are able to use the facilities throughout the week, although the University sports teams use the changing rooms and bar area on Wednesday afternoons and at weekends.

There are four changing rooms that lead out on to the fields, where there is one football pitch marked out. Adjacent to the changing rooms is the bar area where the players go for lunch after training. There are two small offices, (one for the Manager and his Assistant and the other for the Director of Youth and Youth Team Coach), a kitchen and a bathroom for the staff above the changing rooms. The Physiotherapist (Malcolm Stuart) has his own desk in the Youth Team Office, but is generally based across the field about two hundred metres away, in a cluster of three 'porta-cabins'. These are used as a fitness area, (kitted out with a multi-fitness station and various forms of weights) and physiotherapy room. Stuart also has an assistant, Kim Eaton, whose main role is to be physiotherapist for the Youth and Centre of Excellence teams.

The Youth Teams rarely play their home games at the Training Ground, preferring instead to use the facilities of two local public schools, Ardingly College or Lancing College due to the better playing surfaces. All matches are played on Saturday mornings, with the exception of the FA Youth Cup matches that are normally played midweek.

7.4. c) My relationship with the coaching staff at the Training Ground

My role at the club changed significantly during my three years of fieldwork as highlighted in Chapter 6. Throughout the time I was there, my relationship with the youth team's coaching staff (Martin Hinshelwood and Dean Wilkins) was as at all times as good as I could possibly hope for. I always felt welcome in their cramped office, and the atmosphere within this office was always jovial and was similar to the type found in a football changing room. No one escaped being the victim of light-hearted humour or minor practical jokes from the others in the room. My requests for information or interviews were never turned down by any of the three in this office, and this gave me the feeling as a researcher that I had access to everything that I needed.

As my role as Education Liaison Officer developed, I found that I was speaking to Martin Hinshelwood, either by telephone or face to face, almost on a daily basis. In April of 2001, he asked me to accompany him to a seminar at Highbury (Arsenal Football Club) in London, organised by the PFA, related to the Scholarship Scheme for professional football clubs in the South East. I felt that this cemented a close working relationship between us, and it allowed me to converse with him at length about the issues surrounding Brighton's youth set-up as we travelled to and from the seminar. In addition, I was also able to pick up some valuable information concerning other clubs whilst there. I was also able to attend the seminar with him the following year.

My relationship with Dean Wilkins was equally as comfortable. His approach towards his work was based upon hard work as well as being open to new ideas. He was keen to discuss these ideas with me at any time and at no point did he ever make me feel I was getting in the way. This also reflected my relationship with Malcolm Stuart, although I had known Malcolm for many years on a social basis. Therefore, the only problem that I faced for my research with regard to those based in the Youth Team Office was that the more familiar I became with them, the greater the risk would be of a lack of trust from the Youth Team players. Throughout my research, I went to great lengths to assure the players that anything they told me would remain confidential. However, once the Club employed me, I did say to the boys that if I became aware of any serious breach of discipline, I would be duty bound to tell Dean Wilkins.

7.4. d) Changes at the Club

As with any professional football club, there are often frequent personnel changes within the coaching and management staff, and during the period of my research, this Club appeared to be no exception. Adams left in October 2001 with the Club lying third in Division 2 and after winning Division 3 the previous season. Adams went to Leicester City, a Premiership club, as Assistant Manager by way of promotion (as he was now involved with the management of a team in the country's highest level of club football). Peter Taylor, who had just been sacked by Leicester, was appointed as Manager at Brighton. By May 2002, after seven months in charge and having won Division 2, Taylor left, citing the Club's lack of funds as being the reason for leaving. After a three-month gap of in-decision between seasons, Knight finally promoted Hinshelwood as first team Manager. Therefore, the Club having won two divisions within twelve months had three managers for the same period of time.

When Hinshelwood was appointed, there were concerns amongst the local press (and probably the supporters) that he had had no previous experience. His response to this at the Press Conference was that although he was not a 'big name' he did have a long one! This response epitomised his ability to fend off difficult situations with humour, a technique I found he passed on to the Youth team players. The response from the Press was to laugh with him and to move on to the next question. This highlighted the good relationship the club had with local journalists.

The effects of the managerial changes upon my research were quite significant. When Adams and Taylor were in charge, I rarely saw them and when I did, just a nod of the head was given. They never interfered with anything I was doing. However, when Hinshelwood was promoted, I was now allowed into the Manager's Office and was in a much better position to find out about other aspects of the Club, for example, life in the first team. I now had a better idea about what was expected of a senior player, which in turn helped me acquire a better knowledge of what would be expected of a youth team player who was awarded a professional contract.

The changes not surprisingly also had a big effect upon the youth team players. When Adams and Taylor were in charge, they rarely took an interest in any of them. The situation for those in the youth teams seemed ominous when Adams arrived at the Club.

128

Whilst talking to staff (which included Hinshelwood and Wilkins) in the Club offices, he was asked what his opinion was of the youth players at the Club. He replied, (Field Notes 22/11/02) "I don't give a damn. They're not going to get me promoted are they?" This comment really emphasised the short termism often associated with professional football. Clearly, Adams was not about to chance sacrificing his own opportunity for success by allowing youth team players into the first team. Only very occasionally did any of the third years get a place as one of the substitutes in the first team, and even when they were, they were not often chosen to go on. For any professional club, using youth team players, or players who have come through the club's youth system, is a very inexpensive way of competing – as long as the team gets good results. Adams was more prepared to chance his luck on the loan and transfer market with the money made available to him – and to his good fortune/judgement this paid off.

It is apparent that the issue of not trusting youth team players or giving them time or the opportunity to establish themselves as first team players is a problem not just confined to Brighton and Hove Albion. Journalist David Conn (2000:31) describes how a youth team player (Paul Wheatcroft) at Manchester United faces a similar problem. He states:

> "Wheatcroft believes Ferguson (Manager of Manchester United)
> is a prisoner of the instant success demanded in modern
> football. 'He told me that three or four years ago he might have
> kept us on, but now there is no time to give anyone a chance".

The future for Wheatcroft, like many youth team players looked bleak. And yet at Brighton and Hove Albion, once Hinshelwood had taken over, there was a complete reversal of fortune for many as is highlighted in some of the following sections.

Sadly for these players, Hinshelwood was only in charge for fifteen matches and after ten straight defeats was sacked. He was offered his old job back but with the added responsibility of helping the new Manager, Steve Coppell with the first team. This job he reluctantly accepted, for even though he felt he was offered a reasonable financial compensation package, he still found the whole experience rather humiliating (Field Notes 3/11/02). The effect upon the same youth and young professional players, who had been so keen to see Hinshelwood take over, now faced a period of total uncertainty. For

Hinshelwood, the loss of the manger's job was a blow. He was later to state in an interview with the local paper (Donovan 16: 2003):

> "It will be with me for the rest of my life that I failed as a
> manager of a football club, so it still hurts. It hurts because
> of the position I left the Club in. You are always judged on
> results at that level and if you look at the results then there
> was only one way unfortunately."

From an objective and retrospective point of view, the appointment of Hinshelwood had been a disaster, for the sequence of results was the worst in the Club's history (Rollin and Rollin 2003). His critics would say that; he was inexperienced for this position, (having only acted as caretaker manager for Brighton and Hove Albion in the past for five matches); he relied too heavily upon the youth team players, and although there was no money available to buy players, he had not done enough to bring in players on loan. However, his supporters would say that all the matches he was caretaker manager for he had won, and during the Club's best spell over recent years, (when they played in the Division 1 play-off final in 1992), it was widely accepted that as Assistant Manager, Hinshelwood had played a leading role in the Club's success. During his fifteen matches in charge, many of his best players, including the Club's top scorer for the previous season Bobby Zamora, had missed key games due to injury; injuries meant that he had been forced to use youth players and he had brought in two loan players with Premiership experience, Guy Butters and Paul Kitson, but Butters had under performed and Kitson missed most of the games due to injury.

For the purposes of this work it is not essential to establish whether Hinshelwood's lack of success was of his own doing. However, there are two key points worthy of consideration. Firstly, Adam's reluctance (compared to Hinshelwood's willingness) to use youth players for the first team would seem to be justified. Secondly, the first team opportunities Hinshelwood gave to the youth team players may have given them experience in professional football, but it did not do them any good for their immediate future as after Hinshelwood was sacked they were rarely used during Coppell's reign in charge.

For the Brighton and Hove Albion, the 2002-3 season ended in failure as the Club finished second bottom of Division One and was relegated. However, Steve Coppell still had the support of the Directors and the fans, as he was held blameless for the Club's demise. In fact he was held with high regard for, despite the terrible start to the season, they finished nearly staving off relegation. The Club was delighted when Coppell accepted another one year contract to last until the end of the 2003-4 season. At the start of this season, the Club were joint favourites, according to the 'bookies' to be promoted.

7.4. e) The first day as a full-time 'scholar'

For the six first year players that go to the Club's training ground (University of Sussex) on the 1st July, it is the moment that their dreams of becoming a professional footballer are close to becoming a reality. Their life for the next thirty-four months will be totally immersed in professional football, and many of the demands that top-flight football entails. These demands are made very clear to the players when they arrive on the first day as they sit with the other scholars (2nd and 3rd years) and listen to Martin Hinshelwood, Dean Wilkins, Malcolm Stuart and Tim Stevenson (Club Doctor). It was at this time, 1st July 2000 that my fieldwork at the Club began.

The main concerns for Hinshelwood and Wilkins were linked to the players' attitude to training and their behaviour at the Training Ground, whilst Stuart and Stevenson concentrated on the players' diet and general health. Clearly, this served as a reminder to the second and third years who had received such instructions before. In reality, not much of what the first years heard was new to them either as a lot of what was said they had either been told before whilst attending the Centre of Excellence, or heard from players from the older age groups, whom many of them knew beforehand. The main difference here is that whereas before they would be told that they should careful about what they eat, they are now told that they have to be careful, otherwise they will suffer the consequences. In this particular case, one of the third years, Bobby, returned from the summer break with excess body fat (all players have a medical check as soon as they arrive on the first day). He was therefore required to do extra training until he lost the required amount. There was much hilarity about this amongst the players, although there was a serious side too: the coaches viewed this in a very negative way as this is seen to be linked to having a bad attitude. For a player in his final year, bad impressions can be crucial come the end of the season when their future is decided.

On the first day, all first years receive a ring bind folder that is compiled by the Footballers' Further Education and Vocational Training Society (FFE&VTS) (the educational arm of the PFA). In this are forms that the player and the club must fill in as the player progresses through the scheme. These forms relate to the educational courses that the player is taking, health records, the player's progress and general administration. The PFA's regional representative checks these files twice a year.

The players were also informed of the work rota that they had to perform. This rota included tasks such as: cleaning the changing rooms, cleaning training equipment such as hurdles, vacuuming the coaches' offices and cleaning the medical room. The players worked in pairs, and were often from different year groups. The PFA stress in their guidelines to clubs that Scholarship players should not be asked to do menial tasks, and the tasks that the young players were being asked to do seemed to be contrary to these guidelines. Dean Wilkins however, argued that the players are "expected to clean their own space" (Field Notes 26/10/00). The coaches' offices may be seen to fall outside these parameters and therefore it could be seen as unreasonable to expect youth team players to be cleaning them.

On their first day, the players were told what a typical week would entail. This timetable only changes marginally from one year to the next. (See Table 11)

DAY/TIME	AM	LUNCH	PM
MONDAY	Weights and Sprint/distance running		College
TUESDAY	Technical/Individual Skills e.g. heading		
WEDNESDAY	Speed work & explosive games		Reserve Matches
THURSDAY	Weights & Sprint/distance running		College
FRIDAY	Set pieces * practice match		College
SATURDAY	Matches		1st Team Match
SUNDAY	Training if required		

The daily timetable for the Scholars at Brighton & Hove Albion

Table 11

The first day also included light training, followed by some chores. Their day was completed by mid-afternoon. Throughout the day several first team players, who officially start training a couple of days later, normally come in to do some training on their own, so therefore the new players were immediately in the company of professional footballers. This was the first time the young players had really come into contact with the senior players, albeit for short periods (ten to fifteen minutes) of time, when they would cross each other's path in the weights room or the changing rooms and showers. The impression that came across immediately upon seeing this interaction was that whilst the young players were made to feel welcome, they were also witnesses to the loud voices and humour of the professional players. This would have been totally different to the vocational socialisation processes within the Centre of Excellence, where the only people they mixed with was their peers and their coaches. This now was the embryonic stage of life as a full-time professional football.

7.4. f) Life and relationships at the Training Ground

The timetabled week (Table 11) was fairly structured for the youth team players. They always trained in the morning and spent much of their time trying to improve their fitness and individual skills. The coach, Dean Wilkins, stated (Field Notes 3/7/00) that many of the ideas he uses come from his brother Ray (ex-England international) who at this time was a first team coach at Chelsea. He acknowledged that there is a real trend in professional football circles for players to have their fitness levels measured on a regular basis. He achieved this by taking the boys to the University of Brighton once a month to be tested by sports scientists.

The boys are impressed with Wilkins' dedication towards fitness. Will, a third year, claimed (Field Notes 25/9/00): "One of the reasons we do so well as a team is that we are a lot fitter than the other teams that we play. That's got to be down to Deano (Dean Wilkins)."

Further to this, Wilkins's reputation for his coaching ability amongst the boys and staff was outstanding. Andy, a second year at the time, said he thought all the boys felt that none of them had ever been coached by anyone better. He even went on to say (Field Notes 6/3/01): "Dean Wilkins is much more knowledgeable than Mickey Adams (First team Manager). Our training is varied and much more technical. All they do is two-touch football.

Dick, a player in his second year, commented (Field Notes16/1/03) that Wilkins's sessions were always interesting, and no one ever got bored. He claimed that Wilkins was the best and most knowledgeable coach he had ever had. He also said that all of the youth team players rated him very highly. In a match day programme (14/9/02), Hinshelwood discussed the value of having Wilkins at the Club:

> "I'd like to applaud the work Dean Wilkins has been doing as
> the club's youth team coach. It's not an overnight process and
> Dean's hard work since becoming youth team boss is starting
> to reap rewards. He has taught the players well and introduced
> them to good footballing habits. Dean's recently passed his
> UEFA 'A' Licence and in my opinion he is the best youth team
> coach in the country – and we're very fortunate to have him."

The success of the youth teams would seem to confirm Hinshelwood's sentiments. For the 2000/01 season, the results of the two youth teams were outstanding. The Under 17's won their league and were only beaten twice throughout the season, and the Under 19's came third in their division and were thereby able to qualify for the Southern Premier

Division which consists of the top four clubs in the South East Division and the top three in the South West. In this Division they finished third. In the FA Youth Cup, the Under 18's reached the last sixteen. This season was followed by further success in the 2001/2 season in which both the Under 17's and Under 19's finished second in their respective divisions, and the Under 19's finally finishing fifth in the Southern Premier Division. The Under 18's went one stage further than the previous year group in the FA Youth Cup by reaching the last eight, finally being beaten by eventual winners Aston Villa.

In my final season of research (2002/03), the Under 17's again won their league (the second time in three years). The Under 18's were knocked out in an early round of the FA Youth Cup and the Under 19's finished mid-table, but went on to further success in the mid table play-offs.

The knock-on effect of all of this success meant that the mood at the Training Ground amongst the youth team players was extremely positive and this manifested itself through the good humour that was a consistent feature of life there.

This atmosphere was not just restricted to the youth team players. When I began my research at the beginning of the 2000/1 season, the Club had finished the previous season with a fourteen match unbeaten run and the expectations for the next season were full of hope. These expectations proved to be realistic and as a result, throughout the first two seasons relationships between the players were excellent. In fact, many within the Club saw this as the main reason for success.

As my role as Education Liaison Officer developed by September 2001, I was seeing all the players on a weekly basis in a classroom as part of the Core Skills course. It was therefore easy for me to ask them to write answers on pieces of paper to specific questions, always ensuring that they did not write their names on the paper. One of the questions I asked them during my second year of research was how did they relate to the first team players.

On the whole their responses were fairly well balanced between those that were positive and those that were not. A typical positive answer was given by John, a second year at the time, who wrote (Field Notes 10/11/01) that "they are good, always willing to help". Another was given by Dick, then a first year, who said that he always really looked up to the first team players, particularly those who played in his position and if he asked for advice they would give it. However, there was an underlying feeling of resentment amongst some of the others. Andy, a second year, wrote (Field Notes 10/11/01):

> "I find it difficult to relate to many of the first team players, in particular the older pro's. …Some are very aggressive towards you, especially on the pitch. Some pro's try to bully you, especially the youngsters (the younger youth team players) but you must get on with it and do your best."

Steve, another second year, felt that most team players seemed to have a different sense of humour to the youth team players. He described them as often being childish, for example, trying to grab the youth team players' genitals whilst in the showers. He concluded that the youth team players' sense of humour tended to be much more sophisticated. Danny, an eighteen year old, who was a full time professional, but tended to train with the youth team players, complained (Field Notes 11/9/00) that it wasn't just the first team players that had a strange sense of humour but also the club physiotherapist. He would pick on youth team players and make them feel uncomfortable by 'belittling' (Field Notes 11/9/00) them though sarcastic jokes, thinking he was being amusing.

I was keen to find out more about the role of humour at the Training Ground, and I chose to ask the players if they felt their humour was different to the full-time professionals when I saw them in their year groups the following week for their Core Skills class. The overall opinion (although one must be fairly sceptical about making generalisations concerning group opinion as dominant members often influence others) appeared to be that it was the older established players who had the most basic humour as opposed to the younger professionals who were more akin to the youth team players.

There were also some other factors that came to light as a result of the year group discussions. Paul, one of the first years complained that some of the older players did not respond to new health and fitness ideas, and that he regarded some first team players attitudes "as an absolute joke" (Field Notes 17/11/02); whilst Kerry, another first year, thought one of the first team centre-backs was not only overpaid but also never even spoke to any of the youth team players. In the second year discussion, Steve felt that although many of the first team players are good fun and easy to get on with, the mere fact that the youth team players want to play for the first team instead of them means that in some way they should be regarded as rivals. All of the third years agreed that the first team players were very moody, and their relationship with them changed on a daily basis, although in general they did quite like them.

There seemed to be a contradiction here regarding the extent to which the youth team players were acquiring a professional football habitus On the one hand, from their time at the Centre of Excellence, the players were developing similar behaviour patterns, had similar haircuts and wore similar clothes and when they had been signed on as scholars, had shown similar styles of humour and attitude towards football. Yet they seemed on the whole to be fairly disdainful of the behaviour and humour of the first team players. The conclusion I came to was that the youth team players felt in some ways superior to the senior players and despite the success of the first team did not really see them as role models. The habitus they were developing was being shaped more significantly by the youth team coaches, each other and their role models who played in the Premiership. The whole atmosphere of the Training Ground generally appeared to involve around humour for a significant amount of time, although all players gave me the impression that they took training very seriously. I was very mindful of the fact that during my first two years of fieldwork, the Club had been very successful at all levels, and that this enabled people to act in an upbeat manner. One could not be sure if people would be acting in the same way if the Club were going through a bad spell.

I was very aware of the close relationship between all youth team players. Bobby, a third year said that (Field Notes 18/9/00) "We always wind each other up, but no one ever gets picked on", and Will, a fellow third year, said that (Field Notes 25/9/00) "the whole group get on really well"'. Many of them had known each other a number of years, as the majority of them had represented the Club at lower age groups. In addition, a large percentage of the boys had either played with or against each other on numerous occasions. The issue of their close relationship is highlighted by individual interviews that took place with many of the youth team players for the first team's match day programme. When asked to comment on what they thought was the aspect of the club that they most liked, many stated it was the camaraderie they had within the youth team. (One player said Martin Hinshelwood's sense of humour!)There was certainly some gentle rivalry between the three age groups, and to an extent the boys within the same age group behaved in an almost identical manner. For example, one group throughout their time at the club were much more boisterous than any of the others. They would often have explosive arguments or physically fight with each other, but then would immediately go back to behaving normally. This showed a surprising level of immaturity - particularly as none of the other groups ever appeared to do this.

There was one aspect of behaviour form the youth team players that stood out from all others with regard to the way they treated each other. Throughout my research, I never once heard one player criticise another's ability. They all appeared to have a great respect for each other as footballers. Each year I asked the second and third years which third year players they thought would be offered full professional contracts, they were often reluctant to offer any guesses. When they did, the reason they usually gave for why some were chosen rather than others was because they were the coaches' favourites and not because they were any better than those they felt would be rejected. Also, on the two or three occasions when I made a light-hearted joke about one of the player's ability, the others looked at me in disbelief and immediately sprung to his defence. I realised that this type of joke was taboo.

The issue of favouritism usually started to intensify as players entered into the second year. The coaches often used some second years (and very occasionally, first years) for the Reserve team. Those who were chosen regularly for this were often seen to be the favourites of the coaches. On some occasions, second years were selected as part of the first team squad. When this happened, little doubt was left in any of the other players' minds that that person would almost certainly be offered a contract at the end of his third year. This issue did not appear to affect the relationship between the players themselves, although they were sometimes teased by the others about being the coaches' favourite. For the coaches, the players who were chosen were obviously the ones who they thought were doing well, as they would never admit to having favourites. This point is even more pertinent, as one of the youth team players is Hinshelwood's nephew. I very rarely heard any player mention this particular issue as being a problem, despite the fact that the nephew represented the Reserves in his second year and the first team in his third year. I chose not to ask the players if this did create difficulties as I felt that it might stimulate resentment towards the player. The reason I feel that his success within the club did not become a problem with the others was because he was a popular member of the group and he was seen by his peers to be a good player and deserving of his opportunities. Another example of players' closeness came when Steve (a first year) was selected for the Reserves in the place of Nathan (a third year). Steve said (Field Work 6/3/01) that he had very mixed emotions about this, as on the one hand he was delighted to be selected, but on the other, it not only meant that it was 'humiliating' for Nathan to lose his place to a first year, but it also came at the time of year when the third years were going to be told if they were going to be offered a professional contract. Steve actually took the trouble to apologise to Nathan for this. Nathan was to find out a few weeks later that he was being released.

The coaches' relationship with the players was also a very close one. Wilkins (Field Work 2/8/00) felt that foremost he was a coach, but in many ways he was a father and a counsellor, and without being explicit said that he had to deal with a very serious domestic issue for a player the previous year. Hinshelwood's attitude about his role and his relationship with the players as Director of Youth is similar to Wilkins'. He also stated (Field Work 24/8/02) that he was a 'Dad' to them and also a friend. He felt that one of the most important aspects of his job was that he must be approachable. When asked, all of the players thought that this was the case.

7.3. g) Lifestyle

Over recent years, much has been written about the lifestyle of professional footballers through autobiographical and biographical accounts between the early 1970's and mid 1990's. It is commonplace for retired footballers to write (for example Adams 1997) about how they used to spend much of their spare time drinking and gambling. There is little doubt that football has changed over recent years; players are now much more concerned about their bodies, healthy diets and carefully planned fitness regimes in order to keep at peak performance. This may be due to a number of reasons: for example, lack of success in international football at both club and national level, the influx of foreign players, coaches and managers into English football and the influence of role models (for example David Beckham). I was keen to establish how what appears to be an over-riding attitude in top-flight football had affected the lifestyles of the youth team.

From those involved with the management of the youth team, there seemed little doubt that they were in-line with the more modern school of thought. Hinshelwood stated (Field Notes 24/8/00) that "one of the reasons that players don't make it is due to the social pressures put on them by their mates. They have to be strong-willed with themselves, particularly with their friends." He added that his attitude towards the youth players and their drinking habits was that he was happy for them to go out drinking on a Saturday night, but certainly didn't want them going out during the week.

On one occasion, Paul, (a first year) was seen at a nightclub the evening before a game by Wilkins. His immediate response was to send him home and the following morning, Paul was told that he would be banned for two games. On another occasion, Kerry arrived at the Training Ground on Monday morning with cuts to his face and a black eye as a result of a fight at a party the previous Saturday night. As this was the second occasion that this type of thing had happened to Kerry, he was moved out of the family home in a nearby town and into digs in Brighton. He was also told that he was under curfew until the end of the season and was not allowed out of the house after seven o'clock at night. This was seen as second warning and if there was any further trouble, he would be told to leave the Club.

Moving into digs can create its own problems. When Bobby arrived on the first day back for his final year as a scholar, although the Club blamed him for this, Malcolm Stuart (the Physiotherapist) said (Field Notes 5/9/00) that he found that players who stayed in digs were often the ones who had problems with their diet, and therefore he had some sympathy for them. Stuart also said:

> "At the moment we've got three in digs and to be honest
> two of them are not being given the right food. It's everything
> with chips. The result is that according to our fat counter
> when checked they are often overweight,. They will have to
> be moved."

Stuart believes that life is a lot easier for those players that are able to live at home. He argues that parents usually take a real interest and are totally supportive to their sons. So when the boys give their parents a list of food that they should and should not eat, the parents tend to make sure that meals served at home are based upon this advice. Stuart is sure that if the Club paid the host families of those living in digs a higher rate of pay, then they would be more likely to make more of an effort to ensure the player gets the diet required.

Although I fully realised it would be naïve to suppose that the players would always tell me the truth, I did get caught out into believing them when they had lied to me. Towards the end of my first year of fieldwork, the third years had all assured me that they never went out to a club at night -time during the week. I found out that they had done just that as they were seen out by an acquaintance of mine. When I challenged them about this they asked me to promise that I would not tell the coaches. I assured them that this would be the case. (If this had happened during the third year of my research when I was fully employed by the Club, my response may not have been the same as I feel that my professional duty may have to have taken precedence to my heavy involvement with the day to day running of the youth set up.)

The conclusions I drew from this episode and subsequent discussions with the players were that social pressures are to some too difficult to ignore, and that the players will play this cat and mouse game with the coaches. It is a high risk to pay if they are caught, as being classed as someone who has the wrong attitude could make the difference between being taken on at the end of the third year or not. Also, a player would certainly be dropped for the next game, and losing a place in one of the teams for any reason can be irreparable.

It was evident that although drinking alcohol was not a major part of their lives, it was seen as an essential ingredient to a good night out. This attitude is very much in line with an article by journalist Tim Rich who claimed (2002): "When Liverpool lifted their first trophy under (Gerard) Houllier, he noted that the only players drunk at the post-match celebrations were British."

The issue of the attraction of fast food, alcohol and peer culture (outside of the professional club environment) was a strong one. Hinshelwood claimed he always warns players about the outside pressures of doing what their mates want them to do (Field Notes 10/3/02), and that the players must have the strength of character to say no. However, often the pressures of high street consumption to these players proved irresistible.

7.3. h) Education

During the three years of my of field work, I was able to research the development of five year groups, from the three that were at the club when I arrived in July 2000 to the other two new groups that began in 2001 and 2002.The educational qualifications they had already achieved by the time they arrived at the club were as follows:

Year of Enrolment	Number of students with 5 or more GCSE's at 'C' grade or above	Number of students with fewer than 5 GCSE's 'C' grade or above
1998	4	2
1999	6	0
2000	3	3
2001	1	4
2002	4	2

GCSE results of players coming onto the Scholarship Scheme

Table 12

Therefore, from a total of 29 scholars, 18 (62%) had five GCSE's or more and 11 (28%) had fewer than 5. These statistics compare favourably with the national figures for scholars at all professional football clubs participating in the Scholarship Scheme. For the 1998 cohort (Burns 2002) (only year group figures currently available) 55% had five or more 'C's at GCSE, compared to Brighton & Hove Albion's 1998 cohort that had 60%. Even allowing for the general improvement of GCSE results throughout the country in recent years, the results of Brighton players still compare favourably. Their results are well above the regional average for Year 11 pupils in general. According to the study ('Regional Trends' 2001) carried out by the Government, 54.8% of Year 11 pupils taking GCSE's achieved five GCSE's or more in 2001.

Prior to the summer of 2000, virtually all of the youth players at the Club had traditionally taken the BTEC National Diploma in Applied Science (Sports Studies). Only those who chose a more vocational course, for example bricklaying, did not take this. The National Diploma qualification is worth the equivalent of three 'A' levels and is graded:

Pass - Equivalent to approximately three 'E' grades at 'A' level

Merit – Equivalent to approximately three 'C' grades at 'A' level

Distinction – Equivalent to approximately three 'A' grades at 'A' level

The content of this is made up entirely of coursework, and the boys would attend lessons every Thursday from 9am until 4 pm at Sussex University. A teacher who was employed by an educational company based in Wigan took the lessons.

In September 2000, barely a month after I had embarked upon my fieldwork, I was asked by Martin Hinshelwood if I could get some of the players onto courses at my College. Some of the first year parents, after hearing the talk given to them by Keith Waldon (FFE&VTS regional representative) in June, had insisted that the Club should arrange tuition for the boys in chosen 'A' level subjects. The youth team coaching staff did not particularly welcome this request, as they felt it would be difficult to avoid players missing training at different times in the week. The previous arrangement worked well as all of the players missed Thursday together. However, two of the players' parents were insistent.

I was able to accommodate the players and all got the subject choices they told me they wanted. Four of the third years, having looked at the College prospectus, decided that they wanted to do General Studies 'A' level as well as the European Computer Driving Licence, whilst the other third year, Rob, decided to complete his NVQ Level 2 in Bricklaying. All six second years decided to complete the BTEC Diploma in Applied Science as they had already completed one year of the two year course. The first year timetable proved more complicated to arrange. Three players wanted to do the BTEC Diploma, as they heard from the second years that it caused them few problems in terms of travelling (the lessons were held at Sussex University, only half a mile from the training ground), and one player, John, decided to take the NVQ in Bricklaying. However, Andy and Steve, whose parents expressed the wish that their sons were allowed to study two 'A' levels each, chose English and Physical Education, and Mathematics and Physical Education respectively. (For a full list of course studied, see Table 13).

With the exception of Andy and Steve, the best way to describe the attitude of the young players and coaches towards educational courses at this time is through a quote from Parker's research (1996:268). According to him, during education courses were "seen more (by the coaches) in terms of their disruptive impact on weekly routine than their importance on broader aspects of trainee experience".

There is no doubt that as time progressed, players and coaches changed their opinion about this and all seemed to react more positively to this aspect of the Scholarship Scheme, but at this time Hinshelwood and Wilkins were just relieved that it was organised in such a way that training missed in the morning was kept to a minimum. Although Hinshelwood was still concerned about the effect this may have upon the players. He said, with a hint of sarcasm, (Field Notes 18/9/00): "I sometimes think people forget we are running a football club here. If they find that they can't cope with juggling all of this education and their football, don't go blaming me".

The educational programme for the boys was finalised by mid September. Those who attended my College, the four third years doing General Studies and ECDL and the two second years doing PE 'AS' level, all seemed to enjoy the experience of coming back into mainstream education as they were able to join the regular classes that were taking place. Scott felt that (Field Notes 2/10/00): "It's great to get away from the training ground for while. Sometimes it can get quite intense there. It just means you can get a change of scenery."

This positive attitude amongst the players seemed to have developed all within the space of a few weeks, and by the second year of this fieldwork the coaches were extolling the virtues of the education provision available at the club. For the coaches it was easy to understand why their attitude towards the education programme was more positive. It was no longer their job to help set up the programme, which meant they had more time to spend on the football component of the Scheme. Also, the parents of the players were satisfied that their boys were being offered a range of subjects to study, and this reflected well on the Club. In addition, it transpired from the coaches speaking to the FFE&VTS representative that the educational course results of the youth team players from Brighton and Hove Albion were one of the best in the country for a football club. Overall though, there appeared to be a genuine belief amongst the coaches that the education programme was an essential part of the Scheme. I was unconvinced that this was the case before the fieldwork began.

For the youth team players, there were other reasons why the education programme became popular. At the beginning of the 2002/3 season, there was the prospect of moving into a study centre at the Withdean Stadium (where the first team played their matches) for most of the 'A' and 'AS' level classes. As this was a mile and a half closer to the training ground than the College where they normally had their lessons, my feeling as Manager of Education and Welfare was that the Scholars would much prefer this. However, the prospect was met with much lack of approval. Barry (a third year), enquired (Field Notes 16/9/02): "Is it true we have to go to Withdean for our lessons now? 'Cos if it is, it's out of order. How am I supposed to meet any girls if I don't go to College?"

As my response at the time was of uncertainty, I was asked again on several occasions afterwards by a variety of players, until I finally decided to assure them that if there was going to be a change of arrangement, it would not be until the following season.

My reasoning behind this postponement of change was two fold. Firstly, the educational and sociological advantages of mixing with other students within an academic environment are strong. The Scholars had mentioned before their reservations about spending too much time with the first team players. Secondly, their self-esteem at the training ground was not always at its best. They were the trainees, and trainees are at the bottom of the social hierarchy.

During the second and third year of the fieldwork, when the results of the various educational courses started to filter through, I sensed that for some of the youth team players this increased their feeling of superiority over the first team players, who they regarded as less academic in comparison (Field Notes 4/4/01). I had no way of knowing what the qualifications of the first team players were, and I did not feel at liberty to ask, and so this feeling of superiority by the youth team players may well have been unfounded. However, the key issue here is that youth team players were seeing educational qualifications as an important part of an individual's overall achievements. One of the attractions of the educational courses to Hinshelwood and Wilkins was that they could be fitted around the times of the football training and matches. This was not so easy with the vocational courses.

From December 2002 and particularly towards the end of the 2002/3 season, Joe asked if I could ensure that he did a bricklaying course the following year at a College in the north of Sussex. This request was also made by a player who had been offered a scholarship for the 2003/4 season. The PFA representative had advised against this type of vocational course for the young footballers as other people on the course would be involved with this work during the rest of the week. For the footballers, it would involve day release with the remainder of the week dominated by football. In addition, when I told Dean Wilkins of the request he was particularly unhappy. He said (Field Notes 28/2/03):

> "You have to understand that this does not do the players any good.
> It means one whole day away from training. I don't mind if they do
> Academic courses, as they miss two afternoons but they can train in
> the mornings. I'm not going to tell them they can't do this, but it's
> not going to make their lives easy. I hope they and their parents
> realise this."

Here was a very important issue. The boys were for different reasons, all being persuaded to do academic courses and to avoid vocational courses. Wilkins recognised that the provision of academic courses at the Club was a good marketing tool, but more important to him was the fact that boys undertaking vocational courses caused him an inconvenience. Had the academic courses been difficult to fit in, as was the case the year before this fieldwork begun, then these would certainly have been viewed in a less favourable light.

7.3. I) The Core Skills Programme

The Core Skills Programme is a compulsory part of the Scholarship Scheme, Any Club seen by the FFETVS not to be providing this for the youth team players would, according to Mickey Burns (Chief Executive of FFETVS) (Field Notes 25/4/01), lose all funding for the Scheme. The Programme consists of twenty-two topic areas that are to be covered throughout the season. The content of the programme consisted of the following modules: Laws of the Game; Sportsmanship; Role Models; The Image of the Game; Media Skills; Dealing with the Public; Dress, Conduct and Manners; Behaviour in Public; Social Skills; Driving Skills; Nutrition and Diet; Sports Science; Avoiding Alcoholic Abuse; Psychology and Sport; Lifestyle Skills; Drugs Awareness; Financial Planning; Avoiding Gambling Abuse; Relationships; Pastoral Care; Emergency First Aid and Lifelong Learning.

Each year group has a separate session on each area lasting for an hour a week. The resources are provided for by the FFETVS and consist of videotapes, teacher notes and overheads.

The general purpose of the Core Skills is to provide the Scholars with information and guidance on how to cope with the pressures associated with being a professional footballer, (for example, 'Media' and 'Dealing with the Public') as well as life beyond professional football (for example 'Lifelong Learning').

During my second year of fieldwork, I was responsible for delivering this course to the players. The previous year, only a few of the modules had been completed by Dean Wilkins, and guest speakers he had managed to bring in. However, with my new added responsibility, it was the perfect opportunity for me to meet the players on a regular basis, and it enabled me to get to know all the players very well.

Despite my best efforts, it became clear to me that the players, who had to attend these sessions on Friday afternoon, would really rather not be there, although they never complained to me. On the one hand, this may have been because they were worried that I may inform Dean Wilkins and that bad feedback would not be viewed kindly by the coaching staff, or it may have been because they were too polite. My feeling was it was probably a combination of the two, although I regularly reminded them that I would normally only report them to Dean Wilkins if they failed to turn up. I did have some sympathy for them not wanting to be there as they were all really keen to go home and relax after having trained all week and with the prospect of a game the following morning for one of the youth teams (Under17's or Under19's).

Throughout the year, I managed to cover all of the modules (except Driving Skills) either by myself, or through arrangement of a guest speaker. (For example, a local journalist covered 'Media Skills' and the Club Doctor covered 'Avoiding Alcohol Abuse' and 'Drugs Awareness').

During these Friday afternoons, I often asked them to reflect and write down on paper their own progress. I did this for two reasons. I explained to them that firstly, this was to give them an opportunity to reflect on their own progress and to talk to me if they had any problems, and secondly for my own research purposes. Some appeared keen do this, as this seemed to act as a vehicle for releasing any tension, whilst others would regard it as a chore. It was successful for me as it did give me another method of obtaining information.

One of the modules I found most revealing was 'Lifelong Learning'. Although I did not intentionally present this as a session to discuss alternative plans if they were not taken on, the subject did become a major area of conversation. During the second year of fieldwork, the third years were all very reluctant to even talk about educational courses as it would be an admission of self-defeat. The following year I decided to teach this module a lot earlier in the academic year as I appreciated that the time I originally took this was far to close when the third years were to learn of their fate.

As my role of Education Liaison Officer /Manager of Education & Welfare developed, it became increasingly apparent how highly Hinshelwood and Wilkins were regarding the educational element of the Scholarship Scheme. In November 2001, Paul, a first year at the time, missed one of my lessons, claiming that Wilkins had him asked to do extra training. When I broached Wilkins on the subject, he said that he had done no such thing and by way of punishment, dropped Paul from the Under 17 team for the next game. Wilkins told him that he did this because he lied and because he missed the lesson unnecessarily.

The following season, all of the first years missed a PE 'AS' lesson with another teacher because the teacher had been five minutes late. They claimed that they had waited and then decided to go home. Hinshelwood and Wilkins reacted swiftly. They made all of the Youth Team come in on Sunday for training, and they said that the only reason why they had not dropped them all from the Under 17 team was because there were so many of them. In order to tighten up procedure, all players regardless of year group were told that they were expected to be in the College library from 1pm until 5 pm, unless they were attending lessons.

Both Hinshelwood and Wilkins felt this action had to be taken, particularly as in their opinion, the players had developed 'a sloppy attitude' (Field Notes 3/2/03) to life in general which was being reflected by their performances on the pitch. As I was only able through time commitments to watch some of the games, I was unable to establish whether I could agree with such a sentiment.

7.3. j) Psychology

During the third year of fieldwork, Dean Wilkins decided to employ a psychologist to speak to the youth team players on a weekly basis. The players' reaction to this was in general, unbeknown to Wilkins, scathing. The players made their views clear to me during the Core Skills sessions, and they told me that they did not feel that anything the psychologist said would help them as footballers. When I asked if they had mentioned this to Dean Wilkins, one of the third years (Dale) told me (Field Notes 8/11/02) that they did not want to hurt his feelings whilst a first year (Sean) said (Field Notes 8/11/02) that he would be too scared to say anything. This lasted for four months but stopped due to the financial restraints that the Club faced. The fact that it had to stop was a disappointment to Wilkins who was convinced of the value of such sessions.

When Steve Coppell arrived at the Club, it was not long before he employed the services of a psychologist to help the first team in their efforts to fight off a relegation battle. His comments in the match day programme notes explained why he had done this (2003:4):

> "The squad of players have been working with a sports
> psychologist friend of mine Rob Forzoni, and the theme
> of his recent work has been the concept of 'inches' cumulatively
> improving an inch at a time, in all areas, to make an overall
> significant effect."

As I had the opportunity to hear one of the sessions that took place I asked one of the senior first team players what he thought of this idea. He replied (Field Notes 10/2/03):

> "To be honest Al, I don't need all that shit. I'm a professional
> footballer. All this is new to me and if I can't get myself
> up for these games I shouldn't be wearing the shirt. It might
> do some people some good but not me. I treat every game
> like a cup final.....just ask my missus."

It would be wrong to jump to conclusions here and suggest that the established professional footballers were set in their ways, as opposed to the youth team players who were keen to take on new ideas. Some professionals certainly gave the impression that they found these sessions useful, and my overall feeling was that individuals (whether they be professionals or youth players) had their own opinion about their relevance.

149

Therefore this was not an area in which one could make any sweeping statements about the relationship between players' opinions about sports psychology and the vocational socialisation of being a professional footballer.

7.3. k) Results of Courses

The results of the educational and vocational courses were fairly good compared to the national averages within the Scholarship Scheme. At Brighton and Hove Albion between 2000 and 2003 there was an 80% pass rate (28 out of 35) at 'AS' or 'A' level, and a 100% (12) pass rate at BTEC National Diploma (see Table 13).

The only courses that were not completed were for the European Computer Driving Licence (ECDL) or by those who left the Scholarship Scheme before the full length of its duration.

The retention rate was particularly good when compared to other football clubs. The FFE&VTS Report (2002) shows that for the 1998-2001 cohort, 28% of courses are not completed. (No figures were available for 2002 or 2003).

7.3. l) Offers and Rejections and leaving by 'mutual consent'

Towards the end of the third season at the Club, the Scholars were informed of their fate. They were summoned to the First Team Manager's office and told by the Manager if they were to be offered a full time professional contract. Also in the room were the Director of Youth and the Youth Team Coach. Martin Hinshelwood informed me that although the Manager has to make the final decision, he is always heavily influenced by the other two in the room, no matter who the First Team Manager is at the time.

Bobby	3rd Year	General Studies (A level)	Thursday pm	'E' Pass
		ECDL (Computing)	Monday pm	Ongoing
Nathan	3rd Year	General Studies (A level)	Thursday pm	'D' Pass
		ECDL (Computing)	Monday pm	Ongoing
Will	3rd Year	General Studies (A level)	Thursday pm	'D' Pass
		ECDL (Computing)	Monday pm	Pass
Scott	3rd Year	General Studies (A level)	Thursday pm	'E' Pass
		ECDL (Computing)	Monday pm	Ongoing
Rob	3rd Year	NVQ Construction	All day Monday	Pass
		Bricklaying Level 2		

Dave	2nd Year	BTEC Diploma Applied Science	All day Thursday	Pass
Les	2nd Year	BTEC Diploma Applied Science	All day Thursday	Pass
Alan	2nd Year	BTEC Diploma Applied Science	All day Thursday	Pass
Mark	2nd Year	BTEC Diploma Applied Science	All day Thursday	Pass
Neil	2nd Year	BTEC Diploma Applied Science	All day Thursday	Pass
Jim	2nd Year	BTEC Diploma Applied Science	All day Thursday	Pass
Andy	1st Year	English 'AS' level PE 'AS' level	Monday evening 3-4pm Monday & 4-5pm Thursday	'D' (Pass) 'D' (Pass)
Steve	1st Year	Maths 'A' level PE 'AS' level	Thursday evening 3-4pm Monday & 4-5pm Thursday	'B' (Pass) 'B' (Pass)
John	1st Year	NVQ Construction Level 2 Bricklaying	All day Monday	Pass
Mick	1st Year	BTEC Diploma Applied Science	All day Thursday	Pass
Dale	1st Year	BTEC Diploma Applied Science	All day Thursday	Pass
Barry	1st Year	BTEC Diploma Applied Science	All day Thursday	Pass

Courses studied and results achieved by scholars at Brighton & Hove Albion 2000-1
Table 13

Dave	3rd Year	General Studies 'A' Level ECDL (Computing)	Monday & Thursday pm Monday pm	'D' Pass Ongoing
Les	3rd Year	General Studies 'A' Level ECDL (Computing)	Monday & Thursday pm Monday pm	'E' Pass Ongoing
Alan	3rd Year	General Studies 'A' Level ECDL (Computing)	Monday & Thursday pm Monday pm	'E' Pass Ongoing
Mark	3rd Year	General Studies 'A' Level ECDL (Computing)	Monday & Thursday pm Monday pm	'B' Pass Ongoing
Neil	3rd Year	General Studies 'A' Level ECDL (Computing)	Monday & Thursday pm Monday pm	'E' Pass Ongoing
Jim	3rd Year	General Studies 'A'	Monday & Thursday pm	'E' Pass

151

		Level		
		ECDL (Computing)	Monday pm	Ongoing
Andy	2nd Year	English 'A' level	Friday pm	'D' Pass
		PE 'A' level	Monday & Thursday pm	'D' Pass
Steve	2nd Year	Maths 'A' level	Monday pm	'E' Pass
		PE 'A' level	Monday & Thursday pm	'B' Pass
John	2nd Year	NVQ Construction Level 2 Bricklaying	All day Monday	(3 year course)
Mick	2nd Year	BTEC Diploma Applied Science	All day Thursday	Pass
Dale	2nd Year	BTEC Diploma Applied Science	All day Thursday	Merit profile
Barry	2nd Year	BTEC Diploma Applied Science	All day Thursday	Pass
Simon	1st Year	NVQ 1 Plumbing	All day Thursday	Left 1/10/01
Dick	1st Year	Leisure & Rec. AVCE	Monday & Thursday pm	Dropped 1/6/02
Lee	1st Year	PE 'AS' level	Monday & Thursday pm	'U' Fail
Kerry	1st Year	PE 'AS level	Monday & Thursday pm	'E' Pass
		English 'AS' level	Monday & Thursday pm	'E' Pass
Paul	1st Year	PE 'AS' level	Monday & Thursday pm	'D' Pass
		Business 'AS' level	Monday & Tuesday pm	'U' Fail

All students also do Core skills on Friday pm

Courses studied and results achieved by scholars at Brighton & Hove Albion 2001-2

Table 14

Andy	3rd Year	BTEC Diploma Applied Science	Monday & Thursday pm	Pass
Steve	3rd Year	BTEC Diploma Applied Science	Monday & Thursday pm	Merit profile
John	3rd Year	NVQ Construction Level 2 Bricklaying	All day Monday	Pass
Mick	3rd Year	PE AS Level	Monday & Thursday pm	'U' Fail
		ECDL	Monday pm	Ongoing
Dale	3rd Year	PE AS Level	Monday & Thursday pm	'D' Pass
		ECDL	Monday pm	Ongoing
Barry	3rd Year	PE AS Level	Monday & Thursday pm	'U' Fail
		ECDL	Monday pm	Ongoing
Dick	2nd Year	BTEC Diploma Sports Science	Monday & Thursday pm	(2 year course)
Lee	2nd Year	BTEC Diploma Sports Science	Monday & Thursday pm	(2 year course)
Kerry	2nd Year	PE 'A' level	Monday & Thursday pm	Left Scheme 1/11/02
		English 'A' level	Monday & Thursday pm	
Paul	2nd Year	BTEC Diploma Sports Science	Monday & Thursday pm	(2 year course)

		PE 'A' level	Monday & Thursday pm	'D' Pass
Harry	1st Year	PE AS level	Monday & Thursday pm	'D' Pass
		Business AS level	Monday & Thursday pm	'D' Pass
Sean	1st Year	PE AS level	Monday & Thursday pm	'C' Pass
		Business AS level	Monday & Thursday pm	'U' Fail
Graham	1st Year	PE AS level	Monday & Thursday pm	'B' Pass
		Business AS level	Monday & Thursday pm	'D' Pass
Joe	1st Year	PE AS level	Monday & Thursday pm	'U' Fail
		ECDL	Thursday pm	Pass
Carl	1st Year	PE AS level	Monday & Thursday pm	'U' Fail
		BTEC Diploma	Monday & Thursday pm	(2 year
		Applied Science		course)
Derek	1st Year	PE AS level	Monday & Thursday pm	'E' Grade
		ECDL	Thursday pm	Ongoing

All students also do Core Skills on Friday pm

Courses studied and results achieved by scholars at Brighton & Hove Albion 2002-3

Table 15

During my first year of fieldwork, I planned to ask the third years at the earliest stage possible, who they thought would be taken on at the end of the season. I therefore began to ask them their opinions as early as September of their final season on the Scheme. The responses were quite varied, to the extent that some were much more cautious in their discussions with me than others. This variation did not surprise me, as some I had known for a number of years, as I had been manager of their district school team, whilst others I had barely met. For example Bobby, who was one who I did not really know, said that he had no idea who would be taken on and that everybody had a fair chance. Similarly Scott, another player who I had only met recently, felt that the coaching staff did have 'favourites' and had probably already made up their minds who they wanted, but he was not prepared to tell me who those 'favourites' were. This again I felt was not a surprising response, as the others saw Scott to as the one person who definitely would be taken on. Nathan on the other hand, who I had known for nearly ten years, had much stronger feelings. He felt he was being hard done by, as he felt he had consistently played well, and yet this was not recognised. He said he was also beginning to lose respect for the coaching staff, as in his opinion they seemed on occasions to be lacking in tactical expertise. Nathan's bitterness worsened throughout the season, particularly when his place in the Reserves for a match in February was given to first year. This to him was the

153

final straw and he actively sought my advice from then on about applying for universities in the United States.

When I asked him about his own chances, he felt that at best it was '50-50'. He had started the season playing for the Reserves, but now was not even a substitute. He said that life changed for him when the Reserve Team Manager, Ian Culverhouse, left at the beginning of the season. Will felt that Culverhouse, who had played in the same position as Will during his career, rated him highly. However, since he left, according to Will, his chances of being taken on at the end of the season had significantly decreased.

Danny was taken on as a full professional at the age of seventeen and therefore was not part of the Scholarship Scheme, but he did spend a lot of his time with the Scholarship players. As I thought he was likely to have a more objective opinion (as he was not in competition with the others), I asked his opinion of which of the third years he thought would be successful at the end of the season. His reponse was (Field Notes 7/10/00): "I can tell you now it will be Rob and Scott. I also reckon I can tell you who will make it the year after. Les and Jim are definitely the favourites, so they'll be taken on."

Danny's predictions proved to be right for both year groups. In fact so too did all of the Scholarship players' predictions, the only variance to this being when I asked each player about his own chances. In the first year of research, Nathan had accepted his fate well before he was told, whilst Will and Bobby waited until the Manager told them before they accepted it. Will was very philosophical and quickly applied for a course at a local university, as did Nathan. Bobby did not take rejection well and moved back home (he had been living in digs) seeming to avoid contact with the other players as much as possible.

In the second year of my fieldwork, all six players felt they had a reasonable chance right up until they were told in May by Peter Taylor, the First team Manager at the time. The four who were rejected (Alan, Dave, Mark and Neil) all said they felt particularly annoyed on two accounts. Firstly, they were upset as Hinshelwood and Wilkins told them that it was the Manager's decision and that this was totally unfair, as Taylor had rarely seen them play. Secondly, that they could have been told sooner, for example in March, which would then have given them enough time to apply for a course at a university.

154

It is easy to understand the players' frustration at being rejected by someone who had only watched them on one or two occasions, and understandable that they really wanted to hear it from the people who could have given an informed opinion, in other words, Hinshelwood and Wilkins. It is also easy to be sympathetic with the players regarding their second complaint. Did the Club really not know what the decision would be until the end of the season?

As a result, Mark and Dave came to see me in a state of panic to discuss what they should do. My advice did not change too much from what I had told them within the Core Skills programme. Both boys had done exceptionally well with their GCSE's and had a Pass in BTEC Diploma (Applied Science) Sports Studies and were likely to get an 'A' level in General Studies. I therefore suggested that they could apply to the University of Bath to do an HND in Coaching (as this course was set up for people with high sporting ability in mind), apply to the University of Brighton where they could do a sport related course, apply to universities in the USA for a soccer scholarship or have a year off and play at a semi-professional level or try to get a trial at another professional club.

Mark and Dave decided to apply to the University of Bath, and were asked to attend for an interview and a football trial as they had limited spaces. Dave did particularly well and was offered a place for September of that year, whilst Mark was told he did well but would have to go on a waiting list. They both decided to reject the offers and concentrate on trying to get trials at other clubs.

I took it upon myself to contact the Head of Education and Welfare at Bristol City Football Club whom I had known for many years, to ask if Dave and Mark could have a trial there. The response was that they could but it was likely to be a total waste of time as the Bristol City had only taken on three of their eleven Scholarship players due to lack of money. Mark also had contacts at Huddersfield Town Football Club, but despite getting a two- week trial, was not successful there either.

Both boys finally decided to play semi-professional football locally and to upgrade their BTEC Diploma in (Applied Science) Sports Studies. Alan meanwhile, had written to every other professional club in England for a trial but without success. He and Neil are also currently playing semi-professional football.

These boys were typical of many players who are rejected by the Club at 16 or 19 in that they do not give up hope. During the three years of my research and the five different age groups that I followed on the Scholarship Scheme, none of the players who were rejected by the Club ever played professional football for another Club. This emphasised their lack of realism with and moreover, their persisting hope.

In September of my third year of fieldwork, I once again asked the third years individually who they thought would be successful at the end of the season. Steve and John were the names that all players including themselves put forward and this was not a surprise. Both players had already represented the first team and the League's representatives had picked John in the Nationwide Division 1 Team of the Week during August. In addition, the other four players had only featured sporadically in the Reserves. On 1st November, Andy, Dale and Barry who were all now in their final year of the Scholarship asked to see me to discuss their future. All had decided that they wanted to leave by Christmas of that year, as they felt they were wasting their time, they knew that they were not going to be offered a professional contract at the end of the season. Andy was particularly adamant he wanted to leave then as he was looking to travel to Australia, before applying for a university place in the USA for a soccer scholarship.

Just before Christmas of that year, at the end of a PE 'AS' level lesson I was taking, Barry told me that Dean Wilkins had called a meeting with the third year parents as he had been told by an unnamed youth team player that some of the third years were considering leaving before the end of the season. Wilkins has apparently said that this type of attitude was giving out the wrong type of messages and no decisions had been made yet. Andy joined in the conversation to say that they all decided to stay on and just try to enjoy themselves, even though they knew the odds were stacked against them being offered a full contract. He also said that he was annoyed that one of his team-mates had chosen to tell Wilkins of their possible plan. By now others had joined the conversation I was having with Barry, and the group now included three third years and four first years. They all agreed that the culprit must be Paul, although the reason they felt he did it was because the team performances were being affected, and as a player he was unhappy with this.

156

Towards the end of January, Andy asked me if he could talk to me privately. He told me that he wanted to go to the north-east for a few days where some of the top soccer universities were holding a trial for the following academic year. However, he knew that if he told the Club's coaching staff he was going, it was equivalent to an admission of loss of hope of being offered a full time contract. We discussed the situation at length and he told me that he felt he 'only had a 25% chance of being chosen by the Club' (Field Notes 23/1/03). He went on to say that he also felt Dale had little chance either, as neither had "received any of the right signals for months" (Field Notes 23/1/03). He want on to predict that Barry would be given a six month contract, as he had been injured most of the season and had therefore no chance to prove himself, and that Mick ("because Deano loves him") (Field Notes 23/1/03), John and Steve would be taken on. Coincidently, Martin Hinshelwood actually gave me exactly the same information the later that day. My response was to suggest that Martin should tell the boys as soon as possible so that they could explore other avenues.

I asked (Field Notes 2/2/03) Hinshelwood why he felt Andy was not good enough and what were his reasons for releasing him. He said that it could be reduced to two key reasons. Firstly that like Dale, he did not think Andy had the ability to go on to the next stage, in other words as a professional footballer, and that secondly, over recent months he had started to cause problems in the dressing room. When I asked him to be more specific, Hinshelwood said that Andy was openly questioning decisions made by him and Wilkins. It occurred to me that this type of behaviour might well have been caused by the negative signals he had been receiving about his overall chances over recent months. When I said this to Hinshelwood, he stated that if that was the case, that was exactly the wrong way to respond and that he should prove himself on the pitch. Hinshelwood then went on to tell me that when he first arrived at the Club to take over the Youth team, there were boys already there who openly criticised the coaching staff and created a bad attitude in the team. His immediate response was to release the three players he felt were causing the trouble.

Towards the end of February, the players had still not been informed. Andy told me that he had spoken to the rest of the third years and he was asking me on behalf of all of them, if I could ask Hinshelwood and Wilkins if they could let them know. Wilkins told me

(Field Notes 27/2/03) that although he really sympathised with the players, there was nothing he could do to speed up the process as the decision was Steve Coppell's (First Team Manager), and he would not be rushed as the Club were currently in a relegation battle. He admitted that as he knew the players very well, he was in a much better position to make the decision than Coppell but he was not at liberty to do so. Although this was essentially true, it did give Wilkins an opportunity to distance himself from tough decisions and he would also be in a better position to sympathise with those players who were rejected.

During my period of research at the Club, two players, Simon and Kerry, left the Scheme before three years had been completed. In both cases it was the player who requested the termination of their involvement, and in both cases the Club agreed. Another player, Kim, had left the Scheme at the end of his second year in order to go to university in the USA and play soccer. He would have been in his third year as I embarked upon my research. According to both Wilkins and Hinshelwood, the player took the right option, as he would not have been offered a contract at the end of his third year.

Simon decided to leave the Scheme after only attending for two months of his first year. He claimed that he was not enjoying it, and that he would rather work for his father who was a carpet fitter and play for his father's team, which was a local semi-professional team. His father had once been a professional footballer, but told me he gave it up in his early twenties due to his 'dislike' (Field Notes 10/11/01) of the first team manager at the time.

When Simon told him he wanted to give up, his father claimed (Field Notes 10/11/01) that he had desperately tried to get his son to change his mind and not to make the same mistake as he had done. However, his son could not be persuaded and so he left.

At the beginning of the next season, Wilkins offered Simon the opportunity to come back to the Club for a trial period of twelve weeks and Simon accepted. At the end of that period, Wilkins and Hinshelwood felt that he had not progressed enough and so released him.

Kerry, who was in the same year as Simon, asked to leave in November of his second year, claiming he had become disillusioned with the Club. Two weeks prior to his request

158

to leave, he had let in a goal (he was a goalkeeper) that Wilkins felt he should have saved. At the end of the game, Wilkins had asked him if he had been wearing his contact lenses and asked Kerry to take them out to prove that he was. Kerry did so but was very unhappy about having to do so as he felt humiliated. Wilkins apologised to him the next Monday at training, as he felt he had been wrong to doubt him.

The following Saturday, the Reserve Team goalkeeper was injured and this meant that the First Team needed another goalkeeper for the away match to Crystal Palace. Kerry had hoped he would be selected, but instead the Management team chose the forty one year old goalkeeper coach, John Keeley.

The final blow came for Kerry when he was substituted (for Harry, the first year goalkeeper) at half time whilst playing for the Under 19's as Wilkins felt he was having a good game. The following Monday, Kerry's father telephoned Hinshelwood to say that his son would not be coming to training that day as he had severe diarrhoea.

This in itself was going against Club policy, as the player is expected to telephone the Physiotherapist to ask for leave of absence. When the Club doctor telephoned to ask Kerry himself what the matter was, he said that he had enough of the Club and wanted to leave as he felt he had been badly treated. In subsequent telephone conversations with Wilkins and Hinshelwood he repeated this request. Hinshelwood's response was to take Kerry at his word and promised to visit his house in order to get a release of contract form signed, despite Kerry's father's plea to allow his son time to reconsider. Kerry finally left the Club at the end of November of his second year.

As Kerry had left, only three players remained in that particular year group. Just before Christmas of that year, Dick suffered a bad leg injury whilst playing for the Under 19's. A long lay-off may well have impeded his chances of being taken on as a professional, particularly as he certainly was not going to able to play again for that season. Paul was now playing regularly with the Reserves, and as the only other second year, Lee, had not featured at all, I asked Paul (Field Notes 4/2/03) whether a lack of players in his year group would increase his chances. He seemed surprised by the question and said that players were never chosen just because there were only a few left in the year group.

The third years during my final year of research were eventually told of their fate on the 31st March 2003. Steve Coppell had told Hinshelwood and Wilkins that they should tell the boys of the Club's decision as it was they who knew them best. (At about the same time, when I asked Steve Coppell for an interview about the Club's youth team, he said that there would be no point, as he knew nothing about the Club's youth team. It was only when I actually wanted to ask him about youth football in general that he agreed to be interviewed.)

The third years were spoken to individually after a morning training session at the Club's Training Ground. They had not been given any prior warning. The outcome had not changed much from what Hinshelwood had told me back in January. That was that John and Steve were both given a two-year and Mick a one-year professional contract. In addition, Barry was told that he would be given three more months (from July 1st to September 30th) to prove that he was worth offering a contract to. This was because he had suffered a long-term injury that had meant he had not played most of his third year. The remaining two players, Andy and Dale, were released.

There was no doubt that Hinshelwood found this aspect of his job very hard. Naturally, he got to know the boys very well over the six years that he had known them. He was quoted in the local paper (Evening Argus, 10/4/03) as saying; "It's difficult because you have the joy for those boys taken on, but then you have the disappointment for Andy and Dale. They have been a credit to themselves, their families and the Club, but you have to make that decision about the next step up."

Inevitably, Andy and Dale were very disappointed, even though they both admitted that they knew they were going to be rejected. However, although when they came to see me (as Manager of Education and Welfare) they both seemed subdued, they were both really concerned about their next move. They were very disappointed with the Club for leaving it so long before they were told. Dale said (Field Notes 6/4/03): "Did you know that Crystal Palace let their players know before Christmas? They've all got themselves sorted out with something else already."

When I pointed out to them that at least now they knew where they stood and that everyone gets rejected at some stage in their lives, they both agreed (Field Notes 7/4/03) that they would rather be in their position than Mick's, who had only been given a one-year contract and would therefore face further uncertainty within a short period of time.

160

They both emphasised that they were happy for the other players, but they did not hold out much hope for Barry who they thought would be released at the end of September. Andy also said that he was surprised that John had not been offered a five-year contract. I was not sure if he said this because he thought John was a really good player or because he was the nephew of Martin Hinshelwood. From his facial expression and tone of voice I concluded that it was the latter.

Andy had sensibly already done a lot of research about going to study in the United States of America (USA) on a football scholarship. When he came to see me on April 6, he had already been offered a scholarship at the University of North Carolina with 100% of fees paid, guaranteed for one year. As this University had a good reputation for soccer, he was very happy. Now all he needed to do was to take his S.A.T's (a public examination to enter universities in the USA). Purely by chance, I was contacted on the same day by a student I used to teach who told me that he had just secured a post in the USA as the university's assistant football coach, and he asked whether I knew of any players who had been released by Brighton and Hove Albion who may be interested in going to an American university. When I told him about Andy (whom he had known as they had both gone to the same school), he said he would be happy to speak to him and offer any advice. Andy, not surprisingly, was delighted. Andy was particularly pleased because he was informed by the coach that as his academic profile was "relatively good" (Field Notes 6/4/03) (English 'A' Level (D), Physical Education 'A' Level (D) and the likelihood of Applied Science BTEC Certificate Merit profile, the equivalent to two 'C's at 'A' Level), some of this could count towards his degree.

Within three weeks of Andy being told he was to be released, Dean Wilkins had arranged for him to have a trial for Cambridge United. He was invited to play for Cambridge United against Portsmouth. He did well enough for Cambridge to offer him a week at the Club in order to have a better look at him. Andy rejected this offer, preferring instead to play for a local County League team and then to pursue the possibility of studying in the United States. In essence, it seemed that the attraction of becoming a professional footballer had all but disappeared. By June, two months after he had been released, Andy had accepted a soccer scholarship at Drury University, Missouri.

When Andy and Dale were told by the Club that their services were no longer required, of the two it was Dale who had seemed the most upset. However, he had also done some of his own research about courses at local universities. He decided to apply to UCAS to take either Information Technology or Media courses.

During my three years of research, of the eight players that were given a professional contract all, except Les, were seen by Hinshelwood and Wilkins to be able to play in a variety of positions at youth team level. For example, they were seen as defender/midfield players or midfield/strikers who could play on the right or left side. Both Hinshelwood and Wilkins felt that modern professionals, if good enough should be able to adapt to different positions. By the end of the fieldwork (May 2003) the eight players who had become professionals over the two years (in other words from the end of year one of my research until the end of year three of my research) had played the following first team matches:

NAME	MATCHES	POSITIONS PLAYED
Rob	13	Striker, Central Midfield
Scott	12	Striker, Right Midfield
John	7	Right and Centre Back
Les	4	Striker
Jim	4	Right and Central Midfield
Steve	1	Left Midfield
Barry	0	
Mick	0	

First team matches and positions played by scholars between 2000 and 2003

Table 16

There is no conclusive evidence from this research that players playing in some positions are more likely to be chosen for a professional contract than others.

7.3. m) Injuries
During the period of research, the only Scholarship player to suffer any real problems over injury was Dale. He was on the wrong end of a bad challenge that saw the guilty player from another club sent off and Dale to incur a broken leg. His injury was so bad that he had to have a metal plate fitted. It took six months of the remainder of his second

season as a scholar to mend well enough to kick a ball again. Before his final year, Dale decided not go on holiday with his friends as he wanted to make sure he fully recovered and was fit enough to start the new season. However, within the first two weeks of pre-season training he broke the same leg in the same place again after a challenge by his team-mate Paul in a friendly small sided game. The first team players immediately paid for him to go on holiday, but the feeling amongst the coaches was that he may now have lost his chance of ever becoming a professional footballer.

7.3. n) A full time professional contract and beyond

For those who are deemed good enough to be taken on after they have completed the Scholarship Scheme, as with any other professional club, it is commonplace at Brighton and Hove Albion to offer the player a contract. For those who were not selected, other options had to be considered. The destination of those who attended and left the Scheme between 2000-2003 was as follows:

NAME	YEAR LEFT SCHEME	DESTINATION	WHERE IN 2003
Bobby	2001	Fireman	Builder
Nathan	2001	University of Brighton	University of Brighton
Will	2001	University of Brighton	University of Brighton
Scott	2001	**Professional Contract**	**Professional Contract**
Rob	2001	**Professional Contract**	**Professional Contract**
Kim	2000	University (USA)	Unknown
Les	2002	**Professional Contract**	**Professional Contract**
Alan	2002	Employed by media company	Employed by media company
Mark	2002	Gap Year & Retakes	University of Bath
Dave	2002	Gap Year & Retakes	University of Chichester
Jim	2002	**Professional Contract**	**Professional Contract**
Neil	2002	Retail	Retail
Barry	2003	**Professional Contract**	**Professional Contract**
Andy	2003	Drury University, Missouri	Drury University, Missouri
Steve	2003	**Professional Contract**	**Professional Contract**
John	2003	**Professional Contract**	**Professional Contract**
Dale	2003	University of Brighton	University of Brighton
Mick	2003	**Professional Contract**	**Professional Contract**

Destination of scholars between 2001 and 2003

Table 17

In my first year of fieldwork, Rob and Scott were offered a two-year and a one-year contract respectively, although at the end of that year Scott was given an extension of another year. At the end of the following season, both Jim and Les were offered a year each upon the completion of their third year. This was no surprise as both had featured in the first team towards the end of the Division 2 Championship winning season. During the 2002-3 season, all four players played regularly for the first team under the newly appointed manager Martin Hinshelwood until he was sacked.

Within five weeks of Steve Coppell being appointed, he had signed six new players (either on full time contracts or on loan). This meant that there were now so many professional players at the Club that some could not even get a game in the Reserves. The response of the Club was to try to let the younger players go out on loan to other Clubs. Rob was dispatched off to Chesterfield, whilst others waited for a telephone call from their agent who was trying to contact clubs for them. The overall result was that none of the players who had come through the Club's Centre of Excellence played a game under the management of Steve Coppell for the rest of the 2002-3 season. Therefore, even after finally achieving a professional contract, the future is by no means certain and this uncertainty can be purely because of the league position of the club as opposed to how the individual is performing.

However, Scott and Danny had lengthy loan spells with Southend and Exeter respectively, both holding regular first team places. Hinshelwood was delighted for them and also felt totally vindicated in taking them on as professionals. At the end of the season Scott and Danny were both offered and accepted a further one-year contract – the significance being that there were now six players who had been through the Centre of Excellence and were currently full professionals at the Club.

7.3. o) First team players

It was only during my final year of research that I began to interact with the first team players on a regular basis. My new full time job as the Club's Study Centre Manager meant that I was based at the Club's ground, Withdean Stadium. Under the management of Steve Coppell, the players came to the Stadium the morning before they played a match in order to receive a tactical talk and to train on the pitch. I would then often eat lunch and talk with the players and the first team coaching staff. My relationship with them was also enhanced as few became interested in the Study Support Centre and asked if I could get them onto part-time educational or vocational courses.

In some ways, the range of courses they were interested in highlighted their range of educational and sociological backgrounds and personalities. One player had difficulties in reading and writing and was keen to rectify this in order to increase his opportunities of employment once he had completed his professional playing career. Some were interested in vocational courses such as plumbing and bricklaying whilst another was looking to remain in professional football by becoming a physiotherapist. He asked if he could study part-time as a mature student on a Higher National Certificate course in Sports Therapy. The Club Captain, who was to retire at the end of the season, was promised a full-time post at the Club within the Commercial Department by the Chairman. The player, Paul Rogers, had come into professional football at the relatively late age of 27, and had previously been a broker working for a firm based in London. His strong personality and the fact that he was a well-respected player amongst his peers made him an ideal captain, although his early career outside of professional football made him very atypical as a professional player. This in itself aptly demonstrated the lack of vocational socialisation that had taken place within the sport for this player.

7.3. p) What the coaches and players think it takes to become a professional footballer

Throughout my research, it became increasingly apparent that the person with the most influence over who would or would not be offered a professional contract was Martin Hinshelwood. From the youngest age group at the Centre of Excellence (the Under 9's), to the eldest (the Under 16's) Hinshelwood would decide with the team's coach who was to be offered an extension of their contract at the Centre. In addition, throughout the time a player spent at the Club as a Scholar, it was Hinshelwood, in partnership with Dean Wilkins, who decided if a player was good enough to last the full three years. At the end of the three years, although in theory it was the responsibility of the first team manager to decide who was to be offered a full professional contract, in practice, they only acted upon the advice of Hinshelwood and Wilkins.

I was therefore intrigued to know what Hinshelwood thought were the requirements for an aspiring professional footballer to actually make the grade. He said when making a decision about a player's future at whatever level, he would always ask himself the question, can he or has he the potential to make it on to the next level? In addition, he said (Field Notes 24/8/00) that in his opinion, aside from natural talent, it was all about the attitude of the individual. He claimed that:

> "They must have a love of the game. They can't play at it.
> They must be able to cope within a football environment
> and all that it entails. It could be their livelihood. They must
> be able to deal with the social pressures – for example their
> mates. They must be strong willed with their friends."

When I asked Dean Wilkins the same question (Field Notes 2/8/00), he emphasised that it was a combination of factors. He said that "They must have ability and a real determination. There must be a will to succeed. There have been players with ability but have not made it because they didn't want it enough."

To me the most salient feature of these conversations seemed to be that the player's attitude was seen as equally important as his ability. In general, most of the youth team players' opinion did not differ much from this point of view either. In an exercise I did with all of the youth team players as part of their Core Skills, each wrote answers to a series of questions I put to them regarding professional football. One of the questions was, "What do you think you need in order to succeed (at professional football)?"The words that were most common within their answers were: 'dedication', 'commitment' 'focussed' and 'desire'. Often these words were preceded by the word 'show', as if it was a case of proving to the coach or manager about how seriously a player was treating the game. Very few included physical attributes such as skill or levels of fitness, for even though they had been taken on the Scheme did not automatically mean that they had yet reached the standard required for either of these at first team level.

There were other comments that seemed to be written as a joke, but nevertheless expressed an underlying concern of the boys, for example: "be loved by the staff (like Steve)", whilst others felt that they were not being given enough opportunity, for example: "Just be given the chance to show what I can do, and not be sub all the time".

166

When I asked Andy why he thought he was not going to be chosen (Field Notes (28/1/03), he said: "One of the main reasons is because I'm not big enough. You tell me one player who has been offered a pro-contract over recent years here who is small." I could not agree with this sentiment as I could actually name two of the four who been taken on over the last two years who were two of the three smallest full-time professionals at the club.

7.3. q) The future of the Brighton & Hove Albion Football Club Youth system

During December 2002, Martin Hinshelwood asked me if I could assist with the writing of the Club's 'Youth Development Document'. This document was now a requirement as set out by the Football League for every club that wished to have an Academy or Centre of Excellence during the time period of 2002-2006. No funding would be available to any club that failed to produce this. The aim of this was clearly to ensure consistency amongst clubs, and also to establish quality assurance procedures.

Clubs now have to have policies on management and administration, facilities, staffing, their technical programme, health and education and welfare. All these areas have to have itemised costs and clearly stated future objectives. There is also a requirement for the Chairman and Chief Executive of each Club to produce signed statements supporting this document.

The requirement for each Club to produce such a document is a perfect example of how accountability within professional football has increased over recent years. Failure to produce this document to the standard laid out by the Football League would probably lead to reduced funding for the Club's youth system. Brighton & Hove Albion's original 'Youth Development Document' was considered to be close to the standard required. However, in order to have the Document fully approved, Martin Hinshelwood decided to invite Steve Hetzke (Football League, South East Youth Development Monitor) to the Club to discuss where improvements could be made. Although this meeting was initially to discuss minor detail, what followed gave an interesting perspective on what might be the future of youth football over the next few years.

Hetzke (Field Notes 25/3/03) asked the question "Is the system we currently have one of excellence or are we just accommodating kids?" He went on to say that perhaps a way forward would be to join age groups together and thereby take fewer numbers. For example, discard the Under 9's, Under 10's and the Under 11's and continue the Under 12's. He questioned why it was so important to run three sides. He added that at the more senior side of the youth system, many of the clubs in the north did not have an Under 17 team, preferring instead to keep to Under 18's and Under 19's Hinshelwood said that he could not agree with such changes. To begin with, he felt that all players who play for the Brighton and Hove Albion, at whatever level, eventually leave the Club as better players than they were when they first arrived. According to him, so many players were benefiting from the current system that it would be a tragedy to change it. Hinshelwood stated that few Clubs had third year scholars and this did not help those players who were late developers. Hetzke on the other hand felt that Clubs should be encouraged to release third years at the earliest opportunity if the Club had decided not to offer them a professional contract.

Hetzke's overall view of professional football clubs across the country was that 95% of them would scrap their youth system if they did not receive external funding. He did emphasise however, that top Premiership clubs were keen to promote their youth system and that some had put in up to £2 million per year towards it. Hinshelwood interjected to state that he did not believe that Brighton and Hove Albion would consider scrapping their own youth system, citing the fact that the Club had paid £208,000 towards it during the 2001/2 season.

Hetzke stated that currently there are some clubs, for example Bournemouth, that do not actually run a Scholarship Scheme. Their youth team players aged 16-19, attend a local sixth form college on a full time basis and train with the Club at specific times. In this way the Club are faced with minimal expense.

The main issue that Hetzke was keen to discuss was the necessity for all clubs to do the paperwork required in order to prove that the Centre of Excellence and the Academies are run properly, and that the Clubs are accountable to ensure that this is the case otherwise future funding would surely be in doubt. Both Hetzke and Hinshelwood concluded by agreeing that most clubs did not value their youth system nearly as much as they should and the future of English football would suffer badly as a result.

Less than one month after this meeting, a letter (11 April 2003) was sent to all Club Chairmen from the Chairman of The Football League, Sir Brian Mawhinney. This stated that there were problems with the future funding of the Scholarship Scheme:

> "It is with deep concern and regret that I have to advise you
> that the Government's contribution has so far not been
> forthcoming. The immediate implications are that the final
> quarterly payment due later this month via Sport England will
> be 60% less than the figure you would normally expect to
> receive. Clubs who qualify for the full grant will therefore get
> £13,800 instead of the usual £34,500 quarterly amount."

He went on to say that despite meetings with the Minister for Sport, Richard Caborn, and the Secretary of State for Culture, Media and Sport, Tessa Jowell, the Government could not confirm when their contributions would made available.

This seemed to confirm Hetzke's fears that the youth systems of many clubs would surely be in jeopardy without the much-needed Government support.

For Brighton, in recent years the youth system has brought some success to individuals. Over the past five years, the Club can boast to having twelve players that have come through the Club's youth system who have gone on to be given a full professional contract. However, four have since left professional football and none currently hold a regular first team football place. Only one current first team player (Kerry Mayo) at Brighton and Hove Albion has come through the Club's youth system, and he has been a full professional for ten years.

This general issue has regularly been discussed in local newspapers over recent years. For example, one journalist (Lindfield 2003:52) wrote:

> "Chairman Dick Knight tells the Falmer inquiry (the Club is
> currently looking to build a new stadium) the stadium is needed
> so we can continue with our schools of excellence. But what
> happens to the graduates of these schools?"

He goes on to say:

"Martin Hinshelwood may have helped dig his own grave by relying too heavily on our younger players, but the complete absence of them now seems to be equally unfortunate. What sort of message is it sending out to the kids desperate to play for their home team?"

I asked Martin Hinshelwood what his thoughts were on this matter. He said (Field Notes 4/3/03):

"Just look at the Club over the past four years. We spent three years fighting for promotion and this year trying to stave off relegation. The manager wants instant results in these situations and they don't feel they have the time to blood in youngsters. On top of that we've had four managers in three years. There's been no consistency. Also the first team players we've got at the moment are the ones that brought us here from the Third Division. They are finding the First Division difficult themselves. In order to use youngsters, you really need some players who are experienced at the level the team are playing at. We haven't got that."

7.3. r) The final word

Upon nearing the completion of this fieldwork, I managed to arrange an interview with the Club's First Team Manager, Steve Coppell. Coppell is respected throughout the country as a successful manager just below Premiership level, particularly in Division One that involved being in charge of Crystal Palace through three different spells. However, he is best known for his playing days at Manchester United and for England (for which he gained over fifty caps). He also is one of the few professional footballers to have held a degree whilst playing and his autobiography 'Touch and Go' (1985) describes how he was able to balance football with academic work. During this interview (Field Notes 28/7/03) I was able to broach some key issues with regard to young people going in to professional football.

Before the interview began, he was keen to point out that he was not that familiar with youth team football in general and therefore warned that he might not be able to give me the information I required.

On the issue of what was he looking for in a young player making the final step through to first team football, he said that obviously every position had different demands and so in some ways it was difficult to generalise. However, he felt that personality was very important and he would be keen to see if the player had the desire and hunger to succeed. This was not always apparent from just talking to the player, as one only really discovers such characteristics when the person is playing. He felt that players these days should have certain physical attributes, and be physical and competitive. He also stressed that ideally a player should have pace in order to be a top player.

Coppell said that he thought that players coming through to professional football had improved due to the clubs' academies and centres of excellence. Since these youth systems had been introduced, there have been many more qualified coaches who knew more about the game. Players are now more finely tuned and young players today are technically better. This was also due to a change in coaching style of recent years, which has seen a change in approach; for example, in this country we no longer encourage the 'long ball game'.

Since Coppell joined the club the previous autumn, he had chosen not to use any of the youth team in the first team. This, he felt, could be easily understood, as during this time the club had been involved in a relegation battle and he had wanted to rely upon experienced players. However, I asked how well he thought he knew the youth team players. He replied that although he did not often see them play, he asked the coaches after each weekend how they had played, and so he was confident he was keeping abreast of their progress. Consultation to him was important.

To date, my research had shown that there appeared to be more boys entering into the profession with a sound academic background. As someone who had gained a degree whilst playing, I was keen to find out if Coppell felt his own academic achievements had helped him in his football career. His reply was that he thought it definitely had as people naturally regarded him as bright and he was not going to tell them otherwise. He knew of many people in professional football who were cleverer than him, but who he felt were

171

not given the same opportunities due to their lack of academic background. In his opinion, good academic achievement brought about high self-esteem, and a lack of it the opposite.

Although he had no coaching qualifications himself, he thought that these days it is difficult to get on without them. He had not taken any, as after spending 10 months involved in football (the length of a season) the last thing he wanted to do was to go on a course. However, he thought that courses were excellent for getting coaches to interact with each other so that it made one think about different ways of doing things. Ideally, he would like all of his coaches to go away and see how others coach, as it would very stimulating.

On the theme of coaching, he totally rejected the idea that a top coach should have a professional playing background. Many of the ex-professionals he had seen coach or manage just did not have presence. He also felt that it was often a pre-requisite towards getting a top coaching qualification, but this was no longer the case.

As Coppell had used the services of a sports psychologist whilst he had been at the Club, I asked him if he felt this was now essential in professional football. He replied that he felt it was helpful but not vital. To him it was a fresh face saying the same thing as him but in a different way and it only had a certain amount of value. He highlighted a sporting example, whereby in the British Open Golf Championship in 2003, all the top players had a number of advisors on their pay roll including sports psychologists. However, the player who eventually won (Ben Curtis) had none.

As a person who had been involved in recruiting players to the clubs he had served at, I wanted to know if he had experienced or knew of any illegal approaches from one club to another with regard to the sale of youth team players. He replied that it went on all the time and that it was rife in professional football. He added that changes to the system should be made. For example, he did not agree with the rule that players must live within one and a half hours' travelling distance to attend an academy or centre of excellence. He stated (Field Notes 28/7/03):

> "What if there is an outstanding young player who lives
> in the Torquay area. That player may not be able to
> progress to his full potential because he is not playing

with players of similar ability. Also, what happens to
players that live in rural areas that are not within one and
a half hours of a club?"

My final question was how important did he think family background was for a young player hoping to become a professional? He replied that a supportive family is very important and that it can be an immense help. A family like this will help the player with their self-belief and determination.

CHAPTER 8

OTHER CLUBS

So far, all of the primary research for this publication has been based upon one professional football club - Brighton and Hove Albion. One of the problems of undertaking research of this nature is that it is impossible to assess whether the conclusions that can be drawn from one club are common to others. Ideally, in order to obtain a more balanced view, systems at a number of clubs would need to be taken into consideration. Whilst the longevity and depth of research comparable to that that was carried out at Brighton and Hove Albion would be advantageous, it would be virtually impossible to complete without a team of researchers (and even then, consistency between researchers over interpretation of material can cause problems of its own). However, in order to partially overcome this problem, two other clubs have been selected for small-scale case studies. The two clubs, Bristol City and Charlton Athletic, were chosen purely on the basis of close personal contacts within these clubs, the value of which within this context was huge. Access to relevant information was made easy and developing relationships that were based upon trust was unnecessary, as these had already been established. Both Clubs had Academies as opposed to a Centre of Excellence (the difference of which is discussed in Chapter 4) and these had been established since 1998. Incorporated within the Academies are Scholarship Schemes for the sixteen to nineteen year olds, although clubs with academies actually sign players up to the age of twenty-one. In addition, some unpublished research by Owsley (2000) at Bristol City, including her participant observation at the Club, and a report on (Garland and Chakraborti (2001)) an initiative to promote racial equality by Charlton Athletic and Greenwich Council, added to the information I was able to gain.

CASE STUDY 1 – BRISTOL CITY

a) Location and status

Bristol City is distinct from any other professional football club in the South West of England or neighbouring South Wales, as it is the only one that has Academy status. The closest academies to Bristol City are Reading, which is approximately sixty-five miles to the east, and clubs in the Midlands, for example Aston Villa and Coventry, which are all in excess of eighty miles away. Therefore, with regard to youth football, Bristol City has a special attraction to all nine to thirteen year olds that live within an hour's travelling distance of the Club and all fourteen to sixteen year old boys that live within an hour and a half. The special attractions that an academy brings are that the youth team fixtures are against Premiership youth teams; more attention is given by clubs to liaising with the players' schools and to the players' educational well being; there are better training facilities; and finally the facilities must include a sixty metre by forty metre indoor playing area.

According to Peter Coleman, Head of Education and Welfare and a senior youth team coach, (Field Notes 28/4/03) Bristol Rovers had the stronger youth system of the two clubs in the city before Bristol City gained academy status in 1998. However, since that time, this has no longer been the case as he feels Bristol Rovers has not placed as much emphasis on their youth team. For example, he thought it likely that Rovers did not spend the entire £138,000 grant for its youth system in an appropriate way based upon the terms of the funding.

Despite the obvious advantages of holding Academy status, the price to the Club does not come cheaply. Coleman stated that it costs the Club £400,000 per annum. To put this into perspective, Brighton and Hove Albion (that was to play in the same division as Bristol during the 2003/4 season), contributes approximately £100,000 towards its Centre of Excellence – an amount considered generous by the Football League Youth Development Monitor for the South East, Steve Hetzke. This in itself seems to demonstrate Bristol's commitment to its youth policy because of the benefits it can bring.

b) Attending the Academy

The boys, who attend the Academy, train in the evenings during the week and play for the Club at the weekend. The Under 9's, 10's and 11's train twice a week for three hours and play eight-a-side for their matches, whilst the Under 12's through to the Under 16's train five nights a week for three hours and play eleven-a-side for the weekend matches. In total, the Club have fifteen teams that play at weekends, and this includes the girls' teams. The relationship between the girls' and the boys' teams is much closer here than at

Brighton. Often, the girls will train with the boys, although normally the girls will be one or two years older than the boys they train with, as the standard of the girls' football is seen as a lot lower than the boys'. In comparison, at Brighton, the boys and girls train at different venues and never cross each other's paths.

Similarly to those who attend Brighton & Hove Albion's Centre of Excellence, the boys are allowed to play for the school team and schools' representative teams, although Bristol City would prefer it if they just played for the Club. This decision is left to the school, the player and his parents.

c) The requirements to become a professional – the Club's view

When I asked Peter Coleman what he thought was needed to become a professional footballer, he stated (Field Notes 28/4/03):

> "If I knew for sure, I'd be a very rich man. But I think that what you are really looking for in a pro' is that they must be good athletes with a determined attitude. That does not necessarily mean they are the best players."

He went on to emphasise the importance of the 'correct attitude', and that often a coach could spot this from a player as young as nine. He felt that players should not even be considered if their attitude is 'wrong', and argued that the Club had never been proved to have made a mistake over this, as no player who had not been taken on or had been discarded by the Club because of having the 'wrong' attitude ever became a professional footballer. When I pressed him further on what the 'wrong' attitude was, he said that generally it meant not being seen to able to cope with a professional football club environment and the restrictions on lifestyle that go with it. (How one would detect this in a nine year old would be open to question). During the season 2002/3, two first years had been discarded because of their unacceptable attitude and overall, Coleman is convinced that once a player is seen as a problem, even if the situation is resolved in the short term, the difficulties that come with that player never really go away. In his view, it is far better for both the player and the Club if they part ways as not doing so only prolongs the agony for both parties.

176

The Club maintain that players who stay in lodgings are more likely to have difficulties keeping to diets and maintaining a healthy lifestyle than those who live at home – a point made by the Brighton and Hove Albion physiotherapist, Malcolm Stuart. For those players who had been taken on, it meant going against what the Club's expectations were, which were clearly given to them when they joined.

Bristol City produces a list of attributes that the young players should aspire to. These attributes are sub-divided into four groups: common technical attributes (for example shooting and dribbling), common attributes – understanding when, where and how (for example, creating space and supporting the player with the ball), physical attributes (for example, power and mobility) and mental attributes (for example, concentration and confidence). This list is given to all of the coaches and the young players. From a more technical viewpoint, the Club have also produced a sheet which is headed 'Principles of why a player is playing a position and how to play the position'. For this, each playing position found within a football team is given a list of up to twenty-two principles that a player playing in that position should have. This consists of technical ability (for example heading) as well as psychological aspects (such as being calm under pressure). Peter Coleman claims this list is particularly useful when scouting for new talent.

One of the most important issues when selecting a player, according to Coleman, is the player's background. If a coach or a scout fails to take this into consideration, the Club could end up wasting a lot of time and effort. He sees the parent's role as crucial here, quoting an example of a player who was recently released by the Club because his father, an ex-professional himself, was creating problems by openly criticising the coaching staff.

He also felt that a player must have 'stickability'. In other words, the player must want to stay at the Club despite setbacks. He should learn to accept change as well as criticism. Managers and coaches come and go and in some cases they will have different views on the same player. Someone doing well under the previous manager may suddenly find that his position at the Club has become a lot more tenuous as he is not rated highly by the new one – as many players at Brighton and Hove Albion have found out to their cost. He adds that undoubtedly players are criticised by staff from time to time and they have to learn to accept this without getting too upset. However, it is the coach or manager's job to ensure that players progress and are suitable for professional football. Coleman says that the Club's job can be put simply into the following words 'Find, develop and sign'. Dave Burnside, the Academy Director, claims that there is a link between a player's attitude towards education and his attitude on the pitch. According to Owsley (2000:12):

> "Dave has witnessed traits such as footballers who are lazy in
> training also being lazy in their studies, and those who work
> hard in college, very often being the same boys who work hard
> on the training field."

Here, once again, is evidence of a coach using his own psychological analysis of a player as a basis for judging his suitability for professional football. In addition, this quote highlights an issue raised by Hinshelwood and Wilkins at Brighton and Hove Albion - that there is a link between football performance and effort given to academic or vocational studies. Burnside (ibid.) develops this link between the two by stating that he sees the role of education as actually helping the player on the pitch as, according to him, it can lead to a more intelligent player.

d) Head of Education and Welfare

Coleman had been at the Club since 1990 on a part-time basis as Director of Coaching and Youth Development Officer before taking the job on full-time in 1993. In his new post as Head of Education and Welfare, which he has held since 1998 (since City gained Academy status), his responsibilities are not too dissimilar from any post based at a Centre of Excellence. However, whereas an Education and Welfare Officer at a club which has a Centre of Excellence would tend to deal mainly with the educational aspects of the Scholarship Scheme, his job is far more wide reaching. He makes annual visits to all schools attended by Academy players. During the season of 2002-3 this totalled 120 schools. Often, Coleman is required to explain to staff at the schools what attending the Club's Academy entails and try to deal with any misconceptions they may have, either about the system or the Club. In addition, the responsibility he has for those boys on the Scholarship Scheme includes the courses they attend, monitoring of their diet, their lodgings and housing benefit as well as their transport. For the 2002-3 season he also coached the Under 11's. His personal involvement with all of the players is therefore quite considerable.

As someone who has been so involved with young players at a professional football club, I was keen to establish what his views were on the changes that have occurred within recent years and what he thought the benefits were of the current system.

When I asked him if he felt that football with regard to players at a professional level was changing from a working to a classless profession, he said (Field Notes 28/4/03) that at Bristol this was very hard to tell. He did not always know what the profession of the father was, which is what one would need to know if players were to be placed into socio-economic occupational groups. However, he felt that if one were to make the broad assumption that middle-class children were more academic than those from a working-class background and therefore achieved better results at GCSE, then no, there had been no significant change over recent years. Bristol City had for many years seemed to attract boys with a reasonable academic record and Coleman was keen to ensure that that academic progress remained a key part of any young player's future. According to him the idea of a football club academy helped greatly with this process.

Although it appeared that Bristol City did not much have much local rivalry from other professional clubs trying to entice players away from the Club to their own, I was keen to establish if any special favours or treatment were handed out to their most valuable players in order to keep them. Coleman said that the only special treatment that the better players received was the offer of a YD6 (a four year contract at the age of 12) or travel expenses if they lived in Wales and therefore had to pay a £4 toll charge whenever they went back into Wales via the Severn Bridge. He felt quite strongly that he did not want to keep boys who would only stay if the extra demands they made upon the Club were accepted.

e) The Scholarship Programme

For the players at Bristol City, the education programme involved attending Clifton College, a public school that is within close proximity to the Club's Training Ground, from Monday to Thursday between 9.00 am and 12.30 pm. The players were taught separately from the other College students, although they shared the school facilities. In

179

the past, the players were offered 'A' level PE, GNVQ Business Studies, BTEC First Diploma in Sports Studies and GCSE retakes. Over the past two years, all players have been encouraged to take either the BTEC First Diploma or new level 3 courses, (BTEC National Certificate in Sport or BTEC National Diploma in Sport) which have been set up specifically for elite sports performers. These courses have proved such a success that youth team players from Bristol Rhinos (the local professional rugby union club) have joined the classes in a joint venture.

Peter Coleman was very proud of the educational successes the youth team players at the Club have had over recent years, claiming (Field Notes 28/4/03) that Mickey Burns (Chief Executive for FFE&VTS) said that Bristol City was one of the best clubs in the country for high academic standards throughout the Scholarship Scheme. The unpublished reports (2002 and 2003) produced by the FFE&VTS would seem to concur with this. In 2001, the fourteen completing the Scholarship Scheme (cohort 1998-2001) failed only four courses of the twenty-eight taken (2002 figures currently not available). It is clear that the Club is keen to nurture the young players on both an educational and playing front. In a Bristol City Football Club information pack given to scholars and parents it stated (2002):

> "What we hope to achieve generally is a more intelligent sports
> person, one who understands what is being asked of them in terms
> of fitness, nutrition and training methods. This increased
> knowledge and understanding should increase their motivation and
> make them better prepared for their chosen sport."

This issue of the importance placed upon the value of learning for young players at Bristol City is highlighted by some research done at the Club by Owsley (2000). She found in her research (44:2000) that:

> "The Club seems to be aware of the pressure involved in
> maintaining a healthy balance between students' football and
> academic studies. Since the start of the Academy education has
> had a higher profile within the Club…"

One essential ingredient that Coleman believes a professional club should always prioritise in the running of a youth system is team kit, for example tracksuits. He sees this as "the best investment you'll ever make". The reason behind this is that it gives the players a sense of belonging, and the overall effect reflects the level of conformity and collective identity that the coaches like to see towards the Club. (A point also made by Martin Hinshelwood at Brighton and Hove Albion).

f) The Players' Views

Owsley (2000) interviewed the players from the 1998-2001 cohort on the Scholarship Scheme about their experiences at the Club. One of the reoccurring themes of her interviews with the first years was their unhappiness with having to do jobs at the Club. This involved (2000:17): "Sweeping and keeping tidy areas of the ground, polishing the pros' boots, pumping up balls, looking after kit and equipment, etc."

One player said that the only job he did not mind doing was cleaning first team players' boots – this may have been because it is tradition within professional football circles for the youth team players to be paid by professional players to do this. Another said that although he did not like doing jobs, he, like many of the others, felt (Ibid) that "it is an integral part of the discipline of the footballer".

At Bristol City, unlike Brighton and Hove Albion, players are often released at the end of their second year, although as part of the Scholarship Scheme, they are able to continue with the educational element. For example, in 2000 eight of the fourteen players and in 2001 seven of the eleven players were released at the end of second or beginning of the third year. As the players are aware of the Club's policy, pressure inevitably increased during the second year – certainly more so than for their compatriots at Brighton and Hove Albion.

It is not surprising then, that the views of the second years were a lot stronger than those of the first years, particularly as the interviews with Owsely had taken place soon after they were told of their fate. Of the six interviewed, only one was to be allowed to continue the football element into the third year. One of the major complaints was to do with favouritism. Many of those released complained that they felt they were as good as those who had been taken on. One complained that the coaches (2000:23) "only see what they want to see" and if one of the favoured players had a bad game, the coaches would remark on something positive he had done. On the other hand, they were heavily criticised if they had a bad game.

Other disappointments included the feeling that they had been misled, believing at the start that they were signed on for three years rather than two. They also felt unable to approach the Academy Director if they had a problem and that there was a lack of communication between the players and 'the management'.

On the positive side, the boys were keenly aware of the camaraderie they had managed to develop between themselves. In fact Owsley (2000:45) argues that the level of loyalty was more focused towards each other than towards the Club – another feature highlighted with the Scholarship boys at Brighton and Hove Albion. It is clear throughout Owsley's research that the scholars were very happy in each other's company, and they often used their team mates as a source of moral support. Interestingly, as with the players at Brighton, shared humour was seen as a highlight of their time at the Club.

The crucial time for most scholars at Bristol City was clearly the end of the second year, as this was when the crucial decision about their future in professional football was made. Not surprisingly, the one third year who Owsley interviewed and went on to be offered a full contract was very positive about the Club and the Scheme, although he did have some reservations about the way some aspects of the educational element were delivered.

g) Key issues

The most significant way of gauging the success of the Club's youth system is to collate the proportion of boys who have progressed through the junior ranks into professional football. Since 1994, Bristol City has had twenty four players who have played for the Club at first team level and perhaps more relevantly since 1998, when the Scholarship Scheme came into operation, fourteen have achieved this goal.

It appears that like Brighton and Hove Albion, the opportunities of a youth team player depended so much upon the attitude of the first team manager. For example, two of the coaching staff at the Club agreed that the current manager, Danny Wilson's gut instinct was to play full professionals and not to play youth team players. And further still, one of Wilson's predecessors Tony Pullis, was considered by one of the senior coaches to be (Field Notes 28/4/03) "a nightmare for youth team players" as he never appeared to want to consider playing any in the first team. Even though youth team players may not necessarily expect to feature regularly in the first team, it may well affect their 'stickability' if they were totally ignored having been previously considered part of the frame.

Unlike Brighton and Hove Albion, Bristol City has a recent tradition of releasing very few players from its Under 16's, preferring instead to take on most of the players still at the Club to remain until they reach the end of the second year of the Scholarship. The knock-on effects of this are, as Coleman recognises (Fieldwork 28/4/03), firstly that this can create unrealistic expectations, and secondly that the number taken on exceeds the number funded by the FFE&VTS. This second issue creates extra expense for the Club. During the 2002/3 season, the Club paid over £60,000 in expenses for the privilege of having twelve players more than the FFE&VTS quota. However, as long as the Club has a Board of Directors that is happy to fund the youth system to such a level, there is a real temptation for the youth team coaches to delay making career-based decisions about the future of the youth team players until they are eighteen – a full two years after they have left school. To counter this potential problem, the boys who are released at eighteen will almost certainly have had good opportunities to enhance their academic profile – another sign of a successful youth system.

Between 1997 and 2001, Bristol City took on 51 players as trainees (1997 only) or as scholars (1998-2001). Of those, 19 were given a professional contract and for the 2002/3 season, 13 of the 26 full time professionals have come through the Club's youth system. This in itself is value for money for a Division 2 side.

CASE STUDY 2 – CHARLTON ATHLETC

a) Location and status

Charlton Athletic's football ground, The Valley, is based just south of the River Thames, in New Charlton (London Borough of Woolwich). The club's training ground is a few miles away in Greenwich. Charlton currently play in the Premiership, and like Bristol City, the youth system has academy status. The closest professional football clubs to Charlton in terms of location are Crystal Palace (Selhurst), Millwall (Isle of Dogs) and

West Ham (Upton Park). Of these, both Crystal Palace and West Ham have an academy, and according to coaching staff at Charlton (Field Notes: 1/8/03), competition for young players in this area of south-east London is fierce. Charlton Athletic is committed to their youth policy, having spent over £600,000 during the previous season (2002/3) on the Academy, a figure much higher than a club with a centre of excellence would be expected to contribute.

b) Attending the Academy

Upon arrival at the Club, all players are presented with a booklet entitled 'Charlton Athletic -Youth Academy'. In this is information that includes; the aims of the Academy, the Academy facilities, assessment, monitoring and reporting, players' responsibilities, code of conduct, the Academy physiotherapy service, education and welfare, a child protection policy, a grievance procedure and guidelines for parents concerning scouts. The document serves as a comprehensive information guide about the Club's youth system for both young players and parents.

All players train twice during mid-week in the evenings, whilst the Under 12's – Under 16's also train on Saturday mornings. All matches are played on Sunday mornings. Unlike Bristol City, there is very little link between the boys' and girls' teams that represent Charlton Athletic, as they are run completely separately.

c) The requirements to become a professional – a coach's view

I asked Steve Avory (Assistant Academy Director) what he was looking for in a young player as regards his potential to become a professional footballer. He said (Field Notes 1/8/03) that this depended upon the age of the player. For Under 9's to Under 16's he said that players should be able to place their bodies in a good receiving position, be comfortable on the ball and create time for themselves whilst on the ball. They should also be able to play well whilst under pressure from opponents and be able to make good decisions when making a pass. To an extent he felt that the size of a player and their pace are important, but these are more important issues when they are fully-grown. He went on to say: "I've always regarded Arsenal as the yardstick as they have always been the best over recent years. All of their players, from Under 9 to 16, have pace and are full of athleticism. They are also very tall."

Due to the high rejection rate in this sport at this level, Avory felt there was a strong argument for combining the Under 15 and Under 16 age groups, as by this stage the clubs would have a much better idea of who was likely to be successful. The problem of doing this was that the club would be taking a risk by not running an Under 15 team as other clubs may not follow suit. He felt that the result would then be that Charlton may then be seen as a less attractive club to join.

Unlike Bristol City, Charlton did not have a definitive list of skills and requirements that coaches could use to assess potential players by – choice was generally left to the individual's (normally either Mick Brown, Steve Avory or both) subjective view.

d) The Assistant Academy Director

Steve Avory had been at the Club since January 2000, having previously been a Head of Physical Education at a secondary school in Sussex. He had coached at the Club on a part-time basis prior to his full-time appointment and had also coached at Brighton and Hove Albion. One of the highlights of his football-coaching career came when he was chosen to be Manager of England Schoolboys Under 16's in the mid-1990's. Avory therefore had a high level experience of elite youth football, but he had never himself played at professional football.

Avory's line manger, Mick Brown (Academy Director) had a similar background to him, having been a teacher and not played football at a professional level. Avory felt that over recent years, there had been a tendency for teachers to become involved with professional football as they were good communicators and good organisers.

Avory stated that he was not concerned about the results of the teams he coached, with the exception being if one team was continually losing heavily. However, he did admit later on in the interview that as part his annual appraisal with his line manager (the Academy Director), he had agreed to aim for a certain percentage of wins throughout the season. In addition he also has targets to reach for getting players through to the professional stage. At the beginning of the 2003/4 season, there were five players who had come through the Club's Academy who were under 20 and now had professional contracts. (There were also four others who had come to the Charlton at the under 18 level, from other clubs or colleges). In the first team squad for that season there were three professionals who had come through the Club's youth ranks.

According to Avory, the first team manager Alan Curbishley, did not tend to 'get involved' with the Under 9's to Under 16's but did show a keen interest in the Under 16's to Under 19's.

As a person who had a key role in determining which boys came to the Club, I was keen to establish what methods he used to entice highly rated players to Charlton, and what he did to keep them there. He said he felt the key to this was to ensure the player "....must be happy with the coaching environment, that it is a friendly place to be and that parents see it as a welcoming club. I am very conscious that I am seen by the players and parents as being approachable."

He went on to state that he only ever got criticism from the parents when their son was released. On some occasions, parents make a formal complaint to the Club and send a copy to the manager. Avory has never had any comeback from the club for this.

He insisted the only special treatment the best players get is to be offered a four-year contract (YD6) when they are Under 12 instead of a two-year contract for the others that are taken on.

e) The Head of Education and Welfare

The Head of Education and Welfare, Phillip Gallagher, has a full time post at the Club and is also an ex-teacher. The main aspects of his job are to link with the schools attended by those who are at the Academy (from Under 9 to Under 16) and to provide an educational programme for those on the Scholarship Scheme.

Gallagher sends progress reports of the Academy players to all of the schools bi-annually and claims to visit between 80 to 90% attended by the Under 11's (Year 7) and Under 16's (Year 11). Most of the Scholarship players attend a local further education college for the educational component of the Scheme.

When I discussed the issue of the set of academic and vocational results for all Scholarship players that the PFA were considering publishing in the future (and had shared with me over the past few seasons), Gallagher was concerned that the data were

186

unlikely to be as accurate as they should be. He described (Field Notes 1/8/03) how he was asked the results of the Charlton Athletic players on his mobile telephone whilst he was driving a car and could only give the results he remembered. He therefore felt any conclusions that were drawn from this data would probably be misleading.

The main issue that arose during our conversation (Field Notes 1/8/03) was to do with racial groups within the Centre of Excellence. He presented me with the following figures:

AGE GROUP	CAUCASIAN	AFRO-CARIBBEAN	ASIAN	MIXED RACE	TOTAL
Under 9	10	1	0	0	11
Under 10	14	0	0	0	14
Under 11	9	2	0	0	11
Under 12	10	1	0	1	12
Under 13	18	2	0	0	20
Under 14	14	2	0	0	16
Under 15	8	4	0	0	12
Under 16	8	10	1	0	19
Under 17	5	0	0	1	6
Under 18	4	3	0	0	7
Under 19	4	4	0	0	8
TOTAL	103	29	0	2	134

Racial Groups of players attending Charlton Athletic's Academy (2003)

Table 18

He (and later, Steve Avory) pointed out how few Afro-Caribbean players there were in the lower age groups, particularly when compared to the older groups, from Under 15 onwards. He had some possible theories for this. Firstly, that when he came to the Club a couple of years ago, there were even fewer Afro-Caribbean players at the Club, as they were not scouting the local area properly. Secondly, until only recently, all of the Club's coaches and scouts were Caucasian. Thirdly, the schools in Inner London that many Afro-Caribbean boys attend have no formal school matches and are therefore very difficult to scout. Fourthly, the reason for the dramatic change at Under 15 age group could be that many of the Caucasian players came from relatively affluent backgrounds, whose parents were prepared to drive them over long distances (often from Essex) to the

Club to train mid-week and the boys, despite the parental enthusiasm were not actually good enough. Finally, another possible reason for the dramatic change was because the Afro-Caribbean players often came from deprived backgrounds from other parts of London, (many from single parent families) and could not afford the train or bus fare to Greenwich. Once boys got to the age of fifteen, the parent(s) no longer felt the need to travel with them and therefore the cost was halved.

Both Gallagher and Avory felt the Club was not in any way racist and had recently begun to address the problem. For example, there were now two very influential Afro-Caribbean scouts who worked for the Club and as a result many more black players were coming to trials.

Charlton Athletic had been involved in a project based upon the development of anti-racist initiatives at the club and in the local borough (Greenwich). The report 'Evaluation of The Charlton Athletic Race Equality (CARE) Partnership' concluded (Garland and Chakraborti (2001: vi) that the "Partnership was working well towards the ongoing achievement of its own stated aims and objectives". Surprisingly, at no stage within the report is there any mention of consideration for research into racial equality within the Club itself, for example, its own recruitment policy. This can only be seen as a major weakness within the aims of the CARE Partnership.

f) The Scholarship Programme

For the 2003-4 season, the players at the Club's Academy consisted of six first years, six second years and thirteen third years. Six of the third years were however, no longer doing the football component, and were restricted just to completing their third year of education on the Scholarship. Like Bristol City, the Club chooses to guarantee the players only two years of football when they embark on the Scheme.

For this cohort, all the first years were going to study for a BTEC in Sport (at either First Diploma or National Certificate level) except one who wanted to do an NVQ Level 2 in Plumbing. Three second years were to complete their National Certificate in Sport; two were completing 'A' levels and one was to do a Cambridge Certificate in English Language. None of the third years that were no longer doing the football component at the time of this research had informed the Club what vocational or educational course they wished to do in their final year. For those who were continuing with the football, six of the seven were to do a Gym Instructors course, Healthy Cooking and Web Site Design whilst the other player was to complete his Media Studies Course (AVCE).

The daily programme for a player on the Scholarship Scheme attending the Academy is shown in Table 19.

DAY/TIME	AM	LUNCH	PM
MONDAY	Study Programmes 9.00-1.00pm		Training 2.00-4.00pm
TUESDAY	Breakfast & Duties 9.15-10.15 Training 10.15-12.45pm		Training 1.45-3.45pm
WEDNESDAY	Breakfast & Duties 9.15-10.15 Training 10.15-12.45pm		Training 1.45-3.45pm
THURSDAY	Study Programmes (Varied)		Study Programmes (Varied)
FRIDAY	Breakfast & Duties 9.15-10.15 Training 10.15-12.45pm		Core Skills/Meetings
SATURDAY	Academy Fixtures U17 & U19		Watch 1st team match (If at home)
SUNDAY	Rest Day/Injuries in for treatment		

The daily timetable for scholars attending the Charlton Athletic Academy

Table 19

Similar to the two other clubs covered in this research, the boys had a list of jobs they had to do, which according to Phillip Gallacher, (Field Work 5/9/03) mainly required them to be "looking after their own space". For example, this included the cleaning of changing rooms after use and this was done on a rota basis between the players.

g) Key issues

One of the key issues drawn from the fieldwork at Charlton Athletic was the Club's change in recruitment policy and the effect this was having on the youth system in general. A decision was made by the appointment of an Assistant Head of Recruitment to receive more young players for trial, and the actual areas the Club had begun to visit increased. The Development Centres (which involved players in the local area training on a part-time basis) had been increased over recent years. There were now five scattered around London, five in Kent as well as one in Essex and another in north Sussex.

In addition, over recent years the Development Centres and become much more closely linked to the Club's Community Scheme and many of the trialists come through the holiday courses that the Club provides.

Avory was aware that there were more Afro-Caribbean players attending the Club and said (Field Notes 1/8/03) that he always tried to make sure that there was as much social interaction as possible between the players and that they did not separate into ethnic groups. During regular season training this apparently did not occur because the training is intense and there is no time for people to group with their friends. However, he stated (Field Notes 1/8/03) that when the players went on tour he was conscious that the black and white players did not separate into groups. For example, when allocating rooms, he ensured where possible that a black and a white player shared. Avory said (Field Notes 1/8/03) that during the time he had been at the Club he had not witnessed any racial tension.

Avory felt that the longer the Club remained in the Premiership, theoretically the richer the Club should become. In some ways he saw this as being a problem for local talent as the recruitment policy would have to widen still further in order to be sure of attracting the standard of player required. This involves scouting in other areas of Europe (the Club was particularly interested in the Czech Republic at the time this field work was being undertaken) as opposed to USA or Australia, as work permits are easier to obtain for players from within Europe.

Avory commented (1/8/03) that overall, he felt that for those who attended the Academy, there was an even split between those he described as academic and non-academic. He went on to say that whilst he accepted that it was very much a subjective view, he did feel that a certain amount of intelligence and mental strength were needed in order to perform at a professional level. As England Schoolboys manager he had found that the boys who were doing well at school academically, tended to be the ones who understood the more complex tactics.

As far as mental strength was concerned, he spoke of an example of a situation that England international Gareth Southgate had found himself in when he first went to Crystal Palace as a youth team player. (Southgate had attended the school where Avory had been Head of Physical Education). The manager at the time, Alan Smith, told Avory that Southgate had constantly faced a barrage of abuse from the other youth team players as he was seen as different from them because he was regarded as intelligent. As a result, Southgate did not fit in very well with the rest of the group. However, he had been strong minded enough to not let it affect him – and went on to become more successful than any of his peers. Although Avory appreciated that this was an exceptional case, he did use this as an example when talking to players about mental strength and the lengths they sometimes need to go to inside a professional football environment.

Avory did accept (1/8/03) that there were distinctions between 'intelligence, mental strength and academic ability', but according to him often all three went together.

I asked (Field Notes 1/8/03) Avory if he felt that not having played at a professional level lowered his credibility within the Club. He replied that he felt that this had never been a problem to him or Mick Brown (Academy Director), but that they both occasionally heard complaints (usually for parents whose sons had just been rejected) that too many teachers were creeping into the professional game.

Here was an interesting point. This was also true at Brighton and Hove Albion, where there are two full time members of staff (including myself) within the Community Department who are qualified teachers as well as five qualified teachers working as part-time coaches at the Centre of Excellence. Before the Charter for Quality was introduced (1997), at Brighton there was one full time and one part-time member of staff who were qualified as teachers. This increase in numbers within football clubs could well have a significant effect upon football club habitus.

On the issue of the Academy coaches, Avory said that he was happy with the standard of coaching they were providing at Charlton Athletic, particularly now that it was an FA requirement that all had a UEFA 'B' License. In terms of the success rate of these coaches, 12 players from a total of 42, who had been on the Charlton Athletic Scholarship

Scheme (1998-2003), were given a professional contract. This he felt was a good overall rate of success.

Comparisons and contrasts between Bristol City and Charlton Athletic

There are many similarities between the structures of the Clubs' youth systems, purely upon the basis that both have academy status. This includes the high sums of money both Clubs are willing and able to invest into their youth system, which enables them to provide good facilities, the high numbers of coaches and scouts (in relation to centres of excellence) and a full-time education and welfare officer.

There are also similarities within the way each Club operates. For example, both have coaches (full and part-time) who are teacher-trained and there is a real mix between them and ex-professional players. Neither Club encourages nor provides special treatment for their better young players, and coaches from both Clubs interviewed felt that there was a correlation between the intelligence and the ability to succeed in modern day professional football. Of course it may be possible that players who responded best to the coaches and who were deemed intelligent by them stood more chance of being successful, despite not being the most talented players. Indeed, coaches from both Clubs intimated that this might well be the case. One is left with two questions: whether conformity is a pre-requisite to success and does it take priority over talent? From the evidence gathered at the Clubs (and at Brighton and Hove Albion), the answer to both is probably yes.

Despite the similarities of the Clubs' youth systems, they each had their own particular issues that were not apparent at the other Club. At Bristol City, the Club has a large catchment area for potential youth team players, which is good for recruitment but also means young players having to travel long distances (up to one and a half hours). On the other hand at Charlton Athletic, there are many other clubs in close proximity, and so competition for players in the London area is intense. For players already at the Club, the coaches are concerned that ethnic minorities are under-represented at the lower age groups and the Club is currently addressing this issue.

Another major difference between the two Clubs is their status with Charlton being an established Premiership club and Bristol City playing no higher than Division 2 over recent years. As a result, Charlton is able to attract foreign players, (there are currently 8

192

out of 34 in the first team squad) whereas Bristol City has none (Brighton and Hove Albion has one). For young players at Charlton, it could be considered that this reduces their chances of playing for the first team, (see Table 20), as players who have been through the Scholarship Scheme total fewer than a third (10 out of 31) of the total number, whereas at Bristol Scholarship players total half (13 out of 26)

Football Club	Number of players in the 1st team squad	Number of Scholarship players in the 1st team squad
Brighton & Hove Albion	31	10
Bristol City	26	13
Charlton Athletic	34	10

Number of 1st team and Scholarship players in first team squads at all three clubs

Table 20

However, there is no evidence to suggest that if there were no foreign players at the club, the players would be taken up by ex-Scholarship players.

Although this fieldwork does only cover three professional clubs, which all have their own separate issues, there is evidence to suggest that there are common themes running throughout youth systems in professional football clubs and these will be analysed further within Chapters 9 and 10.

CHAPTER 9
DISCUSSION

In light of the fieldwork undertaken for this book, the journey of vocational socialisation that a young player must take in order to make a career as a professional football player can be broken down into three phases: firstly, the player's initiation into football as a sport and the sociological factors that can influence further development in the early phases of the young player's 'journey'; secondly, coping with the direct and indirect requirements demanded by a professional football club at youth team level (at a Centre of Excellence or Academy between 9 and 16); and thirdly, the player's introduction to life based at a professional club as a scholar (Scholarship Scheme) and the processes he needs to go through before, or if, he is offered a professional contract..

1. Football socialisation and sociological factors that can affect development

For any boy growing up in Great Britain in the early twenty first century, coming into contact with football either by observation or participation is almost unavoidable. The extent to which he becomes involved with the sport is dependent upon some key factors, one of the most important of these being the family he is born into.

The results of the small-scale research into family background within this publication would suggest that the sport that has the reputation for being a profession for the working classes (although there is no recent evidence to confirm this) might be broadening out. Clearly, due to the size of this aspect of the study, no conclusions about football in general can be made – it may only point the direction for further research in this area. However, the families of the children attending Brighton and Hove Albion's Centre of Excellence mirrored the socio-economic groups of the working population of Great Britain (see Table 6). In addition, the opinions of the coaches at Bristol City and Charlton Athletic Football Clubs would concur with the view that changes are gradually taking place with the type of background a typical boy attending their Academy may come from – they could come from any group. This is supported by Goodbody and Lee (1999) who discuss the issue of the new influx of the middle classes being attracted into professional football and the increased interest public schools are showing in the sport. Therefore, basing evaluations upon this research, and contrary to the research done by Parker (1996), it seems that football as a professional sport, if not actually moving away from its working class roots, is in fact beginning to embrace a cross-section of our society. Another area within this work that was connected to family background and involved a small-scale study is birth order (see Table 10). This showed that twice as many boys who were youngest in the family were attending the Centre of Excellence than boys who were eldest. Again, it is not possible to make too many broad assumptions concerning birth order and footballers in general because this was only a small-scale study at one club and only eighty per cent of the boys were interviewed, as the others were absent at the time the study was done. One can only guess about the reasons why the number of boys who are the youngest sibling should far outweigh numbers for the eldest. It could be that younger siblings play with the elder ones and therefore are used to playing at a higher standard than one would expect from boys of their own age, but clearly this is only conjecture. Nevertheless, very little research has been done in this area, and the results of this study are worthy of a more thorough investigation.

One area of research to do with birth that is well documented (for example, Paull 1999, Paull and Simmons 1999, Simmons 2002(a) Simmons 2002(b) and Helsen, Williams, Van Winckel and Ward (2003)) is the time of year most players are actually born in. Statistics show there are far more English players who are born in the first part of the academic year than the latter part. The research undertaken for this publication confirmed this for Premiership and Football League players (2002/3), and also for Brighton and Hove Albion's Centre of Excellence players and those who were given a professional contract between 2000 and 2003 (12 of the 24 players offered a contract were born between September and December). Helsen, Williams, Van Winckel and Ward (2003) extended their research to nine other leading European football nations and found similar results. Their explanations for this were firstly that the most important factor was due to variance in size – that the older players are naturally more developed. Secondly, that the older players are likely to achieve more success because of this and this may increase their motivation, whilst younger children are more likely to be de-motivated (and possibly drop out) due to lack of success. Finally, they estimate boys born earlier could have had as much as 700 hours more opportunity to practice than those born later.

195

Whatever the reasons, there is comprehensive evidence that proves the majority of elite players are born in the earlier part of the academic year. Simmons concludes (2002(b): 33) that "The current system may be depriving many players of football but also depriving football of players."

A final point worth considering which is related to the boys' home background is the influence of those from within the family. Six boys at the Brighton and Hove Albion Centre of Excellence had older brothers who were either attending or had attended the Centre themselves. One could assume that the elder sibling may have had some influence over the younger brother in his attraction to the game and helped to develop his ability. Lewko and Greendorfer (1988) argue strongly that the father plays a central role in influencing his child in the sports socialisation process. There is evidence to suggest that this is the case within this research, as it is unlikely to be coincidence that five of the six boys in the focus group in the first year of the Scholarship Scheme had fathers who had played either professional or semi-professional football.

All of the players who are selected for the Scholarship Scheme would, using Bourdieu's terminology, possess the correct form of habitus and the right amount of what Jarvie and Mcguire (1997:186) describe as 'social memory'. The cultural learning that took place to became part of their social memory included conformity in appearance, the type of language they used (for example, football terminology), their humour and demeanour, all of which seemed to develop both consciously and sub-consciously. This process would not have been enough in isolation to guarantee success, as natural ability and improvement of skill levels clearly played a part. However, a balance of these factors – nature and nurture – was certainly required.

An area of potential influence that does not seem to have been strong, as far as the some of the youth team players were concerned, is that of their schools. When asked, none of the boys gave their schools or teachers as reasons for their success in football. Their responses support the views of Lewko and Greendorfer (1988) who claim that schools and teachers do not have very much influence in the sport socialisation of children or adolescents.

Comparisons have already been made between football and other performance-based professions (for example, ballet and classical music), one of the most common being the requirement for young people to become immersed into the socialisation of their chosen activity at an early age in order to stand any chance of success at an elite level. This was certainly true of the focus group at Brighton and Hove Albion, as most of them had been playing in the same teams since they were seven or eight. Only a small number of boys joined the Club for the first time beyond the age of twelve – and those that did so had clearly been playing football for many years as they had attained well developed skills. Most theorists (for example, Byrne 1999 and Richardson 2000) would also state that peers may have a strong influence upon sports socialisation and this research would support this view. However, it became clear from the focus group that a new peer group arose from the best footballers in the area from a very early age (8 years old), despite living in different parts (or just outside) of the Brighton and Hove conurbation. The parents of these boys became good friends and strong relationships developed from there. This group formed the nucleus of the boys that went on to play together for Brighton and Hove Albion for that particular age group, and carried on to the Scholarship Scheme. Five of the six boys have been friends since they were 8 years old.

Indeed, location of residence appeared to be a key issue in deciding which players attended the Club's Centre of Excellence, as over 70% were resident in the Brighton and Hove area, with the remaining 30% of players either being resident along the south coast or near the A23/M23 corridor, which is the main road from Brighton to London. Clearly, from this research it shows that living in urban areas away from the coast, away from the main trunk road and within rural communities, puts boys at a distinct disadvantage.

In addition, the school one attended within Brighton and Hove also had a bearing upon the chances of success. Of the eleven state schools and one public school within the city, two schools were not represented. Both of these schools are situated within deprived areas, and it seems unlikely that the non-representation of boys from these schools was purely chance, although there is no concrete evidence to suggest otherwise. One can only speculate about possible reasons for this. It may be due to the behavioural problems that can be associated the children that attend these schools and therefore the Club is less likely to want such boys to be involved. It may also be because coming from a deprived background often means a lack of a balanced diet and therefore growth through adolescence is detrimentally affected. Of course, the school could also be central to the cause, if there is teacher de-motivation, lack of organisation or lack of extra-mural activity.

2. The vocational socialisation process at the Centre of Excellence

Once a young player has accepted an invitation to join the Club's Centre of Excellence a number of factors will determine his level of progress. One of these is his relationship with others at the Club, particularly his team-mates and his coaches.

From the fieldwork undertaken at the Albion, it is clear that often the best players in the area knew each other before they joined the Club. This may initially have given them a natural advantage over others, as they would perhaps have felt comfortable in the new environment – their position within the peer group having been well established. As a team sport, group cohesiveness is often regarded as a key element towards success and this would have reflected well on anyone who was part of this. However, it was never apparent that there were any form of cliques within the teams, either to myself or to the players I interviewed.

In order to progress through to the Scholarship Scheme, a player needed to be highly regarded by the coaches, both as a player and as a person. It was clear that pure ability was not enough. It was noticeable that the players also had a high regard for the coaches – they at least gave the impression that they did. It was only after they had either been accepted or rejected onto the Scholarship Scheme, that some criticised coaches' knowledge or their ability to convey information. In many ways, this choice of keeping their feelings to themselves represented a level of conformity that was very apparent in other aspects of Brighton and Hove Albion's Centre of Excellence.

For example, the way the players dressed and their general appearance (nearly all had the same style of haircut) seemed very standardised. Of course, wearing Brighton and Hove Albion tracksuits to matches was a requirement set out by the Club anyway. The senior youth team coaches at both Brighton and Bristol City thought that providing players with Club kit gave them a sense of belonging. This in itself developed a level of conformity that was initiated by the Clubs.

However, the importance of being a conformist and fitting in at the Centre of Excellence in itself was not enough to assist young players to rise above the rest of the group in the pursuit of a place on the Scholarship Scheme. Ultimately, the only way to achieve this was is to convince the coaches (in particular, Martin Hinshelwood at Brighton and Hove Albion), that they were good enough to fill one of the six vacant places that were available on the Scholarship Scheme, and clearly the better the player adapted to the socialisation process within the football club the more chance he had.

From a psychological perspective, one element that seemed to be consistent amongst the boys was the high level of motivation. One needs to look no further than the high attendance record at the evening training sessions, where it was a rarity for anybody to be missing. Maintaining this throughout their time at the Centre of Excellence did not appear to be a problem for any, including those who were on the fringes of the teams. The Club encouraged this level of motivation, as a natural by-product of this was an equal level of competitiveness. This came in two forms; firstly, team competition in matches against other clubs, and secondly, competition for their own place in the team. The parents who assumed that their son was better than the one taking his place often accentuated this second form, as signals like these inevitably meant that their son would be unlikely to be offered a scholarship.

Mention has already been made about the effect parents can have upon their son's socialisation into football, but the influence of the parent does not stop there. Parents, as this study has shown, can make the difference between whether their son is successful in moving onto the next stage (the Scholarship Scheme) or not. At both Brighton and Bristol City, examples were given of players who were discarded by the clubs due to the behaviour of their parents. Conversely, a parent who is seen by the clubs to be supportive could have his chances enhanced.

The signals that came from the Club concerning who the likely chosen ones would be were not difficult to ascertain. These included regular selection, the well sought after four-year contract (YD6) when the player was in the Under 12 age group, and playing for the Under 17's at Under 16 level (the final year at the Centre of Excellence).

Various forms of hope and advice were given to those who were rejected at various stages from Under 9 to Under 16. This ranged from comforting, if somewhat hollow, assurances that the Club would still monitor their progress, to other more positive forms such as the Club's desire for the players to train on a part-time basis with the Scholars when they left the Centre of Excellence at 16.

At football clubs with academies in particular (for example Bristol City and Charlton Athletic), links with schools are made as soon as the boys join, in order to take joint responsibility over the child's overall development. This is a positive move in helping the boys to cope with the high possibility of failure. However, for Brighton and Hove Albion, whilst some progress had been made in this area, the limitations of funding and manpower made this difficult to pursue with the same degree as the clubs with academies.

On the issue of equality (Chaudhary 1994, Brown 1997, Khan 2000, Moran 2000, Garland and Rowe 2001 and McCarthy, Jones and Potrac 2003) the problems non-white ethnic groups have within professional football have been well documented. At Brighton and Hove Albion it was very difficult to assess if this was indeed the case, particularly as figures showed that representation of players from these groups at 5% was in excess of the 2.24% of the non-white population for the whole of Sussex (Office of National Statistics 2001). However, at Charlton Athletic this issue was clear to see, for despite there being a high percentage of players from ethnic minority groups represented in the Club's Scholarship Scheme, only a very few were represented in the lower age groups of their Academy. This under-representation was thought by the coaching staff to be possibly due to the problems of the cost of transport to training and to matches and to the Club's scouting policy, which did not used to go into areas inhabited by ethnic minority groups. According to the staff, the Club's policy has now changed significantly as the problem was being addressed. The conclusion that can be drawn from this research with regard to Charlton is that the mere fact that the Club has chosen to seek why ethnic minority groups are under-represented and find solutions to the problem can only be seen as a positive move for aspiring young footballers in south-east London.

3. The continuing process within the Scholarship Scheme

Once a player had been accepted onto the Scholarship Scheme, the level of socialisation intensified as the players were now employed on a full-time basis at the Club. The young players were in daily contact with the first team as they all shared the same facilities. Very few generalisations could be made about the effect the first team players had upon the youngsters. According to the youth team players, some were lazy and cared little about diet, extra training and their general lifestyle, whilst others took these aspects very seriously. The general feeling amongst the youth team was that they themselves worked harder at training than the first team.

Indeed their respect for each other seemed to far outweigh the amount they gave to the full professionals, and their sense of loyalty to each other never appeared to waiver. This was not totally surprising due to the importance of team cohesion that was instilled within their training. This did not prevent them from teasing each other with regard to offensive remarks under the guise of humour. Indeed this humour was an integral part of life at the training ground and an inability to cope with this was seen as a sign of weakness by both peers and coaches.

Competition amongst each other barely appeared to feature, as there were not enough of them to pose a problem for team selection. The only area for tension came when youth team players occasionally took the places of full professionals in the first team. However, I was not party to any discussions with those who lost their place and therefore cannot comment on their reaction to such events.

It became increasingly clear as research progressed which players were likely to be offered full-time contracts at the end of the Scholarship. The signs normally began to surface half way through the second year. The signs would be favourable for an individual if for instance he were selected for the Reserve team (known to the first team players as 'The Brazilians' in a sarcastic comparison to the highly regarded Brazilian national football team) on a regular basis or even for the first team squad. To some individuals, for example Andy who was not one of those who was receiving the right signals, this adversely affected his relationship with the coaches. The situation for Andy then became progressively worse as his attitude was then brought into question by the coaches. It could be argued that the coaches lacked any real insight into why the player's attitude was deteriorating – or maybe they just did not really care (although this seemed less likely).

Coping with rejection was one aspect that players seemed to learn to adapt to. Rarely did it seem that the final decision was a total shock to them. The boys who were rejected were naturally disappointed and some would say that they would start looking at other professional clubs, but none who were rejected during or at the end of the Scholarship ever became professionals with most having to settle for semi-professional football. Malcolm Stuart (Field Work 12/9/03) claimed that he often had to defend the Club when people complained that players they knew, who had played for Brighton at youth team level, should have been taken on. He stated that few players who had been rejected ever went on to play professional football. This was true, but one could argue that unless an individual has a direct contact within another Club it is very difficult to generate interest from elsewhere, particularly as no other clubs are nearby. During the duration of this fieldwork, only one player (Stuart) who had been rejected by Brighton and Hove Albion was offered a scholarship or a contract by another club, and he already had a contact with the new club – his cousin was in the first team. Also, once a player has been rejected by a club at youth team level, they may not be such an attractive prospect for others. Usually relationships have built up between Clubs and their own youth team players over many years, and bringing in players who are new, who had not been with them may not be so appealing to the coach. Publicly, it does not reflect very well on the youth system of the Club if the players who have been with them from an early age are rejected in favour of players from other clubs. For Charlton Athletic in particular, this did not seem to be a problem judging by the number of players who joined at the latter stages of the youth programme.

Of course, making the grade to become a professional footballer does involve high elements of luck, even when players have reached the penultimate stage and joined the Scholarship Scheme. Avoiding injury was an issue that was spoken about at the Club very often, but for one player (Dick), the injury he received will probably be the deciding factor that stops him being offered a professional contract. He was given a lot of sympathy for breaking his leg a second time in one year, particularly by the first team players (they paid for him to go on a week's holiday abroad with a friend after the second

202

occasion), but a senior coach at the Club commented (Field Work 13/7/03) that a full recovery seemed unlikely. Nevertheless, Dick was to keep on trying. As Bourdieu's theories of bodily capital show, there are inevitable comparisons that can be made here regarding the risks and extremes that workers will go to in order to satisfy the employers. However, at this stage the luck factor that affects most players is a change of first team management. Brighton and Hove Albion was similar to many professional football clubs in undergoing many changes in management over a short period of time, although four different managers in fourteen months is an extreme case of such volatility. For any professional player this can have direct ramifications. After a change, some are sold on to other clubs whilst others move from the first team to the reserves (or vice-versa). For the youth team players at Brighton and Hove Albion, the promotion of Martin Hinshelwood created a new dawn and the chance of first team football in Division 1, but this opportunity was taken away by his dismissal.

A new manager is usually linked to a run of bad results from the first team and therefore youth team players are often discarded for more experienced players, as was indeed the case at Brighton. It can also mean the new manager bringing in his own staff, even at youth team level, which in itself can have an impact on the changing fortunes of youth team players. This however did not occur at Brighton.

Due to the high rejection rate in this industry, coping with failure is for most the final stage they have to go through. Even at the end of the Scholarship stage at Brighton normally four from the six in the year group will be rejected. Constructing alternative career plans is therefore crucial in order help the players cope with this rejection. Few of the players were really willing to consider this whilst they were still at the Club. The educational and vocational courses funded by the FFE&VTS were aimed at helping all of the players, at whatever stage they were, to leave professional football. At Brighton and Hove Albion the policy of the coaches was to insist upon the full commitment of the youth team players towards these courses. This undoubtedly played a part in helping them achieve the high number of passes that they did over the three-year period of this fieldwork. The result of this policy was that most of the players were able to move successfully into another career path once they had left the Scholarship Scheme. If one were to regard the investment of the FFE&VTS as a form of security for the young players, then it certainly paid dividends. This approach would certainly be directly in line with the DfEE, that emphasised (1999) the need to have a flexible workforce and multi-skilled as highlighted by Newman and Williams (1995).

The types of course chosen by the youth team players at Brighton and Hove Albion would not be in line with the Monk and Russell's research (2000:67). They stated that in general players tend not to take 'A' levels, preferring to "opt for more less academic courses". Only four of the twenty-eight boys covered in the research did not attempt any 'A' levels (albeit that many took Physical Education or General Studies), and overall there was an 80% pass rate amongst them. This compared favourably with other clubs, but was lower than the national pass rate for 'AS' and 'A' level's generally which, although varies from year to year tends to be between 90 and 94%.

However, the key issue for all the young players involved is: what does it take to become a professional footballer? (See Figure 4). The conclusions of this have to be based upon what the final decision makers (for example, the Director of Football at Brighton and Hove Albion and the Head of the Academies at Bristol City and Charlton Athletic) are looking for. An undeniable fact is that the player must be seen by them to have an exceptional amount of ability and talent as well as the necessary physical attributes; but there are other factors which are just as important.

The player must be a conformist, not just as a person that acts upon the instructions of his coaches, but is seen to be able to fit into the professional football club environment. He should be a good team player and have a strong enough personality not to be upset by the particular type of humour that is an integral part of life at the Training Ground, even if it is directed at him. An inability to cope with this would be seen as a weakness of character. Therefore, being adaptable to the vocational socialisation processes that go on within a professional club is indeed crucial.

Indeed, coaches when trying to identify the players who will ultimately be given a professional contract seek particular aspects of the personality. Parker (1996) in his fieldwork found that (1996:236): "The coaches often talked of the need for trainees to possess certain 'qualities' such as the right 'make up' and 'character' and frequently emphasised the need for players to develop a 'good professional attitude'."

Parker could easily have been describing the conversations of coaches at Brighton and Hove Albion in 2003 with this statement, as there are many similarities with the type of phrases used by the coaches in both studies, in their assessments of personal and individual qualities.

Evidence from this work would also suggest that the masculinist culture that Parker described is also still part of professional football at youth team level. The key areas that he highlighted, (sexual endeavour, conspicuous consumption and socialising), were all to varying degrees part of the culture. However, none of these appeared to be as dominant as those described by Parker and further to this, the importance given to youth team players would allow any of these issues to override their performance on the football pitch – even if for some, sexual endeavour was certainly part of everyday conversation.

There are some aspects of this fieldwork that were strikingly different from Parker's. For the club where he based his research (which was never revealed), he gave a damning account of the lack of welfare the club were prepared to give to the young trainees (1996:272):

> "The Club categorically failed to spell out to any significant degree
> the health and dependency risks that alcohol, nicotine and other
> available drugs posed. Furthermore, whilst recognising the amount
> of spare time and money individuals had at their disposal, they
> declined the opportunity to advise on matters of monetary investment,
> spending and/or general levels of consumption."

At Brighton and Hove Albion, informal and formal reminders of the hazards involved (through the Core Skills programme) were made to the young players about alcohol and drugs. In addition, although players were also spoken to about money matters (including investment) through the Core Skills programme, none of the young players had much to spare due to low levels of income.

Parker also described (1996:237) the lack of detail coaches were prepared to write in the players' log books and wrote of the lack of interest in the players' education courses (1996:268). Again, this was in complete contrast to the youth team coaches (Hinshelwood and Wilkins) who appeared genuinely interested in the youngsters' overall development. Reasons for these apparent contrasts are discussed in the conclusion.

Response to the key questions

The initial question within this work was "What career path does an aspiring young player need to follow in order to become a professional footballer?" The answer to this can be combined with the answer to another which was "What is the vehicle used by professional football to establish young players for the future?" For the successful player at Brighton and Hove Albion, the processes and the means of becoming a professional footballer have been discussed in this chapter, and it begins from the day he is invited to join the Centre of Excellence, through his involvement with the Scholarship Scheme to the day he is offered a full-time contract.

Here comparisons are made between professional football and other performance-based professions (acting, ballet and classical music). The research showed how equally important it is for people at a young age (often before they are 10) to take up acting, ballet or football if they are to have any chance of making a career out of their chosen activity. The vehicle to a successful career in these fields often required attendance at specialised schools or centres, on a part or full-time basis. In addition, as all are competitive industries, similar problems materialised such as high levels of rejection and, in some cases, periods of unemployment. All four industries showed evidence of inequality within recruitment.

There are two main requirements in determining if an aspiring footballer is to become a professional footballer. The first of these is a one that is openly talked about by players, parents and coaches – the development of talent. Martin Hinshelwood spoke throughout the research of the need to possess the potential to go on to the next level, for example, from the Centre of Excellence to the Scholarship Scheme. No one would argue with this sentiment, although many would disagree, particularly the players and parents, about who had the ability to do so.

The second area is the central theme of this book. The sub-culture of the professional football club demands that if he is to be successful, the player must mould his behavioural patterns and his personality to suit the specific environment. Here lies the answer to another key question - what are the socio-psychological and sociological factors that assist a young person in becoming a professional footballer?

This work has shown that the likelihood of becoming a professional footballer in the first place can be based upon factors such as: date of birth, family background, the father's involvement with professional football, position in the family, location of residence and schools attended. In addition, the acquisition of a habitus, which grows stronger as the player spends increasing amounts of time within the professional football environment, becomes an essential part of a successful player's make up.

Added to these are other requirements, and these are:

- To conform to and respect the coaches' wishes with regard to behaviour, appearance and lifestyle.
- To be fully reliable.
- To be highly competitive and able to channel this in an appropriate way.
- To be able to cope with possible career breaking setbacks (for example, injury).
- To be able to fully integrate into a professional football club environment, (for example, cope with humour and abuse which are often synonymous).
- To be able to cope with the physical demands placed upon them by the requirements of professional football.

Therefore, in general terms, the requirements to become a professional footballer include the mixture of talent and a specifically acquired habitus, which is often linked to a character and personality that is strong enough to overcome any barriers that are presented to him.

There is some evidence to suggest from this study that football culture is changing. The youth team players at Brighton and Hove Albion generally had a deep disrespect for the full time professionals who paid little attention to diet and new training techniques. Some were also unimpressed by the basic level of humour shown by the older professionals within the training ground environment.

Sugden (2004:8), when describing the alleged misconduct of Leicester City players at the Spanish resort of La Manga, argued that despite the continuing disgrace professional footballers bring upon themselves with "gambling, binge drinking, drug abuse, womanising and violence" there are still indications of positive change. He stated that (ibid.): "There are promising signs that the influx of foreign players and coaches, along with the introduction of the football academy/centre of excellence pyramid and with it a

207

more structured approach to academic and social education, is beginning to challenge this self-destructive dressing room culture". Significant changes such as these take a number of years to develop, but if they are consistent throughout elite levels of football, then they will inevitably have a positive effect on the habitus of the professional player.

Figure 4 shows, as a result of this study, the key factors that can affect the chances of becoming a professional footballer. This can be compared with Figure 2 that highlighted

Factors that can affect the chances of becoming a professional footballer

| ▬▬ Psychological | .... Socio-psychological | ─── Sociological |

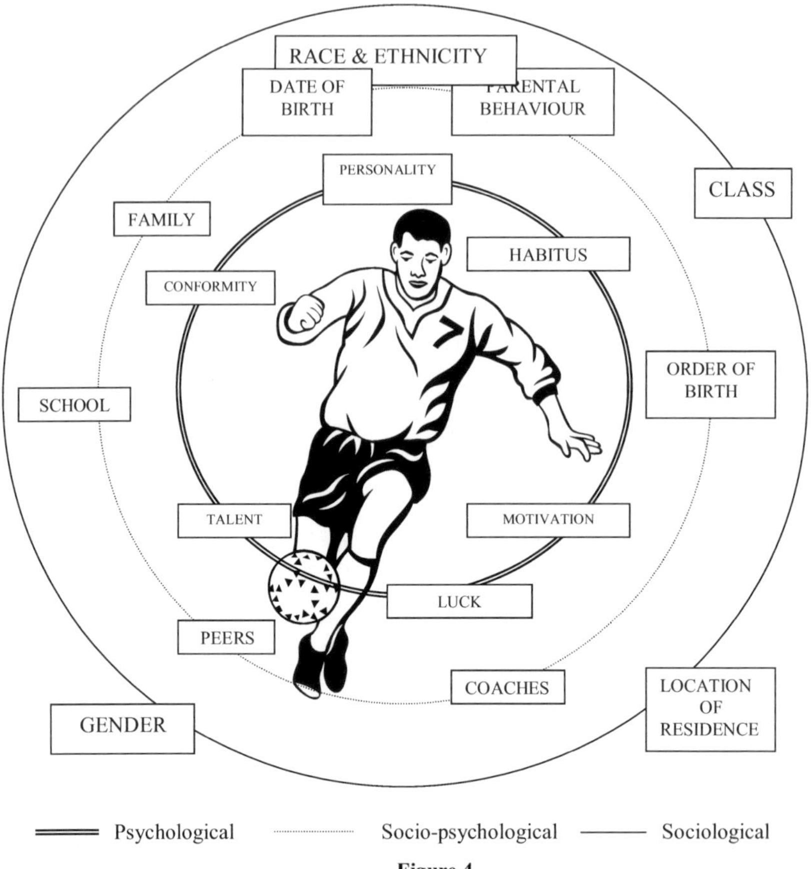

Figure 4

the factors that can affect the chances of an elite performer, the notable additions of which have already been discussed. It should be noted that as in Figure 2, no attempt has been made within Figure 4 to establish an order of importance, for the factors listed as the strength of each could vary significantly according to the individual.

One of the most significant changes between the two figures has been to expand the psychological factors to include others discussed within this research that could be related to it, namely luck and talent. It should be noted here that whilst talent is directly associated with the individual and therefore lies comfortably within this group, it is recognised that luck could conceivably lie within any one of the three groups. For example, the relationship between luck and injury (psychological and other factors), luck and family stability (socio-psychological factors, and luck and location of residence (sociological factors), may all play a part.

Another significant change has been that some factors have been omitted from Figure 4 (self confidence, self esteem, arousal, self efficacy (psychological and other factors) and teachers (socio-psychological factors) that were in Figure 2. This does not necessarily mean that those omitted are of no value, but are rather from this research they are deemed to be of less importance than those that have been added.

Habitus and conformity have been listed as psychological factors, as it can be seen that aspects behaviour can and often need to change, either or both consciously and sub-consciously, in order to adapt to the football club environment.

This has research has shown that parental behaviour, date of birth and order of birth can have an influence on success or failure, although, as previously stated, much more research is needed on order of birth to prove this is something other than a spurious correlation.

The only new factor added within the sociological group is location of residence, as it is clear from this research that where one lives has a huge impact upon the opportunities for an individual hoping to enter into professional football.

One should not lose sight of the fact that only a very small percentage of aspiring young hopefuls, (in Sussex, only one or two per year group) as in any other performance-based profession, will overcome all of the barriers that prevent them from reaching their ultimate goal, which is to become a professional footballer, and this is often dependent upon the character and personality of the individual. This research has given detailed examples of how individuals have reacted to rejection through various stages of the process.

The penultimate key question was to see how Brighton and Hove Albion compared to two other professional case studies. The clubs selected were Bristol City and Charlton Athletic, and although both of these clubs had academies rather than centres of excellence, there were numerous comparisons that could be drawn from all three clubs. For example, the positive attitude coaches had to the education and the welfare of the young players, the structure of the weekly routine, and the requirements the coaches were looking for from individuals who were to be offered individual contracts. The only significant differences between the clubs were the size of their catchment areas and the social make-up of the local inhabitants.

The final question was what can be learnt from this study? The overarching discovery has been to highlight the vocational socialisation processes that an aspiring young footballer needs to go through in order to be offered a professional contract, particularly since the changes that have occurred in professional football as a result of the Charter for Quality in 1997. Where these changes lie in relation to recent Government strategy towards aspiring elite sportspeople can be found in the conclusion of this work.

CHAPTER 10
CONCLUSION

The Government's strategy for the future of sport in this country is set out in 'A Sporting Future for All' (2000), 'Game Plan: a strategy for delivering Government's sport and physical activity objectives' (2002) and 'Learning through PE and Sport' (2003). Although within these publications emphasis is placed upon the necessity of building closer relationships between educational and sporting providers, there is little to suggest that the problems of helping elite young sports people balance their sporting aspirations with their general education have been broached or even targeted.

However, in 2005, the Government plans to introduce a new National Vocational Qualification (NVQ) called a 'Modern Apprenticeship in Sporting Excellence' (MASE) for prospective professional sports players aged 16 and above, and this, like the educational component of the Scholarship Scheme, is to be funded by the Learning and Skills Council (which plans and funds adult education with the exception of higher education, throughout England and Wales,). This new initiative is an attempt to accredit work-based training in this field. The very fact that the issue of elite sportspeople and their education is on the Government agenda is a welcome one.

There is irrefutable evidence that the connection between professional sport and education is becoming prevalent. In 1997 the Government established the 'Playing for Success' initiative in partnership with Local Education Authorities and professional football clubs. This is a study support initiative targeted at underachieving pupils at Key Stage 2 and 3. According to the Government report 'Playing for Success: An Evaluation of the Fourth Year' (2003) this has now extended from 8 in 1998, to 58 study support centres, associated with 12 different sports (of which 45 are based at football clubs). Charles Clarke (Secretary of State for Education) described this scheme as "one of the Government's success stories" (cited in the 'Playing for Success Yearbook – 2002').

It is no surprise the concept of study centres at professional sports clubs has developed in other areas of education. At a local level, Brighton and Hove Albion were awarded £1.7 million in 2004 by the Learning and Skills Council in Sussex for delivering adult learning in Basic Skills and Information Technology, which not only included provision at the Club's own study centre, but also centres at five local semi-professional football clubs. Brighton and Hove Albion were also instrumental in setting up a professional sports employers group, which comprises of the Football Club, Sussex County Cricket Club, Brighton Bears Basketball Club and the Rugby Football Union (through Brighton Rugby Club). The Learning and Skills Council's Director of Operations for Sussex, David Smith, described (2004) the Football Club as "contributing significantly to economic development and the enhancement of opportunities for individuals and communities through harnessing the engaging power of sport to the learning and skills agenda."

There are other examples of how professional football clubs are becoming more increasingly involved with educational initiatives. Arsenal Football Club run an on-line fitness course for adults called 'Health for Life', whilst other clubs, for example West Ham, have as part of their study centre a room totally dedicated to wide range of on-line courses.

Many players from professional clubs also get involved with the new educational initiatives. Foreign footballers in many Premiership clubs visit local schools "in the hope of tempting younger fans to learn foreign languages" (Frean 2003:12). Brighton and Hove Albion first team player Charlie Oatway revealed to journalist Nick Szczepanik (1/3/04) that he could not read or write in the hope that such an admission would encourage adults with similar problems to, like him, take up a basic skills course.

The result of such a plethora of educational activity at professional football clubs helps them to play an essential role within and beyond their local communities as well as enhancing their image. For the young players hoping to enter into professional football, seeing the club involved with such initiatives, particularly at the club itself, is highly likely to assist with installing a positive attitude towards education.

However, there is still much to be done to help the aspiring elite sportsperson cope with the prospect of the unfulfilled dream of not playing to a professional standard. In football alone, thousands of boys are linked with professional clubs with the hope of being awarded a professional contract and yet the vast majority of them will be rejected at some stage between 9 and 19. During that time for many, football has been the main focus in their lives and indeed, it often has to be in order to reach the required standard.

Of course, their future in football may well take the form of playing at semi-professional level, which in itself can be lucrative. However, the commitment to the game offered by boys during their formative years may well have been to the detriment of other parts of their lives, for example their performance at school and their scholastic achievement. As stated, clubs that have academy status do have a full-time Education and Welfare Officer who liaises with the boys' schools, but with often over a hundred boys attending a large number of schools, this can be difficult. (At Charlton Athletic, only two age groups from schools are visited in any one year.). At those clubs that do not have academy status and instead have a Centre of Excellence, few education and welfare officers have full-time posts. Therefore developing links with schools becomes even more difficult, and potentially the danger of under-achievement for boys at school from these clubs increases. The process of vocational socialisation into professional football can be seen to be wasted time for the vast majority who are not able to enter the profession as their preparation for the sport at this level has failed. On the other hand one could argue that the experience that they have been through, even though they have not reached their ultimate goal, has helped them to develop as individuals through sport.

Houlihan and White (2002:166) state that "the government has three objectives for national governing bodies and their clubs: they should take greater account of the social priority of social inclusion, they should improve the quality of their management (particularly the development of talented young people), and improve the quality of their coaching."

Although here the role of national governing bodies and clubs has been identified by the government as one that has an important social responsibility, it is not clear who should take the lead on specific matters such as catering for those who join professional clubs but fail to reach the senior level.

Keech (2003:211) identifies the role schools have within the local community when he states that:

> "The centrality of schools to the development of young
> people's sporting opportunities in the local community has
> meant that local schools have begun to reflect with varying

213

degrees of success, on how to extend and link their provision
with the support of, and to, local agencies."

Keech (2003:220) goes on to discuss the role specialist sports colleges have had in being at the heart of this development.

Perhaps then a fully integrated network should be set up between professional clubs and schools, led by specialist sports colleges, which would focus upon the plight of the young people that fail to achieve their dream, whereby proper support could be directed towards them.

A network of schools would also help social inclusion, for example in the case of Sussex, where children who live in rural areas are rarely recommended to the local professional club and are therefore never given the opportunity to succeed. Such young people would then actually be given a chance; albeit a very small one.

Whatever the solution, society has an obligation to prepare for failure the vast numbers of young people who join professional football clubs and are at some stage rejected. Professional football clubs and the football authorities (for example, the PFA and in particular the FFE&VTS) have a moral responsibility to maintain their commitment to ensure that preparing boys for failure is the cornerstone for youth systems in professional football. Evidence has shown that, to date, the clubs featured within this study are attempting to address the problem. For example, links with the schools attended by players from the clubs' centre of excellence or academy are a key component of recent developments, with the visits of clubs' educational welfare officers to particular age groups.

However, the main challenge is to ensure that public have sufficient public funding, (through for example the Learning & Skills Council), to help assist rejected players with alternative options. If this funding is not forthcoming, it is doubtful whether professional football clubs, from a financial point of view, would put the welfare of rejected players at the top of their agenda.

Limitations of this research

The main limitation of this study was related to the main strength. When the initial fieldwork began, I was not associated with the Club. As time progressed, I became a part-time employee, followed three years later by a change to a full-time employee. Inevitably, access to my field of research became easier and I was party to much more information about the Club and staff than I might otherwise have been.

However, as I became more familiar with other members of staff, particularly the coaches, I was also aware that because we got on well, I was in danger of seeing them in a favourable light. This differed from Parker's experience. He stated that (1996:292): "Throughout the research period, I frequently got the feeling that he (one of the coaches) perceived me as some kind of FA and/or university spy."

Parker had based his research upon him himself taking part in the training and coaching alongside the trainees. This was a stark contrast to my position in the field of study, as I became one of the staff and probably had a closer affinity with them as a result.

The negative responses Parker received from the coaches may have influenced his reporting and so too might the positive responses have affected mine, despite my attempts to be objective.

The conclusion I draw is that both approaches have their advantages: Parker may have got to know the trainees better, whereas I probably had more of an insight as to how the coaches were thinking and was invited to more staff meetings within and outside the Club. Therefore, both in their own way make a valuable contribution to this field of study.

Recommendations for future research

In 1998, when the research for this book began, an F.A. spokesman stated (Field Notes 13/9/98) that Howard Wilkinson had formulated many of his ideas for the Charter for Quality from examples of systems and schemes in neighbouring European countries. It would therefore seem appropriate to contrast and compare the youth structure in this country and how it functions with the systems in those countries five years later.

This is particularly relevant as many English professional teams, particularly at Premiership level, are being filled with foreign players. If the youth systems in other countries are producing better players, then the number of aspiring young footballers in this country facing disappointment will inevitably increase. What will the future for English football be, if the current trend of more foreign players playing at professional level in this country continues?

The evidence from this work shows that there are still many boys who have little chance of becoming a professional footballer for reasons that could easily be overcome. For example, living in a rural area, or being born in the latter part of the academic year can be seen to impede their chances of success. How many gifted boys are not being given a fair chance because of these reasons? In addition, it was surprising to see that none of the Brighton and Hove Albion youth team players questioned felt that their schools had helped them with regard to football in any way. Also, some schools in Brighton had many boys attending the Centre of Excellence whilst others had none. Should the schools play more of an active role in trying to assist their pupils?

Answers to these questions are worthy of further research, for if this vast number of potential players continues to remain untapped, then given the appeal of the professional English Leagues to foreign players, the future for the aspiring young players in this country may be facing a crisis.

BIBLIOGRAPHY
Academic

Alder, P. A., Kless, S.J. and Alder, P. (1992). Socialisation to gender roles: Popularity among elementary school boys and girls **Sociology of Education Vol. 65**

Atkinson, J.W. (1974). The mainsprings of achievement - oriented activity. In Atkinson, J W. and Raynor, J.O. (eds.) **Motivation and Achievement** Halstead

Arthur, M.B., Hall, D.T. and Lawrence, B.S. (1989) Generating new directions in career theory: the case for a transdisciplinary approach. In Arthur, M.B., Hall, D.T. and Lawrence, B.S. (eds.) **Handbook of Career Theory** Cambridge: Cambridge University Press

Bains, J. and Johal, S. (1998). **Corner Flags and Corner Shops. The Asian Football Experience** London: Phoenix

Bale, J and Philo, C (1998). **Body Cultures: Essays on Sport, Space and Identity** London: Routledge

Bandura, A (1977). **Self-Efficacy: toward a unifying theory of behavioural change** Psychological Review 84: 191-21

Barnes, J.A (1979). **Who Should Know What?** Harmondsworth: Penguin

Baumrind, D. (1971). Principles of ethical conduct in the treatment of subjects: Reaction to the Draft Report of the Committee of Ethical Standards in psychological research **American Psychologist Vol. 26 pp 887-96**

Blake, A (1996*).* **Body Language - The Meaning of Modern Sport** London: Lawrence and Wishart Ltd

Boreham, N.C., and Arthur, T.A.A., (1993). **Information Requirements in Occupational Decision Making,** London: Research Series No.8, Employment Department

Bourdieu, P. (1984). **Distinction: A Social Critique of the Judgement of Taste** London: Routledge and Kegan Paul

Bourdieu, P. (1986). 'The Forms of Capital' in **Handbook of Theory for the Sociology of Education** *p241-258* New York: Greenwood Press

Bourdieu, P. (1995). **Sociology in Question** London: Sage Publications

Brustad R.J. (1988). Affective outcomes in competitive youth sport: The influence of interpersonal and socialisation factors **Journal of Sport and Exercise Psychology Vol 10**

Brustad, R.J. (1996). 'Parental and Peer Influence on Children's Psychological Development Through Sport' in Smoll, F.L. and Smith, R.E. (eds) **Children and Youth Sport: A Biopsychosocial Perspective** London: Brown and Benchmark Publishers

Bryman, A. (1988) **Quantity and Quality in Social Research** London: Unwin Hyman

Buffone, G.W. (1984). 'Exercise as a Therapeutic Adjunct' in Silva, J.M. and Weinberg (eds.) **Physiological Foundations of Sport** Champaign Il. Human Kinetics

Bull, S. (1998). **Sport Psychology: A Self Help Guide.** Marlborough: Crawood Press

Burt, R. (1995). **The Male Dancer,** London: Routledge.

Butt, D (1987). **Psychology of Sport** Wokingham: Van Nostrand Renhold

Byrne, T. (1999). 'Sport: It's a Family Affair' in Lee, M. (ed.) **Coaching Children in Sport. Principles and Practice,** London: E & F.N. Spon.

Carron, A.V (1981). **Social Psychology of Sport: An Experimental Approach** Ithaca, N.Y: Movement Publications

Cashmore, E (1990). **Making Sense of Sport** London: Routledge

Chase, M.A. and Dummer, D.G. (1992). The role of sports as a social status determinant for children. **Research Quarterly for Exercise and Sport Vol. 63**

Child, D. (1997). **Psychology and the Teacher** London: Cassell

Clingham, J.M. and Hilliard, D.V. (1987). Race walkers quicken their pace by tuning in not stepping out. **The Sports Psychologist Vol. 4**

Coakley, J.J. (1998). **Sport in Society: Issues and Controversies** Boston, Mass: Irwin, McGraw-Hill

Cole, M. (1989) **The Social Context of Schooling** London: Falmer Press

Coté, J. (1999). The Influence of the Family in the Development of Talent in Sport **The Sport Psychologist Journal 1999 December Vol. 13 No 3**

Cooper (1969). **Athletics, Activity and Personality: A Review of the Literature** Research Quarterly Vol.40 17-22

Cox, P. (1997). Questionnaires as Instruments of Intrusion. In Tomlinson, A. and Fleming, S. (eds.) **Ethics, Sport and Leisure: Crises and Critiques** Aachen:

Meyer & Meyer Verlag

Cox, R (1994). **Sport Psychology: Concepts and Application** Champaign, Il: Human Kinetics

Cratty, B.J. (1981). **Social Psychology in Athletics** NJ: Prentice Hall Englewood Cliffs.

Cox, R (1994). **Sport Psychology: Concepts and Application** Madison, WI: Brown & Benchmark

Cratty, B.J. (1981). **Social Psychology in Athletics** NJ: Prentice Hall Englewood Cliffs.

Creswell, J.W (1994). **Research Design: Qualitative and Quantitative Approaches** London: Sage Publications

Dandelion, B.P. (1997). Insider Dealing: Researching Your Own Private World. In Tomlinson, A and Fleming, S (eds.) **Ethics, Sport and Leisure: Crises and Critiques** Aachen: Meyer & Meyer Verlag

Davis, B., Bull, R., Roscoe, J. and Roscoe, D. (1997). **Physical Education and the Study of Sport** London: Mosby

Dean, J. P., Eichhman, R.L. and Dean, L.R. (1969). Limitations and Advantages of Unstructured Methods.In McCall & Simmons (eds) **Issues in Participant Observation** Massachusetts: Addison-Wesley Company

Denzin, N.K. (1989). **The Research Act. A Theoretical Introduction to Sociological Methods** New Jersey: Prentice Hall

Department of Culture, Media and Sport (DCMS) (2000). **A Sporting Future for All** DCMS April

Department of Culture, Media and Sport (DCMS) and Strategy Unit (2002). **Game Plan: a strategy for delivering Government's sport and physical activity objectives** Cabinet Office HMSO December

Department of Culture, Media and Sport (DCMS) (2003) **Learning through PE and Sport** DCMS

Department of Education and Employment (DfEE). (1999(a) **Meeting The Challenge Of The 21st Century. A Summary of 'Labour Market and Skill Trends 1997/98'** The National Skills Agenda

Department for Education and Skills (2003) **Playing for Success Yearbook 2002** Department for Education and Skills

Department for Education and Skills (2003) **Playing for Success: An Evaluation of the Fourth Year** National Foundation for Educational Research

Duncan, J (1997). Focus group interviews with the elite young athletes, coaches and parents. In Kremer, J, Trew, K and Ogle, S (eds.) **Young People's Involvement in Sport** London: Routledge

Dunn, J. (1984). **Sisters and Brothers** London: Fontana Paperbacks

Eichberg, H. (1998). Body Culture. In Bale, J and Philo, C (eds) **Body Cultures: Essays on Sport, Space and Identity** London: Routledge

Eder, D. and Parker, S. (1987). The cultural programme and reproduction of gender: The effect of extra-curricular activities on peer group culture. **Sociology of Sport Vol 60**

Faulkner, R.R. (1975). Coming of Age in Organisations: A Comparative Study of Career Contingencies of Musicians and Hockey Players. In Ball, D.W. and Loy, J.W. (eds.) **Sport and Social Order** 521-528 Massachusetts: Addison-Wesley Publishing Company

Fergusson and Unwin (1996). Making better sense of post 16 destinations: a case study in an English shire county. **Research Papers in Education March 1996**

Fleming, S. (1997). Qualitative Research into Young People, Sport and Schooling. In Tomlinson, A. and Fleming, S (eds) **Ethics, Sport and Leisure: Crises and Critiques** Aachen: Meyer & Meyer Verlag

Folkins, C.H. and Sime, W.E. (1981). Physical fitness training and mental health **American Psychologist Vol 36**

Foster, S. (1997). 'Harder, Faster, Longer, Higher – a Post-Mortem Inquiry into the Ballerina's Making' in **Border Tensions: Dance and Discourse** Guildford: April 1995 Department of Dance Studies, University of Surrey.

Gain, C. & George, R. (1998). **Gender, Race and Class in Schooling – A New Introduction** London: Falmer Press.

Garland, J. & Chakraborti, N (2001) **Evaluation of The Charlton Athletic Race Equality (CARE) Partnership. Final Report** Scarman Centre, University of Leicester

Garland, J and Rowe, E (2001). **Race and Anti Racism in Football** Basingstoke: Palgrave

Gill, D. L.(1986). **Psychological Dynamics of Sport** Champaign, Il: Human Kinetics

Ginsberg, E. et al (1951). **Occupational Choice** Columbia University Press

Glasstone, R. (1986). Selection and its Influence on the Training of Dancers. In Gleeson, G. (ed) **The Growing Child in Competitive Sport** London: Hodder and Stoughton

Goldthorpe, J. (1987). **Social Mobility and Class Structure in Modern Britain** Oxford: Clarendon Press

Gothard, W.P. (1985). **Vocational Guidance: Theory and Practice** London: Seven House.

Green, L. (1996). 'The Emergence of Gender as an Issue in Music Education' in **Music Education: Trends and Issues** Institute of Education, University of London

Gruneau, R.S. (1975). Sport, Social Differentiation and Social Inequality. In Ball, D.W. and Loy, J.W. (eds.) **Sport and Social Order** 117-184 Massachusetts: Addison-Wesley Publishing Company.

Guilianotti, R. (1999). **Football. A Sociology of the Global Game** Cambridge: Polity Press

Hakim, C. (1997). **Research Design: Strategies and Choices for Social Research** London: Routledge

Halsey, A.H. (1986). **Changes in British Society** Oxford: Oxford University Press

Hardman, K (1973) A Dual Approach to the Study of Personality and Performance in Sport. In Whiting, H.T.A., Hardman, K., Hendry, L.B. and Jones, M.G. (eds.) **Personality and Performance in Physical Education and Sport** London: Kimpton.

Hargreaves, J (1993). **Sport, Power and Culture** Cambridge: Polity Press

Her Majesty's Stationary Office (HMSO) (1996). **Raising the Game** HMSO

Hodkinson, P. Sparkes, A.C. (1997). 'Careership: A Sociological Theory of Career Decision-Making. **British Journal of Sociology of Education Vol. 18, No 129**

Hodkinson, P., Sparkes, A.C. and Hodkinson, H. (1996). **Triumph and Tears: Young people, markets and the transition from school to work** London: Fulton

Hoel, H. and Cooper, C. (2000). **Destructive Conflict and Bullying at Work** UMIST

Holloway, I. (1997). **Basic Concepts for Qualitative Research** Oxford: Blackwell Science

Homan, R. (1991). **The Ethics of Social Research** Harlow: Longman

Hopcraft, A. (1968). **The Football Man** London: Simon and Schuster

Houlihan, B. and White, A (2002). **The Politics of Sports Development. Development of Sport or Development through Sport** London: Routledge

Jarvie, G and Maguire, J (1994). **Sport and leisure in social thought** London: Routledge

Jones, T (1997). **Britain's Ethnic Minorities** London: Policy Studies Institute

Jones, G. (1998). Stress and Anxiety. In Bull, S. **Sport Psychology. A Self Help Guide** Marlborough: Crowood Press pp31-51

Kowalozewski, P.S. (1982). Race and Education **Oxford Review of Education Vol. 8 No. 2**

Kane, J.E. (1976). 'Personality research: The current controversy and implications for sports studies' in Sraub, W.F. (ed) **Sport Psychology: an analysis of athlete behaviour** Ithaca N.Y: Mouvement Publications

Kidd, J.E. (1981). 'Self and occupational awareness as influences on the career development of young people' In Watts, A.G., Super, D.E. and Kidd, J.E. (eds.) **Career Development in Britain** Cambridge: Hobsons Press

Keech, M (2003). 'Sport through education? Issues for schools and sports development' In Hayes, S. and Stidder, G. (eds.) **Equity and Inclusion in Physical Education and Sport** London: Routeledge

Kenway, J. (1993). Parents and Educational Politics **British Journal of Sociology of Education Vol.14 No. 4**

Keil, T. (1981) Social structure and status in career development In Watts, A.G., Super, D.E. and Kidd, J.E. (eds.) **Career Development in Britain** Cambridge: Hobsons Press

Kimmel, A.J. (1988). **Ethics and Values in Applied Social Research** London: Sage Publications

Kwami, R. (1998). Non-Western Music in Education: Problems and Possibilities **British Journal of Music Education Vol. 15, No. 2, p 161-170 July**

Landers, D.M. (1978). Motivation and performance: The role of arousal and attentional factors. In Straub, W.F. (ed) **Sport psychology: An analysis of athletic behaviour** Ithaca, NY: Movement

Law, W. (1981). Career theory: a third dimension? In Watts, A.G., Super, D.E. and Kidd, J.E. (eds.) **Career Development in Britain** Cambridge: Hobsons Press

Lee, R.M. (2000) **Unobtrusive Methods in Social Research** Buckingham: Open University Press

Lewko, J.H. and Greendorfer S.L. (1988). Family Influences in Sport Socialisation of Children and Adolescents in Smoll, F.L., Magill, R.A., and Ash, M.J. (eds.) **Children in Sport** Champaign, Il: Human Kinetics

Long, J and Spracklen, K (1996). Postitional Play: Racial Stereotyping in Rugby League **Bulletin of Physical Education Vol XXXII**

Lumpkin, A. (1994). **Physical Education and Sport. A Contemporary Introduction** St Louis: Mosby

Mackrell, J. (1992). **Out of Line** London: Dance Books Limited

Maidlow, S. (1998). The Experience, Attitudes and Expectations of Music Students From a Feminist Perspective **British Journal of Music Education 1998 Vol.15 No.1 p37-49**

May, T. (2001). **Social Research. Issues, Methods and Process** Buckingham: Open University Press

McCarthy, D., Jones, R.L., and Potrac, P. (2003).Constructing and Interpreting Realities: The Case of the Black Soccer Player on Television **International Review for The Sociology of Sport Vol. 38 No.2**

McCall, G.J. and Simmons, J.L. (eds.) (1969). **Issues in Participant Observation: A Text And Reader** London: Addison-Wesley Publishing Company

McGuire Jr R.T. and Cook, D.L. (1983). The influence of others and the decision to participate in youth sport **Journal of Sport Behavior Vol. 6 No.1 pp 9-16**

McPherson, B.D., Curtis, J.E. and Loy, J.W. (1989). **The Social Significance of Sport** Champaign Il: Human Kinetics.

McQuattie, S (1986). Giftedness in Music. In Gleeson, G (Ed) **The Growing Child in Competitive Sport** London: Hodder and Stoughton

Mitchell, A. Jones, G.B. and Krumboltz, J. (1979). **Social Learning and Career Decision Making** Carroll Press U.S.A.

Monk, D. and Russell, D. (2000). Training Apprentices: Tradition versus Modernity in the Football Industry **Soccer and Society p62-77**

Moran, R. (2000). Racism in Football: A Victim's Perspective **Soccer and Society p190-200**

Morgan, W.P. (1980). The Trait Psychology Controversy **Research Quarterly for Exercise and Sport; Vol.51 p50-76**

Morgan, B.R. (2000). **Young People's choice of post-16 education and training** Unpublished Ph.D. thesis University of Sussex

Morris, T. (1995) Psychological characteristics and sports behaviour. In Morris, T and Summers, S. (eds.) **Sport Psychology: Theory Application and Issues** (pp3-25) Milton QLD: Jacaranda Wiley Ltd

Hellstad, J.C. (1987). The Coach/Parent/Athlete Relationship **Sports Psychologist Vol. 1 No.2 pp151-60**

Murray, L. and Lawrence, B. (2000). **Practitioner-Based Research. Principles of Graduate Research** London: Falmer Press

Nagel, E. (1961) **The Structure of Science** London: Routledge & Kegan Paul

Newman, J. and Williams, F. (1995). 'Diversity and Change: Gender, Welfare and Organizational Relations' in Itzen, C. and Newman, J. (eds.) **Gender, Culture and Organizational Change: Putting Theory into Practice** London: Routledge

Oddey, A. (1999). **Performing Women: Stand-Ups, Strumpets and Itinerants** London: Macmillan

Office of National Statistics (ONS) (1997). **Social Trends** The Stationary Office

Office of National Statistics (ONS) (2001). **Regional Trends** The Stationary Office

Owsley, J (2000). **A Game of Two Halves** Unpublished M.A. (Ed) Dissertation University of the West of England

Oxendine, J.B. (1970). Emotional arousal and motor performance **Quest Vol. 13**

Parker, A (1996). **Chasing the Big Dream. Football Apprenticeships in the 1990's** Unpublished Ph.D. Thesis University of Warwick

Parker, A. (2001). Football Traineeship and Masculine Construction **Soccer and Society Vol. 2, No. 1. Spring**

Patterson, E.L., Smith, R.E., Everett, J.J. and Ptacek, J.T. (1998). Psychosocial Factors as Predictions of Ballet Injuries: Interactive Effects of Life Stress and Social Support **Journal of Sport Behaviour Vol. 21 No.1**

Polley, M. (1998). **Moving the Goalposts: A History of Sport and Society since 1945** London: Routledge

Reid, I. (1998). **Class in Britain** Cambridge: Polity Press

Reilly, T. and Williams, A. M. (2003). Introduction to science and soccer. In Reilly, T. and Williams, A. M. (eds.) **Science and Soccer, p 1-6,** London: Routledge

Reilly, T. Williams, A. M. and Richardson, D. (2003). Identifying talented players. In Reilly, T. and Williams, A. M. (eds.) **Science and Soccer, p 307-326,** London: Routledge

Roberts, K. (1977). **From School to Work**, Newton Abbott: David and Charles

Rodger, A. (1952). **The Seven Point Plan**, London: N.I.I.P.

Sanderson, F. (1996). Psychology. In Reilly, T. (ed) **Science and Soccer** London: E & FN Spon

Sayers, L-A. (1997). Madame Smudge, Some Fossils, and Other Missing Links: Unearthing the Ballet Class. In Thomas, H. (ed) **Dance in the City** London: MacMillan Press Limited

Scanlon, T.K. and Lewthwaite, R. (1984). Social Psychological aspects of competition for male youth sports participants: Preditors of competitive stress **Journal of Sport Psychology Vol 6**

Scanlon, T.K., Stein, G.L. and Ravizza, K. (1989). An in-depth study of former elite figure skaters: Sources of enjoyment. **Journal of Sport and Exercise Psychology Vol. 11**

Schurr, K. T., Ashley M.A. and Joy, K.L. (1977). A multivariate analysis of male athlete characteristics: Sport type and success **Multivariate Experimental Clinical Research Vol 3**

Sheldon, W.H. and Stevens S.S. (1942). **The Varieties of Temperament: A Psychology Of Constitutional Differences** London: Harper Row

Shilling, C. (1993) **The Body and Social Theory** London: Sage Publications

Skinner, B.F. (1974). **About Behaviourism** Vintage Books

Smith, D (2003) **Switched On! Strategic relationship between Media and the Learning and Skills Agenda Conference** 6th October 2003 Brighton: Alias Seattle Hotel, Brighton Marina

Smith, R.E. and Smoll, F.L (1995) **Children and Youth Sport: A Biopsychosocial Perspective** Brown and Benchmark Publishers

Smith, M.D. (1975). Sport and Collective Violence in Ball, D.W. and Loy, J.W. (eds.) **Sport and Social Order** (277-330) Massachusetts: Addison-Wesley Publishing Company

Sugden, J. (1996). **Boxing and Society: An International Analysis** Manchester: Manchester University Press

Sugden, J. and Tomlinson, A. (1999). Digging the Dirt and staying Clean: Retrieving The Investigative Tradition for a Critical Sociology of Sport **International Review for the Sociology of Sport 34(4) (385-397)**

Super, D. (1957). **The Psychology of Careers** London: Harper Row

Super, D. (1981). Occupational Psychology. In Watts, A.G., Super, D.E. and Kidd, J.E. (eds.) **Career Development in Britain** Cambridge: Hobsons Press

Taylor, M. (1996). Research Paper in Post 16 options: young people's awareness, attitudes, intentions and influences on their choice **Education Vol.17. No.3 October**

Taylor, R and Ward, A (1995). **Kicking and Screaming** London: Robson Books Limited

Turner, B. (1996). **The Body and Society** London: Sage Publications

Wacquant, L.J.D. (1995). Pugs at Work: Bodily Capital and Bodily Labour Among Professional Boxers **Body and Society Vol.1 No.1 March**

Walvin, J. (1994). **The People's Game. The History of Football Revisited,** Edinburgh: Mainstream Publishing

Warde, A. (1997). **Consumption, food and taste: culinary antinomies and commodity culture** London: Sage Publications

Weinburg, R.S. and Gould, D. (1995). **Foundations of Sport and Exercise Psychology** Champaign, Il: Human Kinetics

Wheaton, B. (1997). Covert Ethnography and the Ethics of Research: Studying Sports Subcultures. In Tomlinson, A. and Fleming, S. (eds.) **Ethics, Issues and Leisure: Crises and Critiques** Aachen: Meyer & Meyer Verlag

Whitty, G., Power, S. and Halpin, D. (1998). **Devolution and choice in education: the school, the state and the market.** Buckingham Open University Press

Willis, P.E. (1977). **Learning to Labour,** Farnborough: Saxon House

Wilson, B. and Edington, G. (1982). **First Child, Second Child...** London: Souvenir Press

Yin, R.K. (1994). **Case Study Research – Design and Methods,** London: Sage Publications

Yorganci, I. (1997). Researching Sport and Sexual Harassment: The Ethics of Covert Participant Observation and Open Methods. In Tomlinson, A. and Fleming, S. (eds.) **Ethics, Issues and Leisure: Crises and Critiques** Aachen: Meyer & Meyer Verlag

Popular

Adams, T. (1998) **Addicted**, London: Harper Collins

Atkins, H. and Newman, A. (1981) **Beecham Stories**, London: MacDonald Futura Publications

Archer, M (2001) **The World at their Feet** Channel 4 Television

Barnes, J. (1998) **Theatre School** British Broadcasting Company

Bogarde, D. (1985) **Snakes and Ladders**, London: Triad Grafton

Boult, A. (1973) **My Own Trumpet**, London: Hamish Hamilton

Brinkworth, M (1997) **True Stories – Football Dreams** Channel 4 Television 8/7/97

Brinkworth, M. (2000) **Fame School** Meridian Television (Weekly documentary broadcast between January and March)

British Broadcasting Company (BBC) (1998) **Sporting Families** Radio 5 13/12/1998

Burt, J. (2003) A league of our own **The Independent Review 4 March pp4-5**

Cabb, S. (2001) **Football Dream Factory** Channel 4 Television

Carling, W. (1998) **My Autobiography**, London: Hodder and Stoughton

Chaudhary, V. (1994) Asians can play football, too **The Guardian 17th August**

Conn, D. (2000) United's youngsters sacrificed on the altar of instant success **The**

Independent 27th April, p31

Dickinson, M. (2004) Sliding standards in football force Scudamore's late tackle **The Times 9th April p52**

Donovan, M (2003) Sacking still hurts Hinsh **Sports Argus 12/4/03 pp16-17**

Dower, J (2001) **Football Academy** Channel 4 Television 2/6/01

Frean, A. (2003) Footballers help young to score in foreign languages **The Times 17th September 2003 p12**

Garside, K. (2003) Star gazing. **Air. The Thomas Cook In-flight Magazine** Summer

Gilbert, J. (2001) Real Men Wear Tights **The Independent on Sunday. Arts Etc 16th December**

Goodbody, J. and Lee, A. (1999) Soccer scores with public schools **The Times 23rd January, p20**

Herzog, A. (2004) The Rise and Rise of Anna Kournikova **MTV UK (Television) 10th April**

Hudson, A. (1997) **The Working Man's Ballet**, London: Robson's Books

Morrison, R. (1998) Act 1, Scene 1: Enter poverty **The Times 3/4/1998 p35**

Nelson, G. (1995) **Left Foot Forward** London: Headline Book Publishing

Rees, J. (1999) The Mini Michael Owens **The Times Newspaper Magazine 6/3/99**

Rich, T. (2002) Clubs return to youth in pursuit of prosperity **The Independent 10/9/02 p27**

Sugden, J. (2004) Fans who ape their heroes' yob lifestyles **The Argus 29th March p8**

Szczepanik, N (2004) Oatway proving he has the write stuff **The Times: The Game 1/3/04 pp4-5**

Viner, B. (2000) Outsiders who only want to be liked **The Independent – Sport, 21/2/00 p7**

Woolfe, M.(1998) Talented but poor? Here's a role for you **Observer 29/3/98 p22**

Professional

Arts Council (1998) **Work in Dance. A Guide to Careers in Dance for Students** The Arts Council for England

Barwick, S., Jackson, L., Reilly, T., Russell, R., Smith, D., Wilkinson, H., Williams, M. (1998) (eds) The Ajax Way **Insight. The F.A. Coaches Association Journal.**

Issue 3, Volume 1, Spring

Brighton & Hove Albion Football Club **Players & Parents Information Brochure**
(2003) (Unpublished)

Brown, M. (1997) Pele, Maradona, Cruyff…Khan? **The Times Educational
Supplement 7ᵗʰ November**

Charlton Athletic Football Club (2000) **Charlton Athletic Youth Academy**
(Unpublished).

Chuter, R., Heryet, A., Hicks, M., James, M., Levenson, S. and Schofield, A. (2001(a))
How we became the world's most famous Div 3 club **Seagull.** Brighton and Hove
Albion's Match Day Programme (8/12/01)

Chuter, R., Heryet, A., Hicks, M., James, M., Levenson, S. and Schofield, A. (2001(b))
By the Sussex seaside, something starts to stir…**Seagull.** Brighton and Hove
Albion's Match Day Programme (21/12/01)

Conference of Drama Schools (CDS) (1999) **UK Guide to Drama Training** Westlake
Publishing Limited

Coppell, S (1985) **Touch and Go** London: Willow Books

Craine, D. (2003) Every Move He Makes **Dance Now Vol. 12, No.1 Spring p3-18**

Crystal Palace Football Club (2001) **Crystal Palace F.C. Youth Academy**
(Unpublished).

Department of Education and Employment (DfEE) (1999(b)) **Dance and Drama
Awards – Information for Students** Social Inclusion and Student Support
Division DfEE

Football Association (1997) **Football Education for Young Players – A Charter for
Quality** London: The Football Association

Football Association (2003) **Club England Newsletter** London: The Football
Association Issue No. 4

Football League (1997) **Handbook** London: Football League

Football Further Education and Vocational Training Society (FFE&VTS) (2001) **The
Football Scholarship Report** The Football Further Education and Vocational
Training Society. (Unpublished)

Football Further Education and Vocational Training Society (FFE&VTS) (2002)
Statistical Evidence 1999-2002 The Football Further Education and Vocational
Training Society. (Unpublished)

Football Further Education and Vocational Training Society (FFE&VTS) (2003)
Scholarship Guidance Booklet The Football Further Education and
Vocational Training Society Limited (Unpublished)

Forzoni, R. (2001(a)) Motivation in Football (Part 1) The components of motivation
**Insight. The F.A. Coaches Association Journal. Issue 3, Volume 4,
Spring**

Forzoni, R. (2001(b)) Motivation in Football (Part 2) Self-Determining Theory and
Practice **Insight. The F.A. Coaches Association Journal. Issue 4, Volume 4,
Summer**

Glasstone, R. (1980) **Male Dancing as a Career** London: Kaye and Wend Ltd

Hall, R. (2003) Things will never be the same…**Insight. The F.A. Coaches
Association Journal Issue 2, Volume 6, Spring**

Helsen, W., Williams, M., Van Winckel, J., and Ward, P. (2003) Potential Problems
and Pitfalls in Identifying Future Elite Performers **Insight The F.A. Coaches
Association Journal Issue 2, Volume 1 Spring**

Kahn, J. (2000) Asians and Football: Providing Opportunities for Excellence **Insight
The F.A. Coaches Association Journal Issue 4, Volume 3 Spring**

Littlewood, M., Richardson. D., Lees, A. and Peiser, B. (2001) Migration Patterns in
Top Level English Football **Insight The F.A. Coaches Association Journal
Issue 3, Volume 4 Summer**

Incorporated Society of Musicians (1998) **Careers with Music** London: Incorporated
Society of Music.

Murphy, C. (2001) Talent Identification – Are we 'mental' enough? **The
F.A.Coaches Association Journal Issue 2, Volume 4, Spring**

Nicholls, A. (1994) **The Performing Arts** Lifeforce April

Paull, G (1999) Predicting and Developing Football Talent in Children **Insight. The
F.A. Coaches Association Journal Issue 4, Volume 2, Summer**

Paull, G. and Simmons, C. (1999) Season of Birth Bias in Sport: The Football

Association Experience **Insight. The F.A.Coaches Association Journal Issue 4, Volume 2, Summer**

Professional Football Association (1996) **A Kick in the Right Direction** Professional Football Association

Richardson, D. and Littlewood, M. (1999) The Impact of Foreign Players on Youth Development **Insight The F.A. Coaches Association Journal Issue 4, Volume 2 Summer**

Richardson, D (2000) The Influence of 'Significant Others' in the Development of Talented Young Footballers **Insight The F.A. Coaches Association Journal Issue 4, Volume 3 Autumn**

Richardson, J (1995) **Careers in the Theatre** London: Kogan Page

Rollin, G. and Rollin, J. (2003) **Sky Sports Football Yearbook 2003-2004** London: Headline

Simmons, C. (2000) Skill Acquisition in Football 8 to 16 year olds. **Insight. The F.A. Coaches Association Journal Issue 3, Volume 3 Summer**

Simmons, C. (2002 (a)) Science and Talent Identification **Insight. The F.A. Coaches Association Journal Issue 3, Volume 5 Summer**

Simmons, C. (2002 (b)) Opportunity. **Insight. The F.A. Coaches Associations Journal Issue 1, Volume 6, Winter**

Simmons, C. (2003) Visit to the Royal Netherlands Football Association. Koninklijke Nederlandsche Voetballbond (the 'KNVB') **Insight. The F.A. Coaches Association Journal Issue 2, Volume 6, Spring**

Slater, J. (1999) Schools score with £50m soccer bonanza **The Times Educational Supplement 24/9/99**

Smith, R. (2002) Talent Identification and Development in an Academy **Insight. The F.A. Coaches Association Journal Issue 4, Volume 5, Autumn**

Sussex Careers Service (1998) **Drama and Acting** Lifetime Careers

Sussex Careers Service (2002 (a)) **Dance and Dance Teaching.** Leaflet GAF 1 Lifetime Careers

Sussex Careers Service (2002 (b)) **Careers with Musicians** Leaflet GAD 1 Lifetime Careers

837691

Printed in Great Britain by
Amazon.co.uk, Ltd.,
Marston Gate.